I, the Woman, Planted Planted the Tree

A Journey Through Dreams to the Feminine

Pearl E. Gregor

Tellwell Talent
www.tellwell.ca

ISBN
978-0-2288-0229-7 (Paperback)
978-0-2288-0230-3 (eBook)

Table of Contents

Dreams Along The Way
Book One

Section I
Building My House

Section II
Initiation

Section III
Leaving My Father's House

Section IV
The Search for the Mother: Becoming Conscious

Section V
Chopping Open the Frozen Sea

Dreams Along the Way

Book One

The problem is not that each person constructs herself as a story but that she forgets that she has done this!

Dedication

To the emerging Wild Feminine Soul.
Her stories speak to all who have ears to hear.
May you heed Her timeless voice.

Acknowledgements

I must acknowledge my inner voice, soul voice—the voice that would not rest until I wrote.

I am blessed by the love and support of my children and grandchildren and my late husband, Bill.

Every woman who embarks on this perilous journey needs one good friend. The deepest possible gratitude to my friend Verna for her unfailing love and support particularly in those first perilous years.

I am privileged to share parts of my journey with some amazing women and a few very brave men. I honour the many seekers who have journeyed with me in various groups, conferences, workshops and healing circles.

I acknowledge my skilled, talented, knowledgeable and wonderful copy editor, Anne Champagne from Green Words Writing and Editing for her endless patience with details. Her edits, suggestions and conversation are much treasured.

I acknowledge my poet editor, Michael Kenyon, lover of words and all things imaginal. His shaping and shifting one huge tome into a trilogy has been a constant source of delight.

Of course, The Mother resides with me always. I am delighted to acknowledge my pioneer family steeped in the imagery and music of Catholicism. I am a child of Mary, Maia, May, Earth Woman, Inanna and Persephone. I acknowledge the many women of the Assisi Institute and *Seeing Red: The Emerging Feminine in Turbulent Times*. Through *Seeing Red* I learned that the archetype of Inanna lives on in the unconscious of humanity. Inanna emerged from within my being. She lives.

Hear the wind
Feel the moisture
Shrivelled bleeding soul.
Smell life return to the rivers and pastures turn green.
Touch the wild marigold that blooms brilliant yellow
Waters of the storm, flooding, filling, destroying, building.
I need a wild garden
Not clipped and even hedges with sharp angles and symmetry
manufactured by shears
A wild garden where nature shows her wild destructive face
and grins her laughing wrinkled smile in chaotic peace.

Personal Journal 1993

Preface

Why Write Dreams Along the Way?

If I should pass the tomb of Jonah
I would stop there and sit for awhile;
Because I was swallowed one time deep in the dark
And came out alive after all.

−Carl Sandburg, "Losers"

I am caught in a deathlike sleep through years of nightmares from perhaps age nine, and depressions begin when I am 15. When I am 43, I stretch and, pushed by fear, dive into the ocean of the unconscious. I survive the fall. Becoming conscious is difficult work and to birth the Divine Feminine is excruciating. I am my own midwife. There are tears on every page of this dream record.

"Mom, is it always going to be like this?" My young daughter's cry of despair jolts me to the core. Her eyes freeze me.

Rachel sits at the kitchen table. She is a gorgeous, dark-haired, slim, athletic teenager. Tears stream down her face. "Those damn boys. Every time I say anything in class, they make snide remarks:

'You're nothing but a feminist. You need to learn to listen and follow the rules. Your ideas are crazy....' And the teacher never stops them and the other girls say nothing."

She is in Grade 11, studying Advanced Placement English; she has written an analysis of Nathaniel Hawthorne's *The Scarlet Letter*. She is reading from authors such as Starhawk and Merlin Stone.

How long? How long before she just knuckles under—nicely, of course. Always nice. An honours student, athlete of the year throughout high school. Usually friends with girls and boys. Something has shifted, I am all too aware. Please, I plead silently, please, don't give up.

This book is for Rachel, for my sons, and for all the sons and daughters. I did my best, but the culture is stronger than I. Sleeping Beauty, Cinderella, Bluebeard's Daughter. Rachel, soon I will present you with your own copy of *Women Who Run With the Wolves*. I will give you *In a Different Voice,* in which Gilligan makes a strong case for the plight of adolescent girls on the cusp of womanhood. Perhaps in your 40s you too will have the inner strength to push your way out of the patriarchy and remember the Divine Feminine and the Sacred Masculine, the *hieros gamos* or sacred marriage. The god and goddess, the masculine and feminine energy, must be integrated so that together we become strong, compassionate, loving and caring people. The real issue? Recognizing that the Divine Mother, Earth Mother, exists. She has been pushed underground by the patriarchy. I am only beginning to wake up.

That day, my resolve deepened. I did tell her the truth as I knew it. Society says we're equal. And we are, before the law. But the law is an ass. On a day-to-day level? No, not yet. All these years later, I can seriously tell her, "No, we still have much to do, but I know that the Divine Feminine is alive and She is returning. Listen on the wind for Her voice. Listen and watch the hummingbird. Listen to your dreams. Walk on the earth. Sit beneath a tree. Feel the Divine Mother return to her daughters and her sons. And, birth the Divine Mother in you."

I believed I was writing a memoir that would move back and forth among my childhood years, early adulthood, the intense healing years of the 1990s and the writing years post-2004; slowly I discovered the task was to be much larger than memoir.

Intentionality

On February 3, 2016, I declare my intent to move beyond silence and to speak, either through writing, dreams, or in person, with my own woman voice, about the Divine Feminine. I declare my escape from the patriarchal religion of the Pope and the hierarchy. I acknowledge the amazing healing power of the Christ available to all who ask: those churched and those not churched. Divine Love is freely available. Just ask. I share my Catholicism in its deepest, truest intent as what now I think may have been meant by the Christ, who did not found an institution. St. Paul did that. Constantine did that. People did that. Jesus honoured Mary. I should have recognized my inner truth from birth. I came to teach that we are the Children of the Mother. Faith is not beliefs. I have a deep, abiding faith. Beliefs? Well, those change.

My beliefs are much older than I. They spring from the bones of my maternal grandparents, and parents. My DNA arises from these and all the other ancestors of the Kramps and Miller families … deep in the Germanic tribes of Europe. DNA plays a huge part in the collective unconscious of humankind and the personal unconscious of each of us. My DNA, my Germanic tribe, is of the Roman Catholic tradition back to the life and times of Luther. My roots are greening from that DNA of the bones of Hildegard of Bingen buried not far from those of my paternal great-grandparents at Paderborn, Germany.

I am thankful to the songs to Mother Mary in my childhood. For the many times I sang at weddings, and on Sunday morning and at my Aunt Anne's funeral, *On this day, O beautiful Mother, On this day, I give you my love.* At weddings, *Ave, Ave, Ave Maria.* To the peace even in despair found in the grotto in

Midnapore, Alberta. For the grotto my husband Bill built for me on the Gregor Ranch in Leduc County, Alberta. To the grottos of Europe, Ireland, New York State and most especially in Maryknoll Center, New York. To Medjugorje, Fatima and Guadeloupe, the shrines I learned about in the books of my youth.

I, the Woman has been incubating since March 3, 1990. That day I am en route to Wainwright to facilitate a social studies workshop as a part of my consulting work for Alberta Education, Regional Services Branch, Edmonton. I have a serious job. LOL. I am a serious person. Remember both those details. And, by then, I am also deeply into the process of healing and coming to consciousness. Awake. From behind me, a Voice speaks. "Write Dreams Along the Way." Repeat. I drive on. Repeat. I shake my head to clear away the silliness. Again, "Write Dreams Along the Way."

I pull over. Stop the car and get out. Walk around. Get back in. "Write Dreams Along the Way."

I am grateful for the written record of that day and of over 500 dreams. I have a dream website. I studied and read, made notes and wrote. Gave workshops and presented at an Alberta Teachers Conference on Dreams and Wellness. "Does the Deputy Minister know about this?" asked a colleague. "Of course not. I didn't tell him; I took the day off. I am not teaching dream interpretation on work time representing the Department of Education."

I have given conference presentations at Grant MacEwan University (Edmonton). "Aren't you from the Department of Education?" "Yes. I am." That was about 1991.

I have taught about dreams to my grandson's Grade 7 French immersion class. Delightful young people, open to learning. Intent. Interested. In a class discussion about David Almond's "gorgeously weird novel" *Skellig*, my grandson had said to his teacher, "My Grandma teaches this stuff." And so it began. The teacher integrated a dreamwork introduction with the novel. "Sometimes we just have to accept there are things we can't know," says one character, Mina. The book is compellingly mystical. I was never able to figure out what Skellig actually is— is he a human, a bird, a dust bunny, an angel? What? The Grade 7 students didn't seem to ask that kind of "literal" question. They were too intent on sharing their dreams. "What" didn't come up. Each student had written down dreams for 10 days in preparation for the class. We shared dreams and they learned the technique that adults love, "If this were my dream … it might be saying…." The dreamer speaks her dream into the circle and the circle folks use imagination and tell the dreamer, "If this were…." Many ideas are shared and some stick and others are rejected. It is an easy beginning but the rules are very strict. No advice. No telling the dreamer "your dream means." No one knows but the dreamer what her dream might mean. The students were pretty clear as to the meaning of metaphor and symbol by the end of that study.

And workshops? Over and over, those who come say essentially the same thing. "Why have we learned so little about dreams in all our years of schooling, education or life?"

Ah, yes. The Fear. The deep fear of breaking my self-imposed silence is alive and well. But dreams will not be denied. My inner voice is insistent. I may not wish to say anything strange. But dreams come to express the soul, to shatter old beliefs and create new ones.

Perhaps my story will help others … people who get up in the morning, look after homes and children, go to work, help in the community … living with depression is like that. It looks normal. I hid all the horrible stuff. All the while desperately hoping and praying I could hang on another day. Recently, a friend mentioned a colleague's suicide. A neighbour's suicide. "If only I had known…." That's what we all say. So, I do not write so you can **know about** my depression. I write with radical hope. Perhaps you will **heal your own**.

I can tell you that you won't know if someone is suicidal. You can't. If you figure it out, what will you do then? What will you say? Will you say, "Get yourself to a good doctor?" I was told that at the age of 43. I have been seeing "good" doctors since I was 15. At the time of the comment, I was seeing a "good" psychiatrist. Will you tell me, "You can't really be depressed? You don't look depressed." Really? What does a clinically depressed person look like? Or when you hear my story in a dream workshop, will you say, "You should have told me. I would have been more supportive if I had known." Or, like the many doctors I did see over the years, will you suggest the always available pharmaceutical cure? Mask the symptoms and enable the depressive to function at least in public? No doubt the drugs will help you deal with the current day, but not the root causes.

Our culture does not deal well with mental illness. We are afraid. In the many years I sought healing through psychology, psychiatry, prayer and medicine, I learned nothing about dreams. I took several psychology courses in my undergraduate degree. Dreams were mentioned, glossed over and given a biological explanation. The churches? Well my church surely believes in the dreams of prophets and saints from long past. Carl G. Jung built his life on dreams, but he died in 1961, about the time my depression experiences were manifesting in outer illness. What do you know of the work of C.G. Jung? If you ask 10 people tomorrow if they learn from dreams, what will you find? Our patriarchal culture has a very long way to go to learn to dive deeply into the unconscious and learn about the wounds we carry within the psyche. I am grateful for the gift of dreams and the gift of a book on dreams, *Dreams and Spiritual Growth: A Judeo-Christian Way of Dreamwork*.[1] It may well have saved my life.

What about responsibility? I take full responsibility for my depression. Sometimes, when I speak about my life, blame gets splattered here and there. But no, it isn't my Roman Catholic heritage, my parents, my community, my family, my husband, my children. **NO.** It is the agenda of my soul. Yes, I had to unearth my beliefs about sin, impurity, Confession and the role

---

[1] Louise Savary et al., *Dreams and Spiritual Growth: A Judeo-Christian Way of Dreamwork* (Mahwah, New Jersey: Paulist Press, 1984).

of women in the church. I became a flaming, radical feminist. And the reason I write is so that the reader can assume their own responsibility. I have been blessed. Deeply blessed by the symbolism found in the heritage of my childhood church, the love, support, care and concern of my family. By a supportive and loving husband. By a few good women. Ask yourself: What was known about mental illness in the spring of 1961? To judge 1961 in a small rural community by the standards of today with information and knowledge available on the touch screen, is to be self-indulgent, ill-informed and irresponsible. Depression has been my soul's journey. It has led me through deep darkness. And in that darkness, travelling into my personal and the collective unconscious, I found the sweet taste of the breadth and depth of love present to us in the universe. My soul's journey is to WAKE UP. Today I have a home filled with books about dreams, healing, Jungian psychology, depth psychology and spirituality. In fact, I have so many books that one grandson asked with all the seriousness of an eight-year-old, "Grandma, have you read every book in the whole wide world?" No, Noah, I haven't. But I sure would like to.

Don't say anything strange. Don't say anything about wild and crazy inner voices. Be silent. Hmm. That is a perfect description of why it has taken me so long to find the courage to share my experiences. In 2008, my PhD dissertation, *The Apple and the Talking Snake: Feminist Dream Readings and the Subjunctive Curriculum* was published online by the University of British Columbia. I resisted writing it and I resisted publishing. But it's there now. It's time to write the full much more personal story. In a different voice.

This is a story in three books, of spiritual transformation out of the patriarchy through dreams to radical feminism. It is my personal journey through meditation, healing, dreams, depression, becoming whole through journaling and the study of the world of the feminine, and coming to know the Divine Mother. Dreams continue to work within and leave their messages embedded in my body, bones and psyche. By the time

I got to dreamwork in 1988, I was too desperate to give a damn what anybody thought. I would have danced with the devil if she promised healing. This first book will take us to an awakening in 1992. The second book, *Authoring Self,* will begin with that awakening, and the third, well, you will see. Perhaps through my story one other person will learn about dreamwork. Close your eyes. Imagine. And find your own way through the labyrinth.

SECTION *I*

BUILDING MY HOUSE

Chapter One

Last-Ditch Effort

The search of reason ends at the shore of the known; on the immense expanse beyond it only the sense of the ineffable can glide. It alone knows the route to that which is remote from experience and understanding. Neither of them is amphibious: reason cannot go beyond the shore, and the sense of the ineffable is out of place where we measure, where we weigh.

–Abraham Heschel

Strange. Here I thought I was alive when I had merely fallen asleep in life's waiting room.

By my early 40s, depression and I were mortal enemies. The fight had been long and arduous. Beginning when I was a young child, deepening when I was a teenager, now it was reaching dangerous and brutal depths.

Desperate for inner peace, I went with a close friend, Verna, to a Sunday night meditation group based on a book called *The Teachings of the Inner Christ.* We had been friends since the '70s, and had shared a sabbatical leave through our master's degrees at the University of Alberta in 1983–84. Verna will walk this entire journey with me. We have walked together other lifetimes.

That night I wasn't convinced. I preferred praying "inside my closet," not publicly. Certainly not this public channelling of personal messages from the Holy Spirit. I was actually scared stiff. But not scared enough to give it up. Something inside me would not turn away from hope. The intellect may question. But the unconscious is rooted in ineffable ancient personal ideas and collective beliefs that will not be dislodged by mere words on a page. I would learn many new ideas in the coming years. Most powerfully, I'd learn I am one with the universe, one cell in billions. I'd learn something of the many metaphors that live me and find within me the Divine Feminine and Sacred Masculine. In the mid '90s, Mom gave me a book, *Who We Are is How We Pray*.[2] It meant a good deal to me, kind of like consent to celebrate *who* I was becoming. The author focused on matching Myers-Briggs personality types and spirituality with a view to Jung. From this book, I gained inner permission to "pray in my closet" or my inner world. The institutional church would become more and more problematic. Nearly 20 years later, I would be writing a doctoral dissertation from the perspective of the Crone. In April 1988, I had no inkling of the phenomenal changes to come.

It was a million years yesterday. Fall, 1983 Bill leaned over during Mass one Sunday morning, St. Michael's Church bulletin in hand, and whispered, "I think I want to do this," pointing to an announcement of a Roman Catholic Initiation group.

I went with him one evening a week. Since Colin was old enough to babysit, we went for coffee and long talks after every group session. Married nearly 15 years, it was weekly Date Night long before Date Nights for married couples were popularized.

---

2   Charles Keating (Mystic, CT: Twenty-Third Publications, 1987).

Bill was being full-time Dad that winter. Laid off from Kenting Pipelines in April 1983, 10 days AFTER I accepted a sabbatical leave at about 20% salary, he loved being home with four-year-old Rachel, who was in play school just a few hours a week, but being unemployed was hard. But that's a whole other story. His story.

We survived. I taught Education Administration 461 at the University. $600 a month. My sabbatical leave pay was about $600. And unemployment another $600. The house mortgage was $725 since the interest rates had gone from 8 3/4% to 14 3/4%. We learned a lot of new budgeting skills. I marked the grocery store fliers and Bill and Rachel scouted every grocery store in Leduc and sometimes South Edmonton. I won't lie. It was a tense and stressful time and we worked hard trying to ensure the kids' lives and activities were not strangled by the economics of those years, but it could and did get worse.

At Easter, 1984, Bill received the Sacrament of Confirmation. We went that Holy Week to a Mission preached by a visiting priest. My parents were home from their winter in Roadrunner Park in Phoenix, which meant Mom, bless her, was handling the kitchen. Bill loved the Mission. I loved the music. That last evening, Holy Thursday, I went to Confession. I swear that night my soul just shrank. When I confessed to the sin of despair, the priest snorted, told me to get myself to a "good doctor" and to say 10 Hail Mary's for penance. A good doctor? Patronizing, condescending, bloody damn arrogant.... I had been to doctors for 27 years by then. Medical doctors, psychologists, psychiatrists. My soul just flew away. I found Her years later, dried up and dehydrated. It would take a lot of coaxing, love and tears to bring Her home.

There were some fairly serious events in the spring of 1985. At Bill's insistence, I went once more to doctors. Saw the psychiatrist whose diagnosis was clinical depression. The prescription medication did calm me enough to sleep a few hours. My energy was frenetic. When the voices still spoke regardless of the medication, I went back.

"Are you telling anyone? Like your school board?" he asked.

"No. I am not. I may be mentally ill but I am NOT stupid."

He recommended a new drug. "You will have to take two weeks with no medication so that your system is cleared."

He did no intervention other than pharmaceuticals. He made no mention of what I would later recognize as the beginnings of cracks in the self. Splits. My fears of mental instability, of craziness, were not calmed by this professional. I hadn't yet learned the fine art of self. Nor had I learned about the assault begun on the feminine self millennia ago. Think Assyria. Second century BCE. Perhaps centuries earlier.

I remember mostly the icy feelings shivering up and down my body. The hair on my arms stood up. I was a nervous wreck. But I went to teach. I ALWAYS went to work. That was my absolute requirement; staying home brought too much time to think. Work was my saviour.

Somewhere during that time between medications, I approached the school guidance counsellor. "I need a disability leave. How will the board and the superintendent handle that?"

"Give me a bit of time to think that through," he said. Our counsellor was an amazing man. Kind, genuine, compassionate. He came back to my office a few hours later. "No. If you take a leave, you will never return to administration in this district."

One evening in 1990, after our Teachings of the Inner Christ meditation group, a colleague asked, "Do you remember the night at Caledonia Park, about five years ago, when we all went for supper at the Waldorf prior to Education Week Open House for Parents?"

"No, about what it?" I asked.

"You don't remember, for real?"

"No."

"Well, I came to your office and insisted you come for supper. 'You work night and day. You don't eat. You drink coffee and smoke those endless cigarettes.' You finally agreed to come ... after the next task. You would drive your own car. You came. You didn't eat. You drank more coffee. I insisted on driving home with you. On the way you drove through red lights, across the railroad against a red light. Skipped the red light on Black Gold Drive across Rolly View Road."

"Jesus. Why didn't you stop me?"

"I thought you must be trying to scare me," he said.

No. I wasn't trying to scare him. I have a lot of blank spaces where memories should be.

I don't remember what day it was that spring when my Grade 9 social studies class ended and a small group of students approached my desk, "Can we talk to you?"

"Sure."

"Mrs. Gregor, you usually make sense," a boy said, eyes downcast.

Then, looking me straight in the eye, one kind, honest and loving young girl said, "Today you made no sense at all. We think you are sick. We think you should go home." They scurried out.

I went. I stayed at home until the new medication did its work.

In June 1985 when blackouts threatened, and I was unsuccessful in hiding one incident, our school secretary insisted that I see a doctor. In July, I wore a Holter heart monitoring device for a week. The doctors tried to find the source of the continuous palpitations and the blackout sensations. Nothing wrong with my heart. I've lost count of the number of times my heart was tested. I guess medical tests don't show the blocks in the heart chakra.

Early spring 1986, Rachel and I went out to the farm. She slept in the small holiday trailer there while I meandered around. Then, I am lying face down in fresh, raw soil convulsed by racking sobs. Breathing in the soul nourishment of the damp earth as raw breezes caress me. Worms and furry things stop and look. Then hurry forward in their burrowing. Roots tangle deep in moist brown ground. Caterpillar creeps slowly up one canyon, stops, turns and touches down. Every cell of my body longs to settle inside this cave of warmth. Security. Where did this earth come from? How many worms? How many scurrying beetles are joined with granite, now ground of my being? The sky covers and meets the earth. How to join this earth and this heaven. Here on the earth, I can rest.

At home later that Sunday afternoon, I told Bill, "I am going home. I hope you come. I simply can't stay here. I must go home." We did. We moved home, to the farm, in July. But house prices were down in Alberta. We rented out the city house. I would drive the 80-km round trip to work.

Life was chaotic. Trying to make the farm pay. Weaned piglets, healthy when purchased, wound up dead from a highly contagious disease, atrophic rhinitis. We were stumbling through endless problems with finances, health and the remnants of the 1982 massive Alberta recession. In December 1986, when Bill had long-awaited, much-needed hip replacement surgery, even the necessary paid parking at Rehabilitation Clinic at the University was a strain. He had no disability insurance and the patriarchal bureaucracy at Revenue Canada was fighting my income tax claim that Bill was a dependent. It was a mess.

In winter 1987, our son Colin was away in Portland playing hockey. Rachel had finally quit crying at night because she missed him so much. Jason, 15 and romping through Grade 10, seemed fine. Bill's mom was becoming increasingly reclusive; health deteriorating, and sometimes calling late at night, disoriented. Wanting Bill to come and put up the fallen clothes closet rod or get the lump from her mattress. His sister was going through divorce after 25 years of marriage. The long-distance phone bills were killers. A close friend and former Leduc hockey teammate of Colin's had died the previous December 30 in a Swift Current Broncos bus accident. Unable to be there in Portland, ever, meant I worried. A lot.

In winter 1987 I was in my office at the Composite High School. Marion, school secretary, phoned down. "There's a man here to see you. His name is Rod Evans." I rushed out into the hallway to greet a teaching colleague from my days teaching in Grande Cache. Except it wasn't MY Rod Evans. It was the ATB Loans Manager. "You have missed a payment. If you can't pay, we will have to foreclose." I explained I had cleared that with the previous Loans Manager. But this guy was adamant, "We'll have to foreclose."

I lost my temper. Told him to get the hell out. And, in clipped, short syllables, told him that if he contacted my husband, I would not be responsible for my actions. I didn't call Bill. He was having his own problems. I called a lawyer. Yes, it was possible. Even with only ONE missed payment in 13 years? Yes. With such a small amount owing and the huge increase in land values? Yes. I was stunned. Embarrassed. Outraged.

A meeting with the bank manager resulted in a simple solution. We would make up the one missed payment whenever it was possible. Only the residue of my fear and anger remained.

I think you get the picture. I am almost 44 years old. I am a "successful" career woman. A good mother, so my kids tell me. I have the best and most kind and understanding husband on the planet. Good friends. Oh, I have lots of troubles. I just told you all that. But, doesn't everyone? I am now officially declared "clinically depressed." The only solution offered? Medication.

Then comes that day in spring 1988. In conversation with Verna I am relating all my woes, and my constant unanswered prayers, when she asks a simple question: "What kind of angry, avenging, punishing God do you believe in anyway? Do you think, somewhere, deep inside you, depression and chaos in your life is supposed to teach you lessons? As punishment? Where are you with the lessons of sin and all that?"

Then, the farm water well went dry. During the next Sunday meditation, we asked about the well.

The answer? Faith. I had only to believe and the well would fill. Huh? I am 43 here. I have been praying for a bazillion years. "Tell Pearl when she is ready to let go of old, dusty ideas, murky, unclear childish beliefs, then the well will spring forth with water just as the Spirit springs forth with love and faith." Faith?

I had yet to learn that my soul speaks in symbols. Wastelands. I had abandoned my soul. The wellspring within me was dry.

Chapter Two

Early Beginnings

There is an urgency for women. When you have inherited a construct that names, describes, and practices an ideology that women are somehow less important, less necessary, then, the work of defining yourself carries with it a kind of fury.

–Dominque Christina, 2015

The Tribal Child: Weaving the Tapestry

I dropped into the middle of my family story on May 3, 1945. I was welcomed into my perfect world by delighted parents, maternal grandparents, and three adoring older brothers. May is the month of the Mother. It is an energizing, life-affirming month named for Maia, the Greek goddess of fertility. In my Roman Catholic tribe, this is the month we pray daily to Mary, honouring the Blessed Virgin with prayers and flowers at her shrines around the world. Mother, Queen of the Flowers, Queen of the Universe. I sang so many times. "Daily, daily, sing to Mary. Sing…." How easily these songs spring to mind six decades later.

We prayed as a family. The flower of May, the Lily of the Valley. My birthstone is emerald, symbolizing love and success. I am most definitely a Taurus.

I started deep prayer life sometime in childhood when I had the mumps and was desperate to go to the school track meet. Yes. I prayed for miracles. I promised God all kinds of amazing things. I would become a saint. I would even follow in the footsteps of those saints who were into flagellation, wearing spiked belts under their clothing. Mine was a desperate, panicked prayer to the God of my childish understanding who sometimes did favours. I didn't get to that track meet.

Family life included Sunday Mass, mealtime prayer and evening rosary. *The Family that Prays Together Stays Together.* The Family Rosary Crusade. I read anything and everything available. *The Wanderer* included a German language insert in the American edition and I knew that Maternal Grandpa Miller was a German immigrant to the USA and eventually to Canada. My Grandmother Miller was of German descent born in America and died an American citizen. After the death of her parents in 1949 and 1946, I can only assume Mom continued the subscription.

When I was about six, I began to have nightmares about Stalin burning our home and invading our farm. Dad was adamant. "That paper has to stop. She is reading it." The *Wanderer* through the eyes of a six-year-old would be a very scary paper. Now, age 70, I read about its history. The *Wanderer* was founded by two Benedictine monks then serving the Assumption Church in St. Paul Minnesota, in the wake of the political revolutions in Germany in the late 1840s, the dangerous new ideas of the German 'enlightenment' growing in popularity and influence among German Catholics, even German immigrants living in the United States. Attacked by Hitler, accused of treason and threatened, accused by Orson Welles of being "Nazi propaganda," in the 1950s it kept up a relentless attack against the godlessness of Stalin and warned of the spread of communism. It has become a fervent right-wing expression of Catholicism. It fought strongly against the changes of Vatican II and continues the fight for "traditional" Catholicism. It would not like my search for the Divine Feminine.

Fragments of my life. Faint memories. I see a fascination with priestesses. I am a small girl; my three younger brothers are with me in the living room of our new house so I am at least nine. I see myself, chalice in hand, saying Mass with my brothers as acolytes. The priestess. It's not a career my childhood Baltimore Catechism or Sisters of Service correspondence lessons prepared me for. I still have the table that served as the altar though. It sits in the kitchen of my farm home holding grandson Beckett's toys that await his visits with Grandma. He's two.

In the early '50s I made book shelves from wooden B.C. apple boxes. A flour sack, washed, starched and embroidered with yellow stitching around the borders, created the front curtains which were secured with tightly stretched store string. My most prized book? *Nature's Wonder's in Full Color.* Prepared with cooperation of the National Audubon Society, a 1957 birthday present I still have on my study shelves today. I had books about the mystics and a red book, *The Lives of the Saints.*[3] I read whatever was available in the small church library. It wasn't much. Mom must have borrowed some books because when I was about 12 I read about the three young visionaries at Fatima: Jacinta, Francisco and Lucia. I was deeply moved by the miracles and visions of Fatima. The two younger children died very young ... Francisco died at age 11. The story of his devotion and expatiation for "sins" indelibly marked my young mind. Jacinta lived a scant 10 years. The Secrets of Fatima captivated an unbelieving world. Lucia was accused by the local priest of being "an instrument of the devil." She was the subject of continuous harassment and interrogation by many who learned of the apparitions. I believed.

I was a good student and, as a teenager, I made an old sewing machine stand sans machine into a desk. I had the most beautiful

---

3   Rev. Alban Butler, *The Lives of the Saints* (New York: Benziger Brothers, 1887).

wooden dresser with a mirror set inside a carved wooden frame. The dresser was a gift to Mother from her godparents. It had survived the Depression-era train trip from Champion, Alberta to High Prairie and then the wagon ride to Cornwall Creek when Mom was 17. In those years, I craved a French provincial white bedroom set. But coveting "things" was sinful. So, when I found myself paging through the Eaton's and Simpson's catalogues, I confessed to "coveting the possessions of others." Perhaps I was a bit neurotic? Or a scrupulous, fastidious sinner?

I took my First Holy Communion October 12, 1952 together with my cousins, Larry and Kathy. I was a serious child. That morning, as we got ready to go to Mass, Mother put a pot of peeled potatoes on the stove. I reached for a tasty chunk when Dad, usually pretty calm, yelled, "Don't eat that." I shrivelled. Little did he know how guilt-ridden I was about that for years. In 1952, receiving Holy Communion required a three-hour fast. It didn't matter how many hours it took to get to church or any other factor. The Rules were the Rules. Period.

I participated in the sacraments of Confession, later called Penance, at the same time as Holy Communion. It was an excruciating time. I learned about sin and for some bizarre reason focused especially on the sin of impurity. I was filled with shame. I confessed to the sin of impurity … because I scratched my vulva raw and bloody in the night while sleeping. It would be many years before a glimmer of understanding came through the darkness to show me my irrational fear of impurity. Today, we understand such behaviours may arise as the result of molestation. Then, I was deeply attracted to the story of Saint Maria Goretti and even had a colouring book about her life. I only wish I had that book now. It seems impossible that such a book existed, but this is a memory I confirmed with my mom sometime before she died. Thankfully, Mom was willing to discuss anything with me. Well, perhaps not everything. For example, Mother KNEW emphatically that Mary was a virgin and Jesus had no brothers. I tentatively tried a discussion on that topic sometime in the 1990s. Gave up. Decided that some things were just better left in silence. But….

Virginity loomed large in my childhood mind. I read and knew the history of Maria. According to Lives of the Saints, after the death of her father, Maria and her family lived with the Serenelli family. She was 11. The family son, Alessandro, was 19. He stabbed her to death when she resisted his sexual advances. Attempted rape. She prayed for him on her death bed and gave her forgiveness. She prayed for his family and hers. The small community believed her to be "an angel." She was canonized by Pope Pius XII June 24, 1950. In the canonization ceremony, the Pope claimed she, above all, "stands for purity."[4] The story of her life and death concludes that she was an instrument of many cures and miracles including the conversion of her murderer.

So, in the early '90s, when I asked my mom about that colouring book and her thoughts and remembrances of those years, she said, "Dad and I wondered about that because it was so extreme. But we also harboured thoughts that you would become a nun like your aunts. You were a deeply introspective, spiritual, quiet and well-behaved child. You followed all the rules. We thought you were perfect. You were devoted to the Blessed Virgin Mary and had a strong commitment to purity. Little did we know."

Jean and Wallace Clift[5] comment that people often find stories they loved or hated in childhood tell significant information about their inner patterns and beliefs. Thus, my attachment to the St. Maria Goretti story of rape, murder and sainthood takes on immense significance in my healing journey. As a young girl I was pretty certain I wouldn't have the "courage" to suffer the way many of the saints suffered. Praying on nails? It will be October 1993 before I uncover the real Maria Goretti

---

4   Lives of the Saints, Our Lady of the Rosary Library, http://www.olrl.org/lives/.
5   Jean D. Clift and Wallace B. Clift, *Symbols of Transformation in Dreams* (NY: Crossroad, 1984).

story and the history behind it. I can only imagine that my original experience of the text stands in stark contrast to the intention of the adult understanding.

October 9, 1954 our family moved across the yard from the little house into the new house. I know the date exactly because I carved my initials with the date on a large poplar tree close to the back door. I remember crying many nights for years before that because I hurt. My legs hurt. And hurt. And then hurt some more. I got little red pills for juvenile rheumatism. Then one night another nightmare began. There, leering at me out of the top of my small clothes closet, the scarred face of a man with burned, wide, funny chalk-coloured scars down the right side of his face. Years and years and more years. He came out of the top of my small closet. He leered. I ran. And ran. I fell off mountains, cliffs and off nothingness into nothingness. Screaming. My mom put a nice starched white flour sack curtain hung with tacks and a store string over the opening in the closet. She tucked me in at night and always said, "Good night, sleep tight. Don't let the bed bugs bite. And don't put the covers over your head. You need fresh air." I stayed mostly quiet about the nightmares. I prayed. And prayed. And prayed. It's only when I woke screaming that she knew. I guess she thought it was "normal." If I close my eyes even now, 60 years later, that scarred face is vivid. But the fear is gone. Understanding and love kill fear.

The Only Daughter. The Six Brothers

I had wonderful parents. Six brothers … three older and three younger. I remember listening carefully to the radio for one birth announcement. I ran out into the farm yard yelling, "We're gonna call him feather face." My older brother was chasing me yelling, "We are not! His name is Michael Paul." Another brother. Six. It was April 19, 1951. My identity partially formed from, "Oh. You're the ONLY girl. You must be soooooo… spoiled." When somebody cooed and made noises about how spoiled I was, I had thoughts. Dark Thoughts. Like, "How dumb are you?" I never voiced those thoughts. My mother would have been scandalized.

When Dad celebrated his 80th birthday in June 1988, the camera was snapping. Dad and six sons. I can still feel it. I stand there. Mute. Furious. Normal. In fact, smiling. I am 43 years old and still not able to tell anyone what I want or what I need. The words just won't form. Nor do *they* speak. Shouldn't they just KNOW? Sounds petty as hell. But it is the truth. Years later, after Dad is dead, Mom says, "Pearl, I'm sorting through pictures and I can't find one of you and your dad on his 80th birthday."

"That's because there isn't one, Mom."

She frowns. "Hmmm. I wonder why?"

"That's easy, Mom. The big news? The big claim to fame? It was always, 'Oh, my. You have six sons?' 'You have six brothers?' 'Your mom raised SIX sons?'"

I was very proud to have six brothers. Still am. But that June day I was seriously sad and upset. Invisible. I just plain felt invisible. I always felt invisible. Mostly by choice. I guess everyone was used to it. But that day, I was hurt. I look back and see that silent, locked-in, voiceless depressive.

"Why didn't you say something?" Mom was genuinely puzzled.

I sighed. "I just couldn't, Mom. I just couldn't. I kept just wishing someone would figure it out. They never did and now it's too late." I cried then.

My dad was and probably always will be pretty much the most important person in my world or out of it. I truly wish I had learned much earlier to open my mouth and speak.

The truth is, I was spoiled in many ways if that means loved beyond comprehension. Doted on for absolutely certain. For example, there was this billy goat. My older brothers bore the brunt of Billy's bunts. He bunted me only once, Jerry tells me. Then, no more billy goat. Mother knitted, sewed, embroidered and crocheted dresses when I was little and even when I was a teenager. Among all the chores of a rural, pioneer mother with seven kids, no electricity and no running water, she dressed her daughter whenever possible with handmade clothes. My girl cousins simply couldn't understand why when they wanted to play dolls I soon disappeared with the boys. Acceptance. Mom was very disappointed when, after five or six, I liked jeans and flannel shirts the best and wore them always, except for Sunday morning Mass when I sported dresses and a hat. Remember, up until 1962 and Vatican II, women and girls kept their heads covered in church. Oh yes, I was a good girl. Always.

In my teenage years, Bob took me anywhere and everywhere with him. He could always wheedle Mom into letting me go ... with him. When some guy in the community offered me a beer at a dance when I was 15? Bob fixed him with a glare, "She doesn't drink, jerk." End of that problem. I recall vividly one particular time I had asked 15 times to go home, but the guy didn't get it. Once finally home in the yard, car stopped, Dad sauntered out of the house. Came around to the young man's window. "It's Sunday," he said. "You will have my daughter home in time for 5:00 dinner. In fact, you will bring her home when she asks." With that, he sauntered back into the house. Simple.

I loved horses, learned to ride early. My dark bay gelding, Pauncho, was a gift from my parents on my 14th birthday. An uncle protested, "That horse is too wild for a girl." Dad laughed. On his next grain-hauling trip he bought me spurs. "Be sure he minds," he said.

The autumn I was 15, Mom bought me a gorgeous new winter coat. A young man, recently married to an older cousin, remarked, "It must be nice to be A.J. Kramps' daughter." It was. For sure. But that much male energy in a hopelessly patriarchal culture, in a hopelessly patriarchal church meant just one thing. Patriarchal by osmosis. Oh, my parents were partners. They talked often in the early morning and late at night. I could hear the murmurs and was always comforted by that low sound of chatter. I don't suppose the boys knew the conversations since they were all upstairs. My room was on the main floor. Unlike so many husbands, Dad was not, as I recall, a "control your wife" freak. But it was the '50s let's not forget. Mom was a deeply Catholic patriarchal wife and mother. She raised her kids, grew her garden, canned and cooked and worked very hard. She did all kinds of community work. And Dad? He was the Good Provider. They played their culturally defined roles very well. My point is, our home was my haven. But, the patriarchy reigned and....

I got my driver's licence on my 16th birthday. Apparently, that was a big thing. I never gave it a thought. I raced cars against my cousin Larry on a Sunday afternoon when we were in our teens. Beat him too.

"I'll tell your dad you were racing his car," he threatened.

"He won't believe you anyway," I taunted. I was my father's only daughter. Dad took my side on most matters.

I was a seriously outdoors girl. Tomboy. Funny how important that is to girls. It's a big compliment. The opposite label (of course there isn't one) not so good for boys. Never hear an admiring comment about boys being "just as good as the girls." Ha. I understand it now as my attempts to "fit" into the culture around me. To be "one of the boys." I see it all around me now as women side against women in their attempts not to be bullied and intimidated. To be on the winning side. It never works.

I went to St. Joseph's Business College. In the "big" cities, that would have gone unremarked. In pioneer Alberta, things were different. Some of my friends married without graduating high school. From age 18 to 24, I was asked every time I went home: "Are you married (pause) ... yet?"

A benefit of being part of the A.J. Kramps family was parental support for education. Mom was fond of telling me, "Educate a woman. Educate the world." She had wanted to become a teacher. In the 1930s the Depression intervened and she left school at 17, moving with her aging parents from the established community of Champion in southern Alberta to Cornwall Creek—a small tributary of the Big Smoky River—homestead country in the northwest part of Alberta, near what is now the City of Grande Prairie. People came from far and wide to the land made available by the government of the Dominion. $10 for a quarter section. All you had to do was "prove it up." In other words, cut the trees with an axe, pull out the stumps with a team of horses, break up the land with a plough and horses, and—well by now you get the picture. This was damn hard work for people close to 60 in 1933. Education? No. Food and shelter, yes.

You could say Mom was a lifelong learner. She educated herself. She was president of various organizations: The Catholic Women's League, The Women's Institute, the Home and School Association. She attended conferences in cities across Canada. She wrote letters to editors. Read whenever pioneer farm and family time allowed. She expressed her ideas. Mom was definitely supportive of my education ... within patriarchal guidelines, I understand now. The poster on the fridge in the 1970s proclaimed that woman was made from the rib of man so she could stand side by side, not be trampled underfoot. But she deferred to the priests and the Pope's word was law. In those days, women knew their place ... or so I have been told. Often.

My mother was somewhat conflicted by my choices as I strayed from classroom teaching into administration, consulting, and then my own small business. I did overhear her speaking with my niece Michele in the living room of our small farm home sometime in the '90s. It was impossible not to hear the chatter. Apparently, Bill has pretty much raised Rachel since I am "always working." I simmer in the kitchen. Wait for Michele's reply. "Grandma, don't worry. Auntie Pearl's kids are the most well-adjusted of all 27 of your grandkids." Vindicated. Still simmering.

By 1947 our family had moved a few miles east to the Clarkson Valley district. There was a great teacher shortage in the war years. And teacher training? Well, often there was none. Local housewives supervised correspondence. In the fall of 1955, because my brothers and I had not yet received a report card, Mom approached the teacher. "I'll see you after school," she was informed.

That evening, my parents visited my uncle who was on the local school board. My brother Eugene and cousin Loretta were sent to St. Joseph Catholic school in Grande Prairie. Luckily A.J. Kramps Trucking moved grain, cattle, pigs and other supplies several times every day. It was 100 miles round trip. Dad took them to school every Monday morning and home again for the weekend. Eugene tells me he set up a trapline in Bear Creek, which ran through the small town. We were not city children.

The only good part of Eugene being away in school in Grande Prairie was the horse and cutter in the winter. I became the driver. I was 11 years old and in Grade 6.

Of course, Mom thought it important that I learn domestic skills, like ironing and baking and.... One day, I am arguing with her over learning to bake bread. "No, Mom. I can read. If you can read, you can bake bread. I am going outside." Dad smiled. "Never mind. She'll know how to bake bread if she needs to." I went off to do whatever outside. And another time, I declare my freedom. "I am not washing, nor ironing any more of the boys' oil rig stuff. They can stop in Valleyview and do their oily clothes in the laundromat." Mom is aghast. But ... and Dad smiles again and says something like, "Of course they can. They're not helpless." Thank goodness, my declaration of independence stands. These are not the stories other women tell about their lives in big families in the '50s and '60s.

I didn't realize till many years later that, as a woman, I was actually considered inferior to the men. It was a sharp blow. I guess I was delusional. My dad's support was my most valuable asset in aid of my claims to independence throughout my professional life, my marriage and eventually from the dry, dusty, ritualized institutional rules that bound my beliefs.

I feel like Norah in Carol Shields' novel, *Unless*. A college dropout, Norah is sitting on a street corner, with a sign that says, GOODNESS. Norah was a good baby, a good student, a good daughter. Now, she sits on the street corner, with her cardboard sign. I just never had a sign, I guess. If you are a woman, you have committed the original sin of being born female. I worked very hard to be the patriarchal version of normal. I was not successful. I think I get high marks for effort anyway. When I finally figure out that my soul is not in favour of patriarchal normal? What then?

I will come to believe that much of the strength of the patriarchal code lies in its endorsement by one male god. Authority over woman is vested in man by this god. This "advantage" is difficult to overcome since fear of God inscribed in consciousness from birth will repress the impulse to revolt (Beauvoir, 1953). *The Second Sex* was written when I was eight years old. I read it in my 20s but it wasn't until midlife that I came to question the authority of the church. Scripture read from the pulpit and studied in my Baltimore Catechism did not provide for woman as the moral centre. Prior to Vatican II in 1962 scriptural interpretation was the province of the clergy and Catholic laity were "instructed" in Bible understanding. Even though our culture believes it is secular, patriarchal consciousness rests on deeply unconscious religious beliefs in a God made in man's own image, and woman as fatally flawed. The Judeo-Christian cosmology underlying the Western literary canon and Western civilization sees Eve as responsible for the downfall of mankind—a flawed moral centre. Just before she dropped out of university, Norah was reading and discussing Flaubert's *Madame Bovary,* who was forced to surrender her place as the moral centre of the novel. Reading *Unless,* I was Norah. My 15-year-old developing female body brought dawning consciousness of the fatal flaw of being woman. This is the mythology of Eve in the literary consciousness of the Western canon. I have come to believe that Eve's "sin" was becoming conscious. The apple is symbolic of knowledge. Eve recognized her knowing. She was expelled from Paradise. Excommunicated priest, Matthew Fox,[6] proposes that Eve's consciousness of the wonders of creation is

---

[6] Matthew Fox, *Original Blessing: A Primer in Creation Spirituality* (Santa Fe, NM: Bear and Co., 1983).

the Original Blessing. For years I unknowingly participated fully in my birthright of the silence imposed on women since that creation myth was literalized as the downfall of *man*kind.

It will take years for me to recognize how few myths, religions and legends capture authentic female experience. How many of women's ancient sacred images have been demoted to the status of evil? Thus as a woman I am in a double bind, "no longer the complete image of any recognized god and powerless as the subject of one who finds her inferior."[7] And emotion. Oh my goddess. How has it come to be that Western Christianity views emotion as symptomatic of the failings and moral evil of woman? Seemingly no amount of neuropsychology or neuroscience has excavated the unconscious wellsprings of that belief.

When I discover all these self-defeating, unconscious attitudes rooted in my beliefs, as I inevitably do, where will I find the solace or sustenance that my Catholicism provided through years and years? I do not yet know.

I have been accused of making my own religion. Of picking and choosing from a menu of spirituality. I agree. I am guilty. Further, I intend to continue to choose even though the choices sometimes bring deep fear of the outcomes. I recognize that making these choices is inherently "unfeminine" as defined in classical philosophy. This is the Hobson's choice that is no choice at all. To exercise choice, to be active, to be the causal agent in my own life is culturally conditioned as unfeminine. How has it come to be that to think like a woman is to not think at all? This is my dilemma. I am working to become more and more conscious of the Garden of Eden and I hear a Talking Snake.

But I am way ahead of my story.

---

7   Noddings, *Women and Evil* (Berkeley, CA: University of California Press, 1989), 64.

I Am My Father's Daughter[8]

Bill and I met in the post office in Consort, Alberta, March 28, 1969. We were engaged a few weeks later and the first trip home to introduce him to my family was instructive.

"Who'll be there?"

"Well, I'm not sure. Probably just Mom and Dad until maybe Easter Sunday."

We arrived at my home to An Occasion. Good Friday lunch. Fresh local fish of course. As Mom says the blessing, I can see the furtive glances and the silent questions. No, Bill does not make the sign of the cross. He is not Catholic. Vatican II had removed the rules around marrying non-Catholics but definitely not the family stigma.

The following morning, as I leave my bedroom, I hear Mom and Dad talking quietly in the kitchen. "He's not Catholic, Tony."

"You better get used to it," Dad said. "She's going to marry this one."

Bill and I married at St. Joseph Cathedral in Grande Prairie, Alberta, August 23, 1969. We were as different as chalk and cheese. Bill was to become my best and loudest cheerleader. Ever. Quick to anger. Quick to smile. Quick to try anything to support me. I guess he had no idea what a mess I really was.

My dad was more philosophical than Mom when it came to religion. Mom was staunch on the rules. Several things stand out in my mind.

I'm seven or so. My three younger brothers and I together with Mom and Dad are in the cab of the truck. The three older boys in the grain box. We are headed to Sunday morning Mass on a beautiful sunny morning in late June. In my memory I hear singing, "Oh what a beautiful morning. Oh, what a beautiful day" as we drive north to the highway; Jack Clegg is out cutting hay. "How come Uncle Jack doesn't have to go to church?" I

---

[8]   Marion Woodman, *Leaving My Father's House* (London: Rider, 1993).

ask. There is a long pause as Dad considers this. Finally, he says very slowly, "Well, Blink, for all we know, he might be praying up and down every row. And, you know, he is in the biggest church there is."

Another time: "Don't confuse God with the church." Dad was fond of that idea. And yet, when I was at home for the entire winter of 1962–63 and read the Bible through a couple of times, he asked quietly, "Do you think you should be reading that? You know, most people don't really understand it. People make a lot of mistakes based on misreading." Remember that when my parents were growing up, and indeed until after 1962, Catholics were discouraged from reading the Bible. That was the role of the Official Church.

And, in the summer of 1991 when I was visiting at home for a few days with the kids, I left my book on the kitchen table overnight. In the morning, Dad was reading it. He looked puzzled, and asked, "Do you think you should be reading this?" It was Peter De Rosa, *Vicars of Christ: The Dark Side of the Papacy.*

That was the summer of deepening religious questions and discontent. The perfect world, that mythical construction of the perfect family, in the perfect place, with only me as the fatal flaw, began to unravel.

According to De Rosa, the Pope was declared infallible in 1871. I was stunned. Seriously? That's like only 100 years ago. Well, 120. What the hell was he before 1871? That doesn't square with the childhood teaching from … well, not what I thought anyway.

In that moment, reading history, my ever-searching mind threw out massive questions. Another chink, another chunk goes sliding off the belief glacier. Melting. Removed. The tribal beliefs in the church rules were coming undone. 1871. That's when German unification was happening. Studying European History in Grande Prairie Junior College with Miss Hutton in 1966. The Declaration of Infallibility is really a declaration of power of the church in the face of growing nationalism and the Nation State. How could I be so dumb? Damn. Betrayed. Again.

I had not yet discovered the power of myth and mythology. It would take maybe 30 years but deep unconscious beliefs would surface, be cremated and grow again differently. Wider. Deeper. Different. I'd discover inside myself some of the truths the church has enshrined in its liturgy but has forgotten in its life. I'd discover my inner world ... through eons of time.

My early school years were in a log school, via horseback, walking or driving the horse and cutter in winter. We were a pioneer community. Grade 1, I recall like yesterday. I had a ketchup bottle of milk in my lunch. I rode on old Dais behind my brother Bob. In a couple of months, or maybe weeks, the teacher invited this Great Big Man to come to talk to me. He sat on his haunches beside my desk. Placing a green text in front of me, he said, "Can you read this?" I did. "And this?" I did.

Unknown to me, the teacher sent a note home with Bob. The next day, I joined my cousin Larry and his friend, Dale in Grade 2. I don't remember it being a big deal. Larry tells a different tale. "Boy," he said, laughing as we danced together at his 50th wedding anniversary in September 2015, "were Dale and I mad. We figured it just wasn't fair. You were younger than us ... how did you get to just go to Grade 2?" Mostly school was uneventful. I did well. Every report card said the same thing. "Elaine needs to ask questions. She is very quiet."

In Grade 6 it became, "Pearl needs to ask questions. She is very quiet."

What's in a Name?

How did I come to be Pearl? So the story goes, my dad wanted to call me Pearl. Close your eyes. Imagine. It's 1945. It's Crooked Creek, Alberta, one general store, a church and a school. The three sons are 7, 6 and 4. After a difficult pregnancy and having to stay in Grande Prairie some 50 miles from home for 10 days due to spring thaw and complications, my mom finally has a daughter. Elaine? Well, knowing Mom that probably had some literary significance but she never said. Dad, he insisted on Pearl. My godmother Cecilia, my dad's younger, much beloved sister, had more energy than a squirrel and a killer smile. So, I was baptized Elaine Pearl Cecilia and all went just fine. But. Life happens.

Fall 1955. Clarkson Valley School, a little log school about two miles east of home. What are the chances that among the 19 students in spring and fall and 26 in winter when Moon's Mill was in operation, there would be two girls named Elaine? Our community was very small and 250 miles from Edmonton. Teachers were hard to come by. My favourite and BEST teacher ever had left to have a baby. The new teacher spent hours after school picking daisies in the ditches. She constantly mixed me up with my older classmate, Elaine. Her solution? Just call me Pearl. It stuck. After 10 years of being Elaine, I was now Pearl. My classmates made the change easily, as children do. And 15 years later, on my wedding day, my Aunt Anne whispers in my ear, "You will always be Elaine to me." Now, in the midst of inner healing and discovering my soul, I am searching for Pearl.

I could easily have written a memoir called *Quiet*. I will say, however, that now I've reached cronedom, I have learned to speak and to speak up.

As adolescence arrived and took hold, life took a very nasty shift. Strange things began to happen. I spent years hanging on through ugly black days and crazy nightmare nights. My first memories of what came to be diagnosed as "clinical depression" are of the spring of 1960. I miss a full week of school including all the Grade 11 midterm exams. Doesn't matter. Teachers give me my regular term marks. Principal says it is fine. I stay at home, in bed, head under covers. I do remember the iron tonic I was given by the good doctor. Maybe it helped.

Grade 12 was available in Ridgevalley but I wanted to go to Calgary to a private girls' school instead. I asked Mom about it in the '90s as I worked to understand and heal my broken parts.

She thought about it a long time. Finally, she said, "Well, I am not sure, Pearl. You wrote to St. Mary's. You were accepted. You told us you wanted to study piano and voice. Your dad was all in favour of that idea. I suppose too we entertained hope that you might someday decide to follow your aunts, Sister Mary Vincent and Sister Charlotte."

My mom died April 9, 2001. Among her family memorabilia was every letter I wrote home from the private Catholic girls' school in Midnapore, Alberta. Slowly, over the next five years, I went through boxes of memorabilia, letters home from Calgary, Consort, Grande Cache, Edmonton, Leduc and New Sarepta. I owe my mom the biggest debt of gratitude ever.

September 5, 1961, I left home with my brother Jerry and his wife Shirley and baby James to attend Grade 12 in Midnapore, Calgary. I "remember" the exact circumstances because of the pictures in the album. Shirley, James, Cherry, Roberta and I are sitting on my bed and the white suitcase is open.

I don't remember arriving in Calgary that Labour Day evening, 1961. I have no memory whatsoever of my brief time at St. Mary's. In my mind, or maybe it's a nightmare, I am running. And running. I leap over a black wrought-iron fence that surrounds the grounds. Fleeing.

I have Midnapore memories of fear, blackness, fainting, studying and remembering nothing. Avoiding with terror new student initiation. Praying in the grotto, the one place I felt peace. More fear.

I left the girls' school September 28. I arrived via the Greyhound bus at our road end early in the morning. I left my suitcase in the ditch and walked home. I immediately put on my farm clothes and went to the barn and cleaned calf pens. My mother looked very small and unwell. I do not recollect my parents or brothers questioning what was going on. I only remember support and a lot of silence.

In late October, I got on the school bus and returned to the local high school for one fearful and anxiety-ridden day when the walls closed in on me all class, in the hallway and in the gym.

I refused to go back. There was one pretty funny incident. On the bus ride home, a little neighbour girl asked, "What did you do with your baby?"

"I left him in Edmonton," I say.

Well. There. Problem of my three-week absence from Ridgevalley High School solved. Ha. Years later, Mom asked, "Do you think that she ever figured out you did not have a child that fall?"

"Well," I said, "not unless you told her." We laughed. I did leave a child behind all those years ago. Myself. My voice. My music.

I helped a bit with the preparations for my parents' 25th anniversary party November 18, 1961. Mostly though, I slept. The doctors could find nothing physically wrong with me although there were a lot of tonics and discussions of menstrual problems. I menstruated later than my friends and suffered terrible pain each month, a problem later "solved" at the age of 19 or 20 with birth control pills that made me gain 25 pounds. I quit the pills and put up with the pain. The weight disappeared. That became a pattern over the years. Pain, pills, less pain, another problem, pills, less pain, no pills.

After the anniversary celebrations I returned to Calgary with Jerry and Shirley and worked for the month of December in Woodward's toy department. Back at home for Christmas and throughout the rest of the winter I'd get up after my brothers left for school, have hot chocolate and sometimes toast for breakfast, play the piano, sleep some more, tomato soup for lunch, sleep some more and play the piano. I remember Dad asking me most mornings if I wanted anything from the store. "Peppermints," each time he asked. I lived on tomato soup and peppermints. I always set the table for dinner. This "ritual" was important. It represented some major stability. I know I completed a Biology 32 course by correspondence somewhere in there. As I said earlier, I also read the Bible twice but I am not sure what it meant to me. I was simply exhausted all the time. Now I seriously wonder how my parents managed to cope with a 16-year-old daughter, who seemingly had nothing wrong with her, sleeping her way through that fall and winter. I did go to dances some weekends. A friend to whom I tell this story, my most long-time, childhood, forever friend, is shocked. "No," she says. "No." But she does remember one thing. "Do you remember fainting on the dance floor? We used to pick you up and take you home. Now I wonder why we never asked any questions."

When I return to school to complete Grade 12 in September 1962, I survive on Tranxene, Valium. I have only two memories of that year. I'm leaving the gymnasium after my last exam, thinking suddenly, "What exam did I just write?" I can't remember. Second, I refuse to attend my graduation unless I can invite my family of brothers, wives and single brothers. The vice-principal refuses. Soon after that conversation, the principal came to see me. "You never say much, Pearl, and now Mr. Military tells me you will not be attending your own graduation. Would you tell me why?" I explain. "We are a class of six Grade 12 students. Inviting only our parents and one guest? Ridiculous." He agrees. My family goes. It is the first of many stands I will take in my lifetime. I find it intriguing that I have been called upon to take so many stands and viewed by some in the heavily patriarchal male administration establishment of schools and school districts to be incorrigible and stubborn. I prefer to think I learned to simply take a stand on issues that mattered. And, taking a stand, finally, in the life of a depressive? Imperative. Stubbornness is mandatory. I learned it from my six brothers. Seriously? No. In truth, the feminine is strong enough to take a position. It is only the transmogrification of the courageous feminine by the patriarchy that creates the false self that believes it needs manly protection.

I have much to thank my family for. My parents had endless patience. In public, I am quiet, determined and successful. I sing in the small Catholic church on Sunday morning. I pray novenas to St. Theresa the Little Flower. I read. And I do reasonably well in high school and am encouraged by teachers to become a teacher; I graduate with no plans whatsoever. Now, when I go through memorabilia, I find letters to the airlines about being a stewardess. I took no initiative. Thankfully, Mom had some ideas. She suggested business college and so in September 1963 I enrolled in St. Joseph's and lived with my brother Jerry, his wife and two young sons. I walk to college. I play the piano at the college hour after hour. Dad picks me up in front of St. Joseph's College with the grain truck to take me home on weekends. I remember a blue ski jacket and stretch pants. I remember the assassination of John F. Kennedy. I remember with affection the kindly Sister Edwards, Superior.

I do exceptionally well. After graduation, I go work in a large Edmonton law firm for about six months and I get one of the best pieces of life advice from my first boss, Ms. Margaret Lyne, the only female member of the very large law firm. When she requests a raise for me at the end of six months, the boss says, "No. She is too young to earn that kind of money." In breaking this news to me, Miss Lyne says, "Pearl, get out of here. Go to university or else you will work for—holes like this for the rest of your life." When he refused my direct request saying, "You will never get $235.00 per month anywhere," I quit. Went to Calgary, found a job in another law firm … for $235.00 a month. It was the winter of 1965.

These small acts of decisiveness, triggered by overbearing male attempts at unwarranted authoritarianism, would form a pattern over many years. My inner rebel didn't surface often, but when she did, the results were instantaneous. Decisions seem "guided." Each stand pushed me inexorably toward the healing years. When I finally understood the world of my own ...tions, my self-loathing, my relationships with male bosses improved immeasurably. I could say no, and eventually I worked with several very fine men. The operative word? Worked with. Not for. I had learned that focus was necessary. I had learned, from my mother, that the gift of my life, my talents, is the gift of love I must give to others. Love is not gushy, sentimental caring. Love means saying no. Firmly.

Pearl displays
Doug should
too!

this

In June '65, a phone call from Jerry prompts me to go to the offices of GMAC (General Motors Acceptance Corporation) in Calgary and apply for a job in Grande Prairie. "It pays well, and Dad wants you closer to home." So, I apply. By July I have completed a week-long orientation in Edmonton then flown to Grande Prairie to start a new job at excellent pay. I take my beautiful black Standardbred mare to board in Grande Prairie, the accordion Dad bought for me at a pawn shop in Edmonton and in the spring of 1966 buy myself a 1962 red and white two-door hardtop Pontiac. My landlady and friend Joey says, "I so envied you. You were the picture of the successful career girl." Life is grand … except it wasn't.

I was fainting again. Just blacking out. In the most infamous incident, I fainted as I stepped out of the bathroom in our rented suite. There was about a two-inch step down and I fell forward onto a bare cement floor and landed full face. I came to, bleeding and scared. I went to doctors. "There is nothing physically wrong with you." And finally, a psychologist. In a fight with my roommate, she screamed at me, "You are the crazy one. Who else sees a psychologist?" My fears of being crazy are now voiced out loud.

The psychologist did what they did back in 1966. "Your tests show high intelligence. I recommend you quit your job and go to university. And you are afraid to leave your father." He may have told me much more than that. Memories are notoriously bizarre and often untrue. In any case, I do recall clearly wondering why anyone wanted to be smart and I knew most surely that I wasn't nor did I want to be. And what the hell did he mean by fear of leaving my father? I would learn why I drove my mother crazy all the years I was growing up: "Where's Daddy? When will Daddy be home? Why isn't Daddy here yet?" A watch didn't keep any better time than my dad. He was NEVER late. Only in the mind of a small, scared girl child who needed her protector every moment, just in case.

Finally, after multiple years of hints from parents, teachers, bosses and now doctors, I went to the newly opened Grande

Prairie Junior College that fall to begin an Arts degree. The fear, insomnia, blackouts, migraines and general malaise continue. Some days tolerable. Other days a major struggle to force myself to walk up the steps of the old brick building where the college was housed that first year. Fear of failure. I am nowhere near as well read as the students from the Grande Prairie high schools. I feel completely inadequate and very stupid. The psychologist attempts to hypnotize me and take me back to the source of my issues. "You have to be open to this," he says. "No one can help you when you resist." I didn't think I did; but I resisted. I was older than nearly all the students. I lived with a young couple and their two-year-old. The young wife encouraged me day in and day out. She had not had the opportunity to pursue even high school so to her college was huge. I prayed dozens and dozens of novenas to St. Theresa of the Little Flower. One rosary after the next. I was on some kind of medication for anxiety. Getting up in the morning was problematic and going to sleep at night even worse.

The pattern continued throughout my second year of university in Edmonton, where a two-year education program would allow me to teach all but Grade 12. My teaching career began in Consort Junior Senior High School. I was an intern teacher at $21.00 a day in May, 1968, paid less than in the job I had left two years earlier at GMAC. By sometime that fall I was deep in trouble again. The local doctor prescribed a new medication to stop the migraines after I missed a week of teaching. Insomnia plagued me continuously. The druggist said, "Wow. You won't wake up for 24 hours if you take this." I was awake the next morning at 5:00 a.m.

And so it went. Through marriage, birth of children, finishing my degrees. Teaching at New Sarepta. Sometime in 1978, when I was exhausted and unable physically to get out of bed one morning, Bill phoned the school to say I would not be in. "Sorry, my wife says she doesn't even have lesson plans today." The secretary convinced Bill to take me to see a kinesiologist. "Just pick her up and put her in the car if she says no."

By that time, I wanted nothing whatsoever to do with one more doctor. One more well-meaning person with The Answer. One more piece of good advice? One more treatment? One more pill? Stuff it.

Log schoolhouse I attended in Clarkson Valley, Alberta, Grades 1 through 6.

Image © Lavinia Scott, used with permission.

Chapter Three

Cracks in the Granite

One does not become enlightened by imagining figures of light, but by making the darkness conscious.

–Carl Jung

The One-Day Journal April 1986

Somewhere I found the courage to put some of the pain in writing. Not much. Can't admit to much. Life must be fine. I was fine. In a loose-leaf notebook along with job and grocery lists, I wrote simply, "Have just come through another very dark, black period. Severe depression. I have decided to write daily so I can gauge my moods. The world looks lovely again. Dr. S. has changed my medication and the fog has lifted. I have been in school every day. My body moves without severe pain…. I can look back and laugh at myself. So often I feel like driving across the lane in front of a semi. Today I don't."

There are no more entries in that notebook.

Descent into the Darkness

By the summer of 1988, I was too desperate to care where, how, or in what way I could end these depressions. I was exhausted from the never-ending, pounding, pulsating treadmill of gut-wrenching free-floating fear. Tired of nausea, migraines, insomnia, bouts with colitis, loss of balance, fear of failing, nightmares, anxiety, tension and inner self-abuse tapes. And now, with my children growing up, guilt. Guilt that somehow I may be teaching them fear and low self-image. I thought vaguely about the "sins of the father." I received an unrecognized but great gift that summer in the guise of a new job. And I began keeping a Journal For Real. Not just a promise. Not just an idea. Not saccharine sweet. Not just one entry. An actual, written record.

July 8, 1988. I return to my school office to tidy up the remaining details of the budget among other things. There's a large manila envelope with my name scrawled in capital letters across it. It's an advertisement for a consulting position with Alberta Education. I phone Bill. "Go for it," he says. I start praying.

I was called to an interview. I sat in the waiting room of a large downtown office, claiming love and light. Over and over. My mantra. Bill had driven me into the city since the downtown scared the hell out of me. I was perspiring. Shaking. How could I possibly believe I was qualified to do this job? What if I failed? I hate failure.

The next day, the Director of Regional Services called. He offered me a choice of either language arts or social studies consulting positions. It would be a long time before I understood Jung's concept of synchronicity. I began work there in September. Throughout the next year, I was sometimes out of town staying in hotels in places like Whitecourt, Fort McMurray and Lac La Biche, Alberta. Long evenings alone in a hotel room meant the great gift of time for writing, meditating, reading.

Based on the *Being a Christ!: Inner Sensitivity (Intuitional) Training Course* and *The Science of Mind*,[9] I had a long list of exhortations. I am love. I am light. I am…. In my master's degree (1984), I had used the work of Erich Fromm's *To Have or to Be?*[10] to analyse the Grade 9 social studies curriculum. I swear that book started something moving in me. And I was familiar with the I AM of the Bible. Endlessly, I repeated mantras of love … of self. Surrender. Clarity.

I had moments of peace and joy that first summer. I learned Benedictine meditation from books by John Main. Following the instructions, I wrote, prayed and cried. Oh yes, of course. I kept my family looked after because that's what I did. Always. I realize now, the lessons of the patriarchy about the role of mothers are a two-edged sword.

Every new religious, spiritual, or mystical idea, anything unfamiliar frightened me. I searched endlessly through Catholic theology to find sources that either supported or negated meditation. Neither my childhood Catholic catechism nor the Sunday homily mentioned meditation. But I had read the mystics and been entranced with the Seers of Fatima. I began to glimpse that orthodoxy would not serve.

Peace never stayed for long. Sometime that August Bill and I took our small holiday trailer to Gull Lake for the weekend. I descended into a deep depression. Again. I wrote. I meditated. I cried. I felt on the edge of nothingness. Struggle. Hopelessness. The hiding is part of the shame of depression. I had a lovely husband, great kids, a farm home, an interesting new job … and on and on went the tape.

---

[9] Ann P. Meyer and Peter V. Meyer, *Being a Christ!: Inner Sensitivity (Intuitional) Training Course* (San Diego, CA: Dawning Publications, 1983); Kenneth A. Klivington, Floyd E. Bloom et al., *The Science of Mind* (Cambridge, MA: MIT Press, 1989).

[10] Eric Fromm, *To Have or to Be?* (NY: Harper and Row, 1976).

Soon after returning home from the lake, I become physically ill. Diarrhea. Intense sweating. Wave after wave of contorted convulsive twisting in my gut. I threw up endlessly. Sat on the toilet. Finally, on Sunday morning Bill just flatly stated, "Get in the car. I'll help you. What do you need to take? We are going to the hospital." I objected. No. More. Doctors. Bill insisted. We compromised on a Mediclinic. There the doctors sent us straight to the hospital. I was dehydrated and bleeding from the bowel. I returned home five days later, weak, feeling sorry for myself and unable to regain my strength. The doctors said food poisoning. I knew that was impossible since all five of us had eaten the same food. But doctors don't understand depression. I didn't understand the potential outcome of hours of meditation. In the summer of 1991, I would spend two weeks in a Dreamwork Intensive with Father John Rich and Sister Sylvia at Maryknoll Center in New York, where I'd learn about the work of transpersonal psychologist, Roberto Assagioli. When I shared my hospital story with Sister Sylvia, she smiled. "Holy shit," she exclaimed. That is a story for later.

While in the hospital, I read a series of books entitled *Life and Teaching of the Masters of the Far East*.[11] I repeated my long list of affirmations silently hour after hour.

Always a reader, I became even further addicted. I began asking Spirit to give me the name of my special Christ Self that I might know my Inner Christ. One Saturday I tidied the house while asking, "Spirit, give me the name of my Christ Self." As I stood combing my hair and looking in the mirror, the name Aaron came into my head. I assumed I was thinking about our daughter's friend Erin, but suddenly, the name was spelled clearly within me

… A A R O N, and then a voice said, "Read Mathew 13–23." I rushed for my Bible. There I rediscovered all the miracles of

---

[11]   Baird T. Spalding, *Life and Teaching of the Masters of the Far East* (Camarillo, California: DeVorss & Company,1996).

Jesus. I felt an immense rush of energy and joy. It is very strange. I read about miracles endlessly in childhood. Was mesmerized in adulthood and thought I believed. But apparently, only in history. The modern church relies much more on the intellect ... as befits rational Enlightened Man. Bah.

I have pages filled with Bible quotes. Those words guided me in the direction I needed to go. I now understand that is how the unconscious works. It isn't magic. It is intuition. It isn't evil. It is Self leading self and Self speaking to self using my own thoughts. I followed the exhortation of Exodus: *Write this down in a document as something to be remembered.* Exodus 17:14. I entered the eye of the storm.

This book would be based on one big lie if I ignored the actual words I wrote during those days of August, 1989. I was scared stiff. I was Roman Catholic by DNA. Back 700 or 800 years give or take a few. And channelling? Well, apparently the New Age teachings are evil. So said the *Western Catholic Reporter.* Maybe not quite so directly, but my family were concerned. Sometimes I appreciated their concern. Mostly I did not. I was furious. What I need here, folks, is help. Yup. I know, I can't say that. Who in our family says, Help! Oh sure. We help. We are a close family. Except when it comes to emotions and then we are useless. We hide. I was afraid of condemnation if my family knew, really knew, my level of involvement in this new Inner Christ group stuff. That group did not meet in the church. Indeed, were probably not welcome in the church. So, after years of illness, exhaustion, psychologists, education and psychiatrists, I imagined they just figured that I had finally flipped. Totally. "You are so logical, Pearl. You are sooo... good at what you do. Just amazing." Yup. Except I am a wreck. All my life people have come to me. Continually told me I am competent, intelligent, skilled. Always I have cried in silent anguish. If they only knew.

My parents had tried to instil confidence in me. "There's room on this side and there's room on this side" Dad would say as his hands swept back first to the left and then to the right. "If they don't like what they see, they can look alongside me."

Or, "Everybody puts their pants on one leg at a time." And Mom, "Do your best; angels could do no better." But words don't always work. Children learn their own story. I was afraid to go to university, because I was too stupid. I went. I went teaching. I loved it. I thought, well, you have to be smart to get a degree. Then, I got a degree. Then, you had to be really smart to get a master's degree. I got that too. Unwittingly, I subscribed to the "feel the fear and do it anyway" philosophy. Because the alternatives were horrible. Unknown to anyone, I think, I often vomited before I went out of the house to face the day.

I was pregnant with our daughter in 1979. The doctor told me, "You can't handle another child. You need to stay at home and rest. You should not be working. Two children are enough." He knew nothing of our family circumstances. I knew I had to be mentally occupied. Teaching engaged my intellect. Probably the last straw for me then was, "You are too old to have this child. You should have an abortion."

I was 34. I left his office. I railed silently against the stupidity of the medical establishment. I didn't mention the doctor's advice to Bill. I didn't talk depression. I found a new doctor and I learned even more ways to hide the pain. If there are no reasonable answers and solutions to reasonable questions, then shut the hell up.

Now, it's a beautiful morning in August 1988. Our daughter, Rachel, meaning Lamb of God, and Cara-Lynn after my mother, is with me. Mom has come for a visit and is on her way to a Catholic Women's League Convention in Winnipeg, Manitoba. I am unable to explain my channelling, meditation and changing spirituality in any meaningful kind of way. Before going outside on the front step with my morning coffee for my usual cigarette, I explain flatly, "I am going outside to heal my neck and improve my energy level."

I sit down on the crumbling cement steps at the front door. Close my eyes and pray silently. Perfection everywhere now. I ask my Christ Self, Aaron, for assistance. I meditate.

Then, the ineffable. A strange blue light pervades my whole being. My body is lifted. I open my eyes to see unimaginable brilliant beautiful blue/white transparent light flood the yard and fill the mugo pine. Deep. Transcendence. Enveloped. My physical body vibrates and vibrates and ... I am alive. I have no rational explanation for this. It is simply my experience. I am filled. Up. Full. I fly back into the house to undertake what before seemed like endless tasks. Vacuum. Laundry. Cook. Clean. Garden. Mom looks puzzled. She says nothing.

There was happiness and goodness in my life during those many years. I know because I have it written down. August 23, 1988, we celebrate our 19th wedding anniversary. The kids insist that Dad and Mom will go golfing. In hat, golf shorts and T-shirt, all duded up, Bill is an extremely handsome man. That day stands out in my mind because his smile tells the story. The Countryside golf course is beautiful. Jason and Rachel try to teach Dad to hit the little white ball. They laugh and Bill plays it all up as usual. Jason makes us a chocolate Happy Anniversary cake. Colin is on his way home from Switzerland. He arrives safely.

That fall I continue to participate in meditation, reading the mystics, and *Indwelling Presence*,[12] careful to include "appropriate" books that fit with my new-found learning. By appropriate, I mean those with the stamp of imprimatur, the Official Licence of the Roman Catholic Church giving authority that a book or other work is acceptable. I colour within the lines. I play inside the boundaries.

Mass is deeply meaningful; the Eucharist feeds my soul as it always has. The music lifts me up and I sing songs of childhood to the weeds as I go up and down every garden row. I sang in the Choir at Holy Rosary Church throughout my growing up years. I sang at St. Anthony's on Whyte Avenue, in St. Michael's in Leduc. Music soothes my soul; it always has.

---

[12] George Maloney, *Indwelling Presence* (Locust Valley, N.Y., LIving Flame Publisher, 1985).

I am reading *The Science of Mind*. I am well aware it does not bear the imprimatur. I write about forgiveness. I read Father George Maloney, S.J., which does bear the Stamp. And my life is filled with small miracles. I read *Life and Teaching of the Masters of the Far East*. Again. My journal contains long quotes from these books. I meditate on the writings. A Christ is here. A Great Light. On September 21, 1988 at 2:20 a.m. I record amazingly beautiful insights and love energy pours through my very being. After pages of love pour forth, I write, "Jesus, I have a terrible fear of others knowing and understanding my actions. Everyone will be sure I have flipped. The world does not believe God speaks to ordinary people. Just saints. Important people. The world decries spirituality. I am afraid. Heal my fear."

Often fear has overwhelmed me in the past. Tranquilizers just to get through a Sunday afternoon gymkhana. This fear is deeper.

Meditation on a Pinprick

I learn about the chakras and reiki and ancient Chinese medicine. I am deeply lifted and deeply afraid. And the spinning wheel spins. As I try to sleep, I imagine I am facing a wall of darkness. A crack, a tiny pinprick of light pierces the darkness. I try so very hard to see, to know, to understand what is behind those dark walls. I focus on the pinprick. I will go over, under, through that wall. I cannot go on. I have journeyed along this black wall which cuts me off from life. I know if I open this wall, open this door, a more tolerable life will emerge.

I write healing mantras until one day, in my new-found fleeting joy, I show Mom. She says she is "not sure." The Ferris wheel spins wildly. Flips me off.

My mother? Who taught me though childhood to believe in the miracles and the life of Jesus, is unsure. My mom. Who I called from the hospital when the doctors said Colin, then age five, had Perthes Disease like his dad and grandfather, and to whom I said, "Mom, pray." She prayed. Colin left that hospital 10 days later and never ever manifested anything more than 1% loss of rotation in his hip. He skated with The Oilers and I have the newspaper headline, "Oilers rookie scores three." My mom, when my brother Eugene had osteomyelitis as a young boy, prayed and attributed healing, in the days before penicillin, to Brother Andre and the Holy Oil she ordered via the newspaper from the Abbey in Montreal. My mom, whom I heard pray for miracles from Saint Dymphna, patron saint of mental illness, was unsure.

I pretend I am sure. Is there a word stronger than fear?

I meditate in the night. In the morning. While I drive. I listen to music. I pray. Monotonously. Endlessly. I surrender. I imagine a wall. A crack. Behind the cracked wall are the answers I seek. I affirm faith.

December 8, 1988 in evening group meditation I am moved to listen. I have come to call these interior conversations *Promptings.*

Yield your heart to me. You are chosen to use the gift of healing. Come to me with gentleness and love and I will strengthen you. My arms are open wide. Enter into my heart. Use your gifts. Your family awaits this gift of God. Your brothers and sisters are open to receive the gifts of the Holy Spirit. Yield in joy and love for I AM is with you. Ask and you shall receive. Yield to the Spirit within. Share your love. That is all.

Days later I ask again in my journal, "Jesus, why is it so hard for me to believe?"

Earlier that fall, I had been warned by a sister-in-law, Beware of False Prophets. The fear deepened. I read the Bible only to discover that "You will know them by their fruits." So, I wasn't bloody well hurting anyone. I gave myself inner permission to continue.

Chapter Four

The Endurance Run is Ending

*Writing gave me a feeling of control over time and space,
and a faith that I would recover.*

–Laurel Richardson,
"Getting Personal: Writing Stories"

Sometime in all of this turmoil, a box of books arrived in the mail from another sister-in-law. She and my brother were worried. I was participating in all kinds of alternative therapies, religions and groups. In that box of books, was the ONE that would provide me with the beginning tools to heal my depressions. I have given copies of *Dreams and Spiritual Growth: A Christian Way of Dreamwork*[13] away over the years but I continue to keep the original because it is a literary anthropological dig into my psyche. The book makes what I am doing clear—it is written for

---

[13] Louise M. Savary, Patricia H. Berne and Strephon Kaplan Williams, *Dreams and Spiritual Growth: A Judeo-Christian Way of Dreamwork* (Mahwah, New Jersey: Paulist Press, 1984).

everyone in search of an understanding of themselves. Learning to love and accept who you really are is difficult work. I came to understand it as a task for midlife. In Jungian terms, a neurosis is an unsuccessfully resolved conflict with roots in childhood. More importantly, if not resolved it is represented in the current life situation. From Jung's point of view, neurosis ALWAYS provides the opportunity for individuation, for becoming whole. I intended to take that opportunity. Did I have a choice?

The book said I could ask for a dream. I did, and it worked. Subsequently, I would learn to write the dream in present tense, immediately upon waking. I learned to give my dreams a title and include some context in my journal so I would remember what was happening in my daylight consciousness as well as my night-time consciousness. Then, in my reading, I began to find symbols and connections in the strangest places. Synchronicity indeed. The universe works in mysterious ways. Those books were Catholic to the core. Remember, according to some, Catholics are NOT Christian. In my first 43 years I had had endless paralyzing nightmares. But I followed instructions and asked for a dream. A dream came. It's still coming. Transformation continues forever. I had a lot of inner beliefs to dissolve. But my new self was conceived in that dream.

The Landing, December 11, 1988

I am in an elevator in the Harley Court building where my office is on the seventh floor. There are several other people, mostly women, with me but I do not recognize any of them. The door closes and the elevator begins to fall. It falls and falls endlessly and everyone begins to scream and yell in panic. Silently I pray over and over, "Jesus, make it safe," while out loud I repeatedly assure the others that everything will be fine. After what seems like hours, the elevator gently lands. The landing is the clearest aspect of the dream. Ever gentle, softly the elevator came to a halt bouncing like a child in huge feather pillows or lamb's wool.

I understand nothing of dreams. Nothing. I have been talking with Verna of taking a "leap of faith" and buying a computer. My world experience tells me I am being illogical and selfish. Bill and I are flat broke, have an operating loan, a mortgage on both the farm and the house in town. Every month we juggle in order to cover expenses. However, this is something I must do and I must trust in Infinite Abundance. The dream feels symbolic of "leaping" off a cliff but landing safely in something soft like lamb's wool. Jesus is the Lamb of God. Lamb of God, Have Mercy on me, repeated every Eucharistic celebration for 43 years.

I am once more filled with energy and new hope. But it doesn't last. There again recorded is the truth of it. The numbing fear returns. My body screams in pain. I want to kick and break things.

I am very glad to find Father Joe Killoran's address through an article in the *Western Catholic Reporter*. He gave Bill instruction when we were engaged to be married. He also was our parish priest in Grande Cache. Baptized Jason and gave Colin the little green tractor. In fact, he is the guy who told me how to ensure the mugo pine, about two feet high when we moved to the farm, would grow huge. Five gallons of water every day of the summer. That tree is now the biggest mugo in Alberta and has come to be the tree of life following my August experience.

We love this priest. No judgement. Peaceful. Loving. So very kind. He suffered deep emotional stress due to barbed comments from parishioners, his fellow priests and the hierarchy. He doesn't like the authority; we have a lot in common. Authority has come to mean only repression to me. I hang onto the address as a kind of talisman.

Christmas comes and I struggle through with smiles and pretence of joy. I must say, I am very good at this. I bake. The kids are impressed with the stollen, "Almost as good as Grandma's." High praise indeed. I try to explain the traditions. I don't really think they are interested. But they love the bread. Mince tarts. Christmas pudding from my family recipes. We have a very good Christmas Eve. Christmas Day. And underneath it all I feel the sadness that has no words. I am a void. As I write this great, gulping panicky tears flow with bitterness. Why? What in hell is still wrong with me?

On New Year's Eve, Bill and I take Rachel to First Night Celebrations in downtown Edmonton. We create masks and party hats. Her cousins are with her. City Square is alive with fireworks and the night is deliciously cold. Rachel asks on the way home, "Why are we a family of only three, so much?" I think of how Colin angrily demanded to know why we had her so late. "I won't even be home to watch her grow up." He was 14 then and she was five. Of course he was right but the bond between them was and remains incredibly strong. We arrive home exhausted and seemingly happy at 1:00 a.m.

My inner tape runs. I write pages into the new computer. Relive every day since April, nine months ago. I read Richardson[14] who gives me academic credence, external authority for my journal writing. Funny what backstops and footholds I find. Trees. Books. People.

By January 2, 1989, I am in the deepest of black moods. I wonder if all my extraordinary spiritual development is some kind of macabre joke. Remembering the absolute worst of times, I think only of crawling under the bed and staying there forever. I am crying and furious. The new computer doesn't work. I am to be at Gerry's by 7:00 p.m. for meditation. I can't. I can't I can't. I plan in my head. I will drop Rachel off and come straight home. I slam the bedroom door on the way out. I am done with this whole stupid idea of meditation. Calm and civil, I drop Rachel with Yvonne for a few days.

I smile and greet the group. I sit to meditate.

The energy returns again. Stronger. I receive a deeply moving vision of sunflowers, seeds, a forest of trees and a beautiful river of silver coins. I have never since seen the man who voiced

---

[14] Richardson, "Getting Personal: Writing Stories," *International Journal of Qualitative Studies in Education* 14:1, 33–8, 2001.

the vision. Through me came words that left my whole body vibrating.

The Gift of Compassion and Forgiveness

Prompting

> *Beloved child, you have waited for this year and this time to come. It is the time to step forward into the coming age of perfection. This is the end of the endurance run. You and your family will see joy, happiness, peace, prosperity, light, love and knowledge beyond your wildest comprehension. This was the promise made to you when you walked with Jesus on the sand at Galilee. Be at peace, beloved child. That is all.*

My energy soars. It seems that I must be healed. I continue to pray, read, and write. *The New Diary: How to Use a Journal for Self-Guidance and Expanded Creativity* and Natalie Goldberg, *Writing Down the Bones: Freeing the Writer Within.*[15] Instead of the daily diary disaster of the weather, or boyfriends and teenage stuff, these books suggest writing whatever comes up. Well. Whatever comes up gets written and recorded; words, quotes, questions, emotions, memories spew across the page. I write several journals from April to January. Phrases come from many directions. Books, hearing voices, songs. "And the truth shall set you free." These words, they feel abstract. Out there. Nice words. Comforting words. As in Truth in religion.

I began to ask in prayer, "Why so many years of depression? Why all the stress, anxiety, but yet no understanding of why?" I never accepted the psychiatrist's chemical brain imbalance. What

---

[15] Tristine Rainer, *The New Diary: How to Use a Journal for Self-Guidance and Expanded Creativity* (NY: Tarcher/Penguin, 1978); Natalie Goldberg, *Writing Down the Bones: Freeing the Writer Within* (Boulder, CO: Shambhala, 1986).

was his diagnosis based on? I cannot remember the multitude of tests and diagnoses. I pray to understand. I pray to heal the depression once and for all time. I just want off the treadmill. I read dozens more books. I begin to question further the rules of the church. I want to know. I yearn for clarity. I begin to think perhaps I have been on this earth before.

My mantras have changed a little. Now I breathe in peace and breathe out confusion. Pray for clarity. As so many times before, the chaos begins to worsen. Then, again my inner voice, prompting.

Beloved child, so often you see but do not listen. Do not be afraid. First comes the muddying and churning. Then comes the clearing. Listen. Beloved Pearl, you are opening and unfolding to receive the gifts promised so long ago. Open your heart. Open your mind's eye to see the wonderful works of God, the Source of all beauty, joy and knowledge. Your prayers are heard. Many are called but few listen and hear me in the inner silence. You have asked for faith. Know that you have been given faith in full measure. Be still and listen for I AM is always with you. That is all.

I give thanks and soar. But some little event throws me back within days into mass confusion and doubt. This time it is a phone call from our eldest son on January 28. Bill is on the extension downstairs. After Colin and I have chatted for a bit—long distance in 1989 was horrifically expensive—Bill comes upstairs. "I am not certain you should be telling Colin all this stuff."

I lose my temper. "You don't even believe."

He shouts back, "I do so. It doesn't hurt to pray."

And with that I am devastated. Doesn't hurt to pray? I screamed. He screamed back. I stomped off into the living room, tried to calm my doubts. Of course, he only voiced what I could not. Doubt. I had yet to learn that doubt isn't the opposite of faith; rather it is a crucial aspect of mature faith.

Prompting

> *You have put the process in motion. Surrender. Trust. Remember the promises we made to you.*

I share very little with anyone. Even now, nearly 30 years later, even given all the amazing events of my life, I still struggle with fear of ridicule. I am educated in our culture, where rational thinking, logic, and the Enlightenment produce a state of induced amnesia. Inner work, dreams? Well, irrational to say the least. All this I know. I know that I am human. I just want to be healed of clinical depression. Permanently. Is that too much to ask? Our culture's approach to faith? We want proof. Of course we insist that we must have peer-reviewed and replicated results. In 1989 I was working as an Education Consultant. I hadn't yet learned much about quantum physics and I knew precious little about the mind, about psyche. I had built my life on logic. A woman in school and education administration must always and forever ensure cold, hard, irrefutable logic. Channelling does not produce results that can be replicated. Witches were burned at the stake. Joan of Arc was burned as a heretic and eventually sainted. She heard "voices" from the age of 13. Women, it is said, have soul and are irrational. Men are logical.

I didn't know anything about the power of the deep unconscious and our access to our own depths. But that awareness was beginning to build. Slowly.

Well aware of the hierarchy's resistance to and condemnation of what I am doing, I am filled with confusion, doubt and anxiety. I study the Bible only to learn there are over 760 healing instances and significantly more than 250 contradictions. I have never heard much about this from the pulpit even though I have been in Mass every Sunday of my life; in 1989 that would be 2,288 times plus daily Mass when I lived in the city and the depression was the most paralyzing.

For nearly another month I am focused on Maloney's *Uncreated Energy: A Journey into the Authentic Sources of Christian Faith*.[16] It bears the stamp of the Imprimatur. Some of the doubt clears. I may not hear these ideas in the Sunday homily but Catholic theologians write a great many books that never make their way to the masses. Pardon the pun.

Hockey, cross-country skiing, the usual family activities. Nothing more is said between Bill and I about prayer. My writings are filled with frenzied thought. Page after page. I struggle with the possibility that I may yet fall back into an even deeper and more desperate place of blackness. I want to hide my head. I want to run screaming from meetings, from my family. I want simply to cease to exist. I can't make it much longer. Verna tells me carefully and with deep concern that Spirit prepares us slowly for occurrences in the future. I can slow the many promptings I am receiving and ask for more clarity. I am in control. Remember what we have learned, she says. I take a tape recorder with me in the car so that I can record my thoughts. My therapist is my own inner world—Spirit, if you will. Religious belief is very strong. I believe the dream that says I will land safely.

That night Colin phones again. He is much calmer. Playing better. "I love you, Mom," he says. "I am so sorry to bother you with all my fears."

I fly. There is no joy greater than words of love from a teenage son. I sing softly to myself.

So begins another round of questions. I have not yet gotten to the bottom of this pit. I have not yet landed. The inner screaming and yelling continues. Desperation builds again. Verna has read everything I have written and made notes from her own meditation. "No," she says. She's slow and careful on the phone. "You are not yet done."

Search childhood, says the voice, *search little girls alone.*

---

[16] George A. Maloney, *Uncreated Energy: A Journey into the Authentic Sources of Christian Faith* (Rockport, MA: Element Books, 1987).

I am frantic. I believed I was better, but the pain, agony, fear, frustration of this week and this night are impossibly far worse than anything before. I am torn with every level of pain. I cannot think. Breathe, breathe. Keep on breathing. Stifling, convulsive sobs roll over me again and again. I cannot do this.

Somehow, as I lie down to rest, I breathe deeply. I breathe in peace. I breathe in love. I breathe in trust. I breathe in joy. Over and over. Desperate. Determined. I force my mind back into childhood. I let the veil of darkness be torn away and light floods my being. I am one with God. I am in the perfect love and care of God. I yield. I surrender to the Christ Consciousness within. Speak, Yahweh, your servant is listening. Repeat relentlessly. Give me inner knowledge. Unbind my sight. Grant me total love and trust. Strengthen me. Give me courage. My heart hammers madly, agonizingly and then You are here. As I drift, I am again pervaded with a deep inner knowing. Hours go by. I repeat these affirmations persistently. Peace comes over me.

Prompting

Beloved Pearl, child of light, you are indeed one with God and His love and care. You are deeply loved. Your father loves you greatly and would never willingly or knowingly hurt you. You have felt you cannot yet face the years of turmoil and your fears for Colin pervade you. Trust. Trust.

Would not your Father in heaven grant you peace? You must write more of your story for your family so that you may receive your heart's desire. Beloved child, your earthly father has taken care of you with great love. Trust your heavenly Father to do far more. Be at peace for I AM with you. Write. Meditate. Be with God. Your time has not yet come but the endurance run is over. Be at-one-ment. Surrender completely to the Christ Consciousness and rely on your inner power and strength. Fear not.

There Is Much More to the Inner World Than Meets the Eye of the Intellect

January 21, 1989 could well be the most significant day of my life.

These words are taken unedited from my journal.

There were over 500 people for the prayer breakfast at St. Basil's in the city today. Music by the Mustard Seed was inspirational and deeply relaxing. I was not that inspired by the speaker especially when he spoke of Jesus as judge.

I had never been to a prayer breakfast before in my life. I planned to leave when my friend did but somehow I found myself at the front where an older, very tall, strong-looking man and his wife were ministering. I waited a long time. Then the man asked, "Why have you come?"

"I don't know," I said. "I came because I was told to come."

He and his wife prayed over me praising God and giving glory. A great peace and joy came over me. The man told me to place my hand over my heart. When I placed my hand over my hammering heart, his wife exclaimed, "Jesus is here. Jesus is here. Praise God. You are healed. A great insult has been healed. A great hurt. Give it to Jesus."

Hot tears streamed down my face. I sat enveloped in translucent blue electrified energy. Mugo pine blue energy. Meditation and vision in Gerry's living room blue energy. As I drove home I sang the same songs over again. I could have flown. This is the most joy, the most peace, the most alive, expansive, lifted I have felt ever in this life. The lady's words are etched on my mind. Her voice is very clear and light.

It is now Saturday, February 4, 1989. Verna and I meet for breakfast. I hand her all my writings.

Monday after work, we meet yet again. She has read, reflected, thought about the words. She has promptings for me but is reluctant. "Perhaps I misunderstood." We meditate again.

"Tell Pearl to honour the creativity of writing and healing and continue to keep a journal, especially a journal of the internal messages, for these shall be the core of what is to grow in abundance. She will see her word published. She will need to seek knowledge in that area. For now, her writings, as is, will be 'wisdom' for her family. She might meditate on Bible quotations to receive even deeper understandings of that which was written.

"Tell Pearl the fear comes from a large hurt in this life expression that was indeed dislodged from the heart chakra but will still have to be confronted. Look, there is no need for judgement—just seeing and filling with love, then the dark times will be no more. It is no longer possible to hold hardened fear in her heart because too much love and light is there. Tell Pearl to write the early story of what occurred to get her to close herself off from her Christ awareness. Fear is lack of understanding—not seeing what really is present. The purpose of the writing now is healing. Once all the healing is complete she will write what really needs to be said. Tell Pearl her writing will heal all those who have been closed off and who choose to open. Explore when the depressions started. Explore little girl times. Explore mothers and daughters. Explore fathers and daughters. Explore daughters alone. Explore family secrets in the mind of a child.

"Tell her we are with her through all times; that all has been for the learning of compassion and the power of forgiveness. Tell her she is loved and safe and rather than retreat from thought, bring the thoughts into the light for healing. Tell her there is nothing to fear and that she is strengthened by the light of Spirit. This is a time of enfoldment. We did not leave you then and we do not leave you now. You no longer need the ritual to hold on to our touch. You have always known and felt the presence of Spirit but in your anger you could not see, in your pain you would not look, in your sedation you could not feel, in your fear you chose not to hear.

"Now is the perfect time to tell that story for the telling shall free it, you and others. Be at peace, Pearl, meaning faith and old treasures."

The next day, our family attends Mass as usual. I cry softly throughout. The music speaks. "Be not afraid, I go before you always. Come follow me. I shall give you rest.... Here I am, Lord, if you need me.... Dear Father in heaven, come close to us your children." I am overwhelmed by the Presence. Love. The joyous tears flow. Bill and the kids pretend not to notice.

At home, in my chair, pen in hand, I ask incessantly, "What is it you would have me learn?" I sit silently, pen and journal beside me, meditating.

Prompting

Plant the seeds, let them grow.

Water them with your tears,

love them,

nurture them,

and delight in their growing.

Fear not when they wilt a little;

they will thrive in love.

Wilt. Indeed, by the following day, I move slowly, barely able to put one foot in front of the other. A zombie. Repeating over and over my mantras *ad nauseam*. I don't sleep. I feel like Death Valley. I am actually at work. Finally, at noon, I phone Verna. I must be driving her crazy. I have no choice. She agrees to meet with me and our meditation colleague, Gerry, the next evening.

A Chapter Closes While Remaining Open

February 7, 1989. I sit frozen, tongue-tied, still. Empty. I may well be dead. Nothing exists but this room and these two people. I have formed a plan if this night does not go well.

Spirit floods the room. The moment the words begin, tears flood my face.

Beloved child, you are so loved. You come against your own conscious will. You have shown a great trust in opening your heart and sharing your burdens with well-loved friends. Your fear is great. You want always to be with God, Creator, Infinite Source of Love, Wisdom, Understanding, Joy and Peace. You have yet to fully accept your own great good. The struggle has been long and you fear the deepening of this struggle. Your fear will decrease as your demonstration of trust is a great step in reaching your goal.

This moment of truth brings the understanding of what has created these years of depression and despair. I was transformed. From deep within my being came the memory of a childhood assault buried under 43 years of repressed emotions. I have tried thousands of times to find the words to express this experience in understandable words. It is not possible. A translucent blue fire of energy passed through my being, seeming to transform my very cells into peace and harmony. Joy unspeakable. Full of glory. Wave upon wave of pure, deep peace. I will never be the same again. Metaphorically, I had indeed landed in the arms of Jesus and the Lamb of God cradled me gently while the Holy Spirit enlightened me with the power of forgiveness and compassion toward the person responsible for the assault. I seemed to understand in that moment the reason for many of the decisions I

Verna asks for wisdom as to why I feel such a strong emotional surge whenever these interior conversations begin.

Beloved Pearl, you have lived long in fear of something that has been beyond your understanding. This fear is not reality but has been created through experience that you were too little to understand. Your family were unable to comprehend the gifts

had taken in my life. I had built the masculine aspects of my being as understood in our society. I was educated, considered successful in my career in areas where the vast majority were men. I was inflexible, unbending with myself, driving myself with whips, choosing always to repress my emotions for fear of being thought weak or flying into fragmented pieces. I emulated my very strong and quiet father and held my own against my six brothers, at least in my mind. I was undemonstrative with everyone except my own three children upon whom I lavished as many hugs, kisses and as much affection as I possibly could.

that had been given to you. You feared scorn and ridicule and closed off the gifts. This has created great confusion in you. In order to feel loved, and to fit in, you turned away from the inner vibration and followed the world's theory of nerves and mental depression. You were not able to risk the love of your family, you were too afraid. Your father also turned away from the inner vibration of the Spirit and that is why he is so stern. He understands more now. He lived many years in fear of his own great wisdom. The exterior shell of being male was difficult for him. He has gathered around him many loving souls and waits for them to share their learning with him. You have known for a long time.

Is there anything that Pearl needs to know and is willing to know at this time regarding her childhood that would help her?

As I come to see and feel and know this very early experience, I begin to understand my strong adherence to the symbolism of white and purity. My devotion to Mother Mary. My strange religiosity. I was a small child sleeping in her carriage away from the crowd of people assembled for a community picnic. I was just past a year old. When I told my parents, they were stunned. How could this happen? Was I sure? Yes, I am sure. How could they not know? It's easy. This is not about blame. This is about learning compassion and forgiveness. Later, I would assure Mom that silence was for the best. Can you imagine what Dad might have done had he known of this incident? It is better this way. I should add, it serves my soul's purpose. I came to the planet with the goal to learn compassion and forgiveness. Learning begins with self. It has been a very long and arduous road. Fog comes and goes. But, as I step into this hurdle, the road slowly begins to clear.

I am prompted to understand more deeply.

Pearl, you are confusing your family who believes. A kind and loving husband helped you overcome your fears of womanhood. For many years you confessed to self-abuse to block the fear of the early hurt. You learned hardness to block penetration of your being. You learned what you thought was emulation of your father. Long has your mother been concerned for you in your pursuit of what the world believes to be male-dominated activities and interests. You had many arguments with your mother.

Children of Light, your purpose here tonight is to heal all the dark times. To free Pearl and to free him from the anguish. What is necessary at this time is for Pearl to declare her forgiveness of him, of her own vulnerability, to declare her forgiveness of closing off her feminine nature, that aspect of herself that was so closely in touch with the God-light that she has and is. It would be wisdom at this time to do a psychic healing.

As we continue the meditation session I hear myself murmuring, *"That poor man, that poor man."*

Would you show Pearl a knowingness of the convent experiences?

Again, I was given to understand that my trip to the convent for high school was a flight from the world of masculinity and competition. The world of nuns was to be my protection from growing to the light within.

Prompting

Between the walls of the convent the light grew very strong and you retreated back to the world of childhood, to your father and to your room. The fear grew and the pain was felt by your family and they had no understanding of how to respond. In your anger you built walls against all who would come close to you and expressed your fear through your understanding of masculinity and your relationships in an attempt to be like your brothers. The fear only succeeded in closing you away and no one knew how to respond although many made attempts.

Shimmering translucent blue light, vibration after vibration pulsed through my body, surrounded me and seemed to make my very being transparent. I felt some kind of electrical energy ebb and flow over, through and around my entire being. Tears flowed freely, my heart pounded incredibly. I have tried a million times to convey this experience in words. This was an *ekstasis*, or a going beyond myself; it was more than a trance state of consciousness but indelibly left my soul lighter and my body cells changed.

In the convent, I had been searching for a safe place for my feminine nature against the assault. And when God came too close, I simply fainted. I was deeply fearful He would find me. As the Light grew stronger through my prayer, I became very much more afraid. I understand now that there really are only two real emotions. Fear and love. I was afraid of punishment for my impurity. In my childish, interior world, Saint Maria Goretti died to preserve her purity. After this "Landing," my feet did not touch the ground for several weeks.

Fast forward. In 2016, for the first time since my failed publishing attempts in 1989–90, I reread the recorded words—Verna and Gerry present with me in meditation—and finally, the strangeness, the amazement, the fundamental differences between the rules of religion and the mysteries of the universe begin truly to pierce my consciousness. Clarissa Pinkola Estes says: "In mythos the teaching of endurance is one of the rites of the Great Wild Mother, the Wild Woman archetype. It is her timeless ritual to make her offspring strong. It is she who toughens us up, makes us potent and enduring."[17] The father symbolizes the aspect of psyche that is supposed to guide us in the outer world. So I have made a soul bargain, a contract, which Estes refers to as the Bargain without Knowing. My soul knew what She was doing. My Christ Self knew what my soul journey was intended to be and do in this lifetime. If I understand Estes, these inner movements I hear, see and feel are material for my entire life process. She advises I should sit with my Muse. Endurance means to make something. I am making soul.

Promptings

> *Beloved Pearl. There is a deep knowing within you that what occurs to us in life is always of our own nature. To a baby it does not seem possible to be accountable for what occurs to you. At 17 you know that that experience was a completion of a previous life expression but your knowing was confused with the world's misunderstanding. And so you simply told yourself that you must be wrong. Beloved Pearl, the energy from within you has completed the healing that was begun and worked at the charismatic meeting. It is unnecessary to dwell on it longer.*

---

[17] Clarissa Pinkola Estes, *Women Who Run With the Wolves: Myths and Stories of the Wild Woman Archetype* (NY: Ballantine Books, 1992), 389.

Its very vibrations have been healed from the universal records[18] so complete is the energy that has moved through you. There is nothing further that needs to be learned or understood from either the childhood experience or the convent experience. Now is a time for joy. Now is a time for you to blossom forth into the incredible Light being that you know yourself to be. We say to you, beloved child, there will never again in this lifetime or in any other life expression be a darkness within your psyche. You have experienced the complete healing love of Jesus. There will be many times when you will wonder when darkness will come. I say to you, it will never return. For there is no longer a need; there is no longer a confusion. There is only clarity and light. It would be wisdom for you at this time to ask the questions that are more related to your growth into the light of wisdom than your retreat from the Light of God, for that time is complete. It is ... finished.

Beloved child, move forward in keeping with your own impatience and the inner need to grow quickly will be met from within. You have no great need for the ritual but it will comfort your family. You need not fear giving them the book nor do you need to reveal any more than is comfortable for you because you trust in your learning and sharing. You feel your words are not from Spirit but Spirit is within and accessible to you instantly whenever you request. You can write about things not known on a conscious level. You have all past knowledge available, future knowledge is available if you but ask. Your fear as a child that you knew more than the adults was your understanding of truth. Your image of the huge man in Grade 1 was your truth. You have tried to hide that gift but were only successful with some people. Others have truly understood. You must let it go and acknowledge your own understanding of the world, which even as a child was great. You must recognize that understanding in the children that you meet. That is all.

---

[18] Hildegard of Bingen speaks of Akashik Records, Universal Records recorded in the ethereal realm.

In the next few weeks, I discover that my menstrual cycle has normalized. My expression of feminine sexuality is freed immeasurably, as is our marriage relationship. The depression is gone. I now face the daunting task of healing the remaining vestiges of depression.

Doubling Back

I have encountered my soul and must nurture her into full life within my body. This journey has brought me to full frontal contact with my Self as defined by Jung: the divinity within. I have and will continue to find many beliefs that no longer serve my soul. I need a confidante, someone with ears to listen to my questions and doubts. My mother suggested a Spiritual Director. I dismissed that idea out of hand although I did visit one of Dad's cousins, Sister Doreen, a nun at Providence Centre in Edmonton, a trained Spiritual Director. I soon understand that the purpose of spiritual direction is to steer. I want to explore the unknown. I am unable to trust the answers from someone in authority. I have multitudinous layers of questions. I need my own answers.

How is it that Jesus came and expressed full masculine and feminine energies yet Catholicism is totally infused with the dominance of the male god and by extension the male gender? I will study the origins of beliefs, the patriarchal need to dominate evil and to find its source in women. I will read and find the instances of the introduction of sin and salvation. These do not, as far as I can see, follow the Christ of the New Testament. I was blind, and now I see—albeit dimly. Study will bring possibilities and amazing joy along with doubt and uncertainty.

Sandra Schneiders in *Beyond Patching: Faith, Feminism and the Catholic Church* speaks to the choices Catholic women have when faced with their own doubts. One, stay the course with the status quo. No. Two, remain in the church and try to change it from within. That is the choice I make in 1989. Three. Existential despair. That is no choice at all. I move in all directions, spiralling out and in at the same time. Unlearning a life learned. There is no map for this journey. I have my inner guide. I have the teachings of faith from childhood. I no longer have blind obedience nor blind faith.

I will express my soul purpose and explore my own spirituality; I will face my own fears. This is the generation that will set the stage for the emergence of the feminine. I will participate and find my woman soul place in the universe.

SECTION II

INITIATION

Chapter Five

Inanna-Ishtar's Door: Descent and Dismemberment

Nightmares … "A dream unexamined is like a letter unopened."

–Jewish Sage

Children have nightmares and parents console, "It isn't real. It's only a nightmare."

As a child in the 1950s, in a culture with little or no knowledge of the inner world, how would I have possibly understood the potential of nightmares? I knew only fear when the scarred face of a man with burned, wide, funny, chalky white scars down the right side of his face leered out at me from the top of my small clothes closet. I ran and ran. I fell off mountains, cliffs and off nothingness into nothingness. Screaming. I awoke with painful cuts in the palms of my hands from where my fingernails penetrated the skin and drew blood. Now I know the nightmare was psyche's attempt to get my attention. The nightmare was telling me again and again about the inner scars and about potential healing. Nightmares may be the first indication of deeply repressed trauma. I needed to stop and listen. Running served no soul purpose.

As long as I looked to the outside world for answers, I would find none. The inner night world of the unconscious has the capacity to open up in violent fashion the forces that show me the tensions that exist within. My level of consciousness and patriarchal, religious, rational thought chains had prevented me from awaking to new possibilities. Now, after many years of studying dreams, archetypes, symbolism, field theory, and the works of Jung and the new Jungians, I recognize that potential is always present for both destructive and constructive change. In the hands of a skilled psychotherapist, a skilled dreamworker, nightmares can become the gateway to the wounds of childhood. I believe my inner world led me to follow forced moments of deep reflection through meditation and caused the first massive cracks to appear in what seemed to those around me to be a stable system. I was led by my unconscious intuitions to confront my inner world through the violent overthrow of the intellect. Jung calls this the process of individuation. The call of the soul to its purpose. Nightmares serve individuation. The initiatory elevator dream showed me that the descent into the unconscious was safe, but I didn't know then what I know now. My response to the first dream, buying a computer, from a rational standpoint was silly. Intuition tells me that it was exactly the best response. Writing my way to freedom. The nightmares opened the door to my inner world.

Perera presents four perspectives on the myth of Inanna: a story that describes the rhythmic order of nature; initiation into the mysteries of the underworld; sacrifice of upper-world Self to creation of integral consciousness; and, the pattern for psychological health of the feminine for both men and women.[19]

---

[19] Sylvia Brinton Perera, *Descent to the Goddess: A Way of Initiation for Women* (Toronto, ON: Inner City Books, 1981), 173

Nightmares Can Become the Doorway to Dreams

But if a theologian really believes in God, by what authority does he suggest that God is unable to speak through dreams?

–C.G. Jung

In 1992, Marion Woodman wrote *Leaving My Father's House: A Journey to Conscious Femininity*. I was far along in my journey across the threshold to a feminine consciousness when I read that book.

What follows is my Leaving Story as written through many dreams over many years. *The Landing* dream began my inner healing. Now I understand that the decision to write in a journal everything that happened was a profound action that honoured the dream. I would never believe nor accurately remember the dreams and experiences without the written evidence. For several years, the intensity of the healing process batters my multiple identities, shatters old beliefs and creates new ways of being in the world. I struggle with the changes occurring and hold far too inflexibly to old ideas. Why? It feels like the rigid structures around me are breaking down and old grey beard god/man/ kings are grieving the loss of power and control. Is it possible that humans are evolving to realize that power, wisdom, courage, life itself, lie within, where the essence of God resides in magnificent wholeness? We all have a part to play in the animus mundi, the world soul. The purpose of my soul unfolds in painful beauty over the coming years, and seeks its expression in the co-creation of the universe.

In *The Landing* there are many symbols with deep, archetypal significance. The office may symbolize the rational intellect where I have lived long without questioning its irrationally high value in Western culture. Ralston Saul speaks to our entrancement in *Voltaire's Bastards: The Dictatorship of Reason in the West.*[20] In an interview from 1996 Saul says, "It seems to me we have about six qualities, which are: common sense, creativity, ethics, intuition, memory, and reason."[21] Notice where reason comes in the sequence. Dead last.

The seventh floor may symbolize sacramental (sacred) wholeness, as in seven sacraments, seven virgins, seven levels of the inner crystal castle envisioned by mystics, or seven days and nights, the creation of the world in six days and resting on the seventh. The seven lions that pull the chariot of the goddess Inanna. I have found in the last 30 years dozens of references to the symbolism of seven. Chakras, seals of the soul, and…. Strangely enough, several years went by before I realized that in reality my office was on the 8th floor, thus I think the seven is profoundly purposeful.

The unfamiliar women who are screaming in the elevator are the unknown feminine aspects of myself. Yes, I am in a panic. I have prayed since childhood. I have fallen forever in nightmares. This time, the descent ends safely and softly. Now, the dream message says, "You will descend to the unconscious, find fear and panic, but then safety and comfort." Dreams are a metaphor. They tell stories. A journey, once begun, never ends.

Given the 40-plus years of repressed trauma, life does not become perfect overnight, like a Disney movie. My outer life mirrored my inner doubts, which mocked with endless, unstoppable interior voices conversing. So, I did what I had just found works, I prayed differently but incessantly; I meditated and I wrote.

---

[20]   John Ralston Saul, *Voltaire's Bastards: The Dictatorship of Reason in the West* (NY: Simon & Schuster, 1992).

[21]   http://www.scottlondon.com/interviews/saul.html "The End of Rationalism" interview with Scott London 1996. This interview was adapted from the public radio series "Insight & Outlook." It appeared in abbreviated form in the *Ottawa Citizen*, December 16, 2001.

A Crack

A few months after the 1989 experiences, I had a very disturbing dream. My inner guide continued to prompt me, to give loving and gentle peace. But you can't meditate 24 hours a day. The cognitive dissonance between my experiences and my early beliefs thundered. With a brother, I attended a conference in Calgary, Alberta sponsored by a Catholic charismatic group. The speaker, P.J. Wencker, warned of the evils of New Age groups. "I can read your story," she said, "and I will tell you if your healing is from the evil one, the devil. You need to submit to 'authority,'" she said. Raging at yet another authority, I went home with all my notes. Phrase by phrase I refuted her statements from biblical and other Catholic theological "authorities." I got no response to my 26-page letter. I still have the letter though.

I continued to rage inwardly against authority figures, fundamentalism and the constant carping that evil was seemingly everywhere. I questioned my beliefs, my interpretations, and my entire bedrock began to crack. I felt like a question dancing out of control as in the story of The Red Shoes.[22] I was foolish enough to read Douglas Groothuis, *Confronting the New Age*.[23] My inner doubts became chasms as rage turned to thoughts of possibility. Then, thankfully, I read C.S. Lewis, *The Screwtape Letters*.[24] The devil hates laughter.

I rediscovered what I had learned as a child. Many early Catholic saints were questioned, chastised, persecuted, written off as *hysterics*. Burned alive. Prophets, saints and mystics have a tough struggle. We make saints out of really old, really dead, for several centuries dead, people. Time seems to allow us to

---

[22] Clarissa Pinkola Estes, *The Red Shoes: On Torment and the Recovery of Soul Life* (Louisville, CO: Sounds True, 2005), audiobook.

[23] Douglas Groothuis, *Confronting the New Age: How to Resist a Growing Religious Movement* (Eugene, OR: Wipf and Stock Publishers, 1988).

[24] C.S. Lewis, *The Screwtape Letters* (New York: HarperOne, 1942).

re-evaluate our understandings and reach deeper meaning. I discovered that deepening faith carries wisdom that eventually seeps as water through rock. St. Catherine of Siena; St. Francis of Assisi; St. Hildegard; Joan of Arc; and Jacinta, Francisco and Lucia of Fatima. All were endangered by the status quo. The authorities investigated and often these people were threatened with excommunication or far worse.

The writing of Thomas Merton, George Maloney, S.J., Father John Main and particularly anything written about the visions of Blessed Mother Mary comforted me while bringing floods of tears. The writings of Sister Francis Clare and Eileen Caddy brought pockets of profound peace. But in all truth, I was furious. Furious with so-called believers who really didn't believe at all. Hypocrites. Talk of love. Talk of miracles. But, no action, please. In fact, if you read the St. Joseph Edition of the Bible, you will even find the statement that "in modern times, no new revelations are expected from God" or some such drivel. Today we don't burn people at the stake. We simply freeze them out of polite society.

Paul Tillich, in *The Courage to Be*, speaks in metaphors of the soul "being itself" and "non-being" and "ground of being."[25] I find myself nodding as I read Tillich a second time, delighted that my soul has found a language that speaks to it. Stuck in an indefinable present. Moving creatively into an unknown where the only fact I know is that I am alive right now here in this moment. The only question then is "what do I intend to do about this being alive?" One partial answer: the connection between obedience and the self which commands itself provides depth. Another: the command to Be My Own Authority takes on soul meaning. It is not arrogance to follow the dictates of your soul. Fear dissipates.

---

[25] Paul Tillich, *The Courage to Be* (New Haven, Conn.: Yale University Press, 2000).

In summer 2016, finally, after years of self-torture, I tell one brother of my deep pain at what I perceive to be indifference to the significance of this miracle of healing in my life. I tell him of the turmoil arising out of the P.J. Wencker conference. He listens and does not dissolve. I think you might call his a "stunned silence" at the depth of my emotion.

I was reading Sanford, *Dreams: God's Forgotten Language*[26] when the next dream occurred. I had read Mark, Chapter 2 the evening before. In that text, Jesus challenges the Pharisees as he breaks bread with "sinners" and heals a man on the Sabbath. They too had their rules and rituals, to which it was more important to adhere than to follow the simple commandment to love. Not much seems to have changed in 2000 years. Pharisees abound. I renew my relationship with the etymology, or historical meaning, of words that always fascinated me. Over and over in reading I encounter original Greek, Latin or Aramaic meanings. So, from Latin, I find *religuere*, to link or connect to the source. This definition has long been subject to controversy. I choose to use it because the connotation of connection is very important to me. Other authors claim it means to "bind or tie." I do not like that definition. I have no wish to be bound but rather to be connected.

Shortly after I touched the numinous, I discovered that my descent from the seventh floor to the lamb's wool in *The Landing* was, in Jungian terms, the descent to the unconscious. I read Sylvia Perera, *Descent to the Goddess: A Way of Initiation for Women*. I made notes in the margins of 1988. I barely understood it in any way, shape or form. My background in mythology then fit on the head of a straight pin. The margin-writing created a literary anthropology from which I can now be clear on how little I understood. How am I linked? I thought I knew. I thought my source was God. I never questioned the gendered identification. Now, I am beyond appalled. How many women never question

---

[26] New York: Crossroad, 1984.

the illusion of a male god? Hundreds? Thousands? Hundreds of thousands, millions? I was a daughter of the patriarchy.

In 2016, now I am Old Woman, Crone, I recognize the doors I opened in the psyche in 1989. How am I linked? The question should have been, "What is the meaning of Source?" I was about to participate in the dismemberment of initiation through the rites of the Goddess. Learning would require full initiation into the mysteries.

"There is a gate into and out of the underworld later called Inanna-Ishtar's door. Through it others who made the journey to become conscious of the underworld were advised to pass.... She [Inanna] descends, submits, and dies."[27]

I have been alienated from the feminine ground of my being. I will meet the goddess, I will sacrifice my identity as a daughter of the patriarchy.

Perera is succinct: "Our planet is passing through a phase—the return of the goddess—presaged at the beginning of the patriarchy...."[28]

Over the years, my dreams will shake the very foundations of my identity. I will spend years and years integrating and connecting disparate aspects of self. Carl Jung was known to celebrate depression! To the soul, depression means the beginning of the defeat and shattering of ego. The abusive voices within? The angry ego determined to regain its ascendancy but forced to recognize its smallness. My soul voice has spoken to me. Now, like Inanna, I must pass through the seven gates on my way to the depths of the underworld. Only my Western rational mind steeped in fear of hell does not know this yet. Perera's work tells the psychological story of this descent I am on. She describes the domain of Ereshkigal as "seemingly unbounded, irrational, primordial, and totally uncaring, even destructive of the individual....

---

[27] Sylvia Brinton Perera, *Descent to the Goddess: A Way of Initiation for Women* (Toronto, ON: Inner City Books, 1981), 17.

[28] Perera, *Descent to the Goddess*, 15.

[The] destructive-transformative side of the cosmic will ... pitilessly grinding ... heaving forth new life.... Then these forces bring about a hopeless, empty, shattering, numb, barren void or chaos."[29]

So it was and so it shall continue in a feminine story cycle of birth, death, life, rebirth.

The Broken Church, May 12, 1989

I am in an unknown church. Wherever I sit, the people get up and move away. I do not know any of these people. The chairs in the church are totally wrecked. I move around, sitting in various places within the church. The unknown people are very angry. I leave crying like a heartbroken child.

I awake sobbing.

Bill says nothing but my face is wet with tears. My arms and body ache. My inner church, my temple, is in terrible disrepair. I am searching for a new place to "sit." Moving out of my comfortable pew? The rule-oriented aspects of my being are displeased; my dream ego is filled with fear of ridicule? For being different? I have always been different. I hate it. Such anger. Is it really against myself for being so weak? The dream points to my broken inner belief system, to the dissolution of the righteousness of my church self. Angry inner voices say, "Be humble. You think you are right. No one else thinks you are right. You are just arrogant. How can you possibly think like that? You are a fool."

During a 2016 pilgrimage to Galway, Ireland and Celtic goddess sites, I will remember that the etymology of humility is "humus": of the earth. Rich, dark, composted materials make humus, which enriches the soil. Humility of the earth enriches

---

[29] Perera, *Descent to the Goddess*, 24.

my soul. The rocky places of Earth have been enriched by millions of years of bits of organic materials. My soul needs organic bits. I will come to realize that I treasure being different … sometimes.

It is the word "fool" that triggers the *sometimes*. To believe as I do in a world that places high value on money and status—of course, this is foolish. To pay workers more than minimum wage on the farm, when I could move to town and live "cheaper"? Foolish. Install solar power at a huge cost that will require 10 years to pay for itself? Re-create wetlands? Plant 2000 trees? All foolish. To come to know the inner world. To spend so much time, energy and resources on dreams? The list of foolish things is endless. But my soul says a fool with humility is not foolish and I must honour my soul.

When I returned home from Ireland, I put a note above my computer, "Dear Pearl, humility is to love the interplay of forces between limitations and giftedness. You are indeed limited to the human experience of earth and will return to the earth. Dust unto dust. And you are gifted with the Presence that pervades you." My soul spoke to me so clearly.

In 1989, I look outside and blame the church hierarchy, which is steeped in the negative masculine and controlled by the Rules made over centuries. The fear comes from the fact that only now am I questioning. The questions have been repressed for decades, perhaps even lifetimes. Blame is totally useless, so I try not to indulge. The mantra? I am blessed with the learning of this lifetime.

The trouble with Christianity, as Gandhi famously claimed, is that it has never been tried. I have learned to internalize well. My inner hierarchy, ego self, has very rigid rules which push me to ignore my deep knowing. I know, at least intellectually, that the church is not a collection of buildings, rules and rites but rather, on a far deeper level, the collective mystical Christ Consciousness—and that includes every single aspect of Earth. Jew, Gentile, Muslim, man, woman and child not to mention Earth itself. Quite possibly, the universe. The church is symbolic of the universe. It is symbolic of a place of healing where the universal God can heal all the angry people; all the angry aspects of myself. Betrayed. Broken. The dream brings up the challenges to the little ego. I come face to face with my own fears, self rage and confusion. I must come to understand that God is love. I must freely give forgiveness to all those aspects of myself who would criticize, for in their condemnation is their misunderstanding. I must send love to all the children within me and on planet Earth that our fear may be brought to the light of the Christ and be healed. The people within me can no longer sit on the broken chairs. The child within me cries brokenheartedly as the egoic consciousness refuses to stay with her, to comfort and love her. The baptism of the Spirit is not a denominational experience but an inner experience. The Spirit moves like the wind. Where it comes from and where it goes is a mystery. I breathe the wind breathed by the great mystics. I am reading Jean Houston's, *A Mythic Life: Learning to Live Our Greater Story*.[30]

When I look back I see how hard I worked to convince myself. It is critical in dreamwork to write without censorship even when the dream is embarrassing. The *Broken Church* dream is recorded just after my birthday in 1989. I have since spent many hours in meditation, circle work with other women in both the Catholic Church and with a small group of friends. I read many times that if I stay awake, and watch, what I "need" will come to me. This is true. Workshops, books, women's circles, meditation and promptings appeared as I was ready. I seldom "knew" I was ready.

Only with long hindsight do I come to understand the depth and breadth and reality of the healing that has occurred. Integrating wholeness emotionally, mentally, spiritually and physically requires deep transformation of belief systems.

---

[30] Jean Houston, *A Mythic Life: Learning to Live Our Greater Story* (NY: HarperCollins, 1996).

Belief systems create our identities. Changing identity? Almost impossible. I am a Westerner. I wasn't interested in a gradual instant. I wanted instant healing. What I got went and continues to go far deeper.

"The process of initiation in the esoteric and mystical traditions in the West involves exploring different modes of consciousness and rediscovering the experience of unity with nature and the cosmos that is inevitably lost through goal-directed development.... It forces us to the affect-laden, static, and transformative: these depths are preverbal, often pre-image, capable of taking us over and shaking us to the core."[31]

I was shaken. I poured hundreds of words, questions, and ideas into my journal. Dad's words echoed. "Earth is the biggest church we have." Institutional church was becoming increasingly difficult, even painful. The Creed? I had not always *heard* the words. Baptism? Original sin? A punishing, vengeful, wrathful God? I couldn't voice those questions to my family. I kept it to myself.

> *The psyche, if you understand it as a phenomenon occurring in living bodies, is a quality of matter... it is simply the world seen from within.*
>
> –C.G. Jung

It is January, 2015 in Victoria, B.C. I am living in a small studio apartment focused on writing and physical rehabilitation from several TIAs (mini strokes) over four days last April, and rotator-cuff surgery last October. This morning birds are singing in the rain outside my window.

---

[31] Perera, *Descent to the Goddess*, 14.

It is now nearly 26 years since this next dream occurred. I was in the early stages of massive spiritual confusion, struggling to understand what was happening in my inner life in the aftershocks of healing the actual depression. Some dreams, Jung says, are for a lifetime. This early sequence of dreams is surely that. Outwardly, my life seemed unchanged to most friends and family. A few, perhaps three or four, knew better.

The Living Room

I arrive home from somewhere to find the living room has been renovated. It is filled with beautiful new furniture. The colour scheme revolves around rich shades of blues. Royal blues, pastels.... I am surprised and very calm. The dream ends.

By June 1989, I have learned a little about dreams and their relationship to my inner world. I know that symbols are bound up with intuition and emotional apprehension. Symbols point to a meaning that cannot, nor ever will be, fully understood. Dreams are never "finished." My inner world is present and also still coming. How difficult it is to rearrange the room of one's beliefs and inner world. It is particularly confusing for women who have been and continue to be socialized to enact structures, mostly through language, that were not made for "her." Trying to think "otherwise" is close to impossible since the learned systems of representation are so thoroughly patriarchal. But now I can, do and will continue to learn to use my "old crone" status to present another form of womanhood through the use of focal practices like drawing dreams to evoke imaginal worlds. Art, music, dance, experiences. Soul work.

I have long associated blue with the Virgin Mother Mary's mantle. For me, royal blue connotes spirituality, devotion, innocence, and *religuere.* Often, as I meditate, blue swirls around and through me to bring feelings of peace. I think of wisdom and chakras. The Divine Mother appears in a blue mantle. She does not wear pastels. The terror at losing a son precludes any wimpiness on the part of my Blessed Mother. She is the strong feminine. In the face of real trouble, and when comfort is needed, She is strength and courage in the eye of the hurricane. She is the Woman in Red. I have no connection to passivity in the Mother. I learn to use Jung's active imagination techniques to draw swirls of blue. Big sweeping strokes that involve my body.

"Active imagination is a method of assimilating unconscious contents (dreams, fantasies, etc.) through some form of self-expression… The object of active imagination is to give a voice to sides of the personality (particularly the anima, animus and the shadow) that are normally not heard, thereby establishing a line of communication between consciousness and the unconscious. Even when the end products—drawing, painting, writing, sculpture, dance, music, etc.—are not interpreted, something goes on between creator and creation that contributes to a transformation of consciousness."[32]

Using active imagination is very foreign to me. I have long avoided anything like drawing, painting, sculpting. I am not good at it. So says the false self.

Now the whispers inside saying "Come Home" suggest a return to my Self, my inner divinity. When my Inner Voice whispered "Come Home" during Mass in 1986, I knew I needed to go home … to the farm. Now, I believe it more probably meant home to my soul.

Jung used capital letters to refer to the Higher Self, divinity within, as opposed to the personal self. Personal context is important to understanding dreams. Dreams come from both/ and the personal and collective unconscious. Living room, the room where I live inside myself, is filled with deep spirituality

---

[32] Daryl Sharp, "What is Active Imagination?" in Carl Jung Resources, AROPA: The Romanian Association For Psychoanalysis Promotion, http://www.carl-jung.net/active_imagination.html

when I come Home to the many and deep connotations. The story of the prodigal child provides significant meaning because of my life experiences. If this were your dream, your psyche would choose symbols that you might find significant due to your own life experiences. Dreams are individual. One clear message I have learned from dreamwork? Not one other soul, no expert, no friend, wife, husband, parent or sibling will ever know what my dreams mean.

As Lao Tzu said, "New beginnings may come from painful endings." The total transformation of a belief system is life changing, something like water to steam. *The Living Room* dream is far greater than "learning." This is the very root of my existence. These massive internal shifts brought moments of truly existential despair, which is the work of the ego. My very identity was threatened. Who am I if I am not the same Catholic, same woman, same mother, as I was yesterday? I wanted a miracle healing; I surely did not want change. Laughable.

Ego in fact fights desperately to remain in charge. Ego uses every possible mind trick. *The Living Room* surely suggests change and transformation is underway in my psyche. Those are soft words for what was happening within.

Life continues in my external world. I love my work at Alberta Education and I seldom miss a day throughout the entire transformative process. I work in small towns like Whitecourt, St. Paul or Elk Point. Evenings, when my work is finished, I often walk. I have time to pursue this dreamwork and healing obsession. I meet fascinating people who are open, helpful, friendly and often as desperate as I am for deep conversation. I write. Pages.

For example, this week, June 1989, my team is staying in the town of Whitecourt, which is located in a very beautiful, wild, forested part of our province at the confluence of four waterways—the Athabasca, McLeod and Sakwatamau Rivers and Beaver Creek.

Along the Athabasca, I find the perfect place to sit and meditate. I write. I love the water running through me. I am learning that I have an inner river that flows beneath the river, *Rio Abajo Rio.*

My journals are hundreds of pages of thoughts. I am very careful to colour inside the lines while pushing against the boundaries. Prayers and Scripture quotes such as from Genesis 2:10, "A river rises in Eden to water the garden; beyond there it divides and becomes four branches."

An Ode to the River:

I come today, Source of All Branches, love, joy, peace and knowledge, to contemplate You in the joyous singing of your river.

I come to the Source of Life, the rushing, trembling water flowing to its Source, an everlasting cycle of refreshment; a living stream of life.

The water flows creating new life, new joy. The Fountainhead lies high on a mountain as pure snow. Cascading over solid rock it journeys to new life in ever-deepening sometimes wide, often narrow channels. Always it moves back to its origin over solid foundations.

Life rushes, trembles and hisses as golden light shimmers over the surface with love. Gentle breezes flow playfully around me as I watch the silent, ever-steady moving Spirit of God. The river speaks of beauty and life through its living, ceaseless waters. Over rocks and trees. Slowly. Curving. Straight. Rushing. Always searching for the will of its Source.

Show me your ways Mighty River that I might be as solid, as life-giving, as loving and joyful as You. Wash my stones, purify and cleanse the fragments within as I too journey in grace and love to the Fountainhead.

Open my heart and mind like living waters and the whispering small voice of Spirit. Stillness. Guide me to the channel of living water. Flow with the sea of life. I long to know the oneness of heart and mind. I am the flowing river.

Crystal clear. Gushing waters of Mother, moisten the soul. Pour forth. Waters of bubbling laughing life. Joy and peace reign. Wisdom and love are Queen. Harmony with each and every creature. Stand forth upon the Rock. River feeding solitary oneness; movement, touching, seeing, sensing potential energy torrents; endless, birthing, satiating, slaking, wild. Mysterious inner estuaries, hollows, tributaries, rise, roll, surge, spill, basins, rock beds, channels, soul source, pools, ponds, streams, sanctuaries, rising, falling, filling, emptying; washing away the pollution.

The sun holds in the sky until nearly midnight in this Alberta land so close to where I was born. Earth. Home.

To the Fourth Dimension, July 8, 1989

I am with unfamiliar people, one definitely a woman. We are in a hairstylist shop. One person has dark hair and resembles me as a teenager. These are "New Age" people. We begin a meditation. I am on the verge of leaving my physical consciousness and going to the Fourth Dimension. I feel beautifully peaceful. I ask Jesus to lead me by the hand to the fourth time span. I am afraid to go and at the same time want to follow Jesus. A woman sits behind me now with her legs around my body. There is a very elusive sexual energy. I hear the beginnings of very beautiful, soft music. Suddenly I am overcome by fear and I start into the deepest meditation I have ever experienced. I struggle desperately and anxiously. I come back from the depths.

The scene changes. A woman, a professional colleague, whose acidic gossipy tongue I greatly fear, appears. She is very pregnant.

I am loath to write down the dream. I sit with it for several months before I begin to let myself ask questions. I read, write, meditate and the dream does its work in the depths.

My 1989 journal entries show me that I am still suffering from deep free-floating anxiety. I cannot get a hold on its source.

I am physically exhausted and crying a lot. I try to listen to Father Larry Faye's meditation and contemplation tapes. I am unhappy with my shallow faith, my aches and pains, financial instability, unsold Leduc house, the soggy farmhouse basement, the ruined sewer pump, the underweight pigs, low price of cattle and the never-ending bloody work. I "hear" messages in my meditation about "healing the house." I don't understand. I am deeply restless, discouraged, unsettled and fearful. I question the healing experiences of the past several months. Why and how can such deeply experienced peace and healing turn again to fear and anxiety? I pray. I sing endlessly. Monotone. The truth? The *To the Fourth Dimension* dream scares me silly.

It will be 1991 before I slowly begin to realize that the hairdresser represents the beginning of change in my inner feminine. Hair is a symbol of the strength of the feminine power. The hairstylist may represent Real Me or my inner analyst. In childhood, conditioned by the culture of the '50s, I learned to be very carefully socially acceptable. Without ever being told, I learned to please, placate and perform obediently according to the norms of the culture. Underneath the persona or mask of social acceptability lies the authentic person. One dreamwork goal is to uncover the layers of "masks" and find out who you are. This is not a slap at parents. You are a product of both nature and nurture. My experience is just that. Mine.

The motif of unfamiliar people continues. These figures aren't even family but strangers. The dream takes me back to my teenage self, to the days of the first "nervous" breakdown as a 15-year-old in Grade 11. Even though I want to find my inner wisdom and my Self, as symbolized by my attempts to follow Jesus (symbolic of spirituality and love), I become desperately anxious. Dreamwork is not for the faint of heart. Transformation is dismemberment. It requires working through deeply held, unconscious fears. We insist we will "face facts." I think perhaps, in fact, there are no known soul facts. I am trying to face myself.

This dream brings me the gift of possibilities. The beautiful music may symbolize the possibility of harmonious transformation by my inner hairdresser. We listen to classical music, relaxation music, the heavenly choir sings and we are mesmerized. Music soothes and heals the soul, the brain and the body.

What happened to Samson of Biblical fame when Delilah cut off his hair? He lost his power. Why are prisoners subjected to head shaving? To rob them of their identity. Soldiers? Short hair is a sign of the collective, military power over the individual. The power of life and death. Just watch controlling parents insist on their son's haircut. I can tell many stories about hair and my own sons. Jason did the green hair thing in Grade 8. His teacher actually called me to ask, "Why are you allowing Jason to come to school with his hair dyed green?" It was a short conversation. She asked, "Aren't you the President of the Local Alberta Teachers' Association?" Really.

Look around. Turban, skullcap, fez, hijab, wimple. Cover. No cover. Short hair. Long hair.

We have our hair done to "feel" better, to be more "beautiful." We "let our hair down," meaning loosen up, have more fun or forget the silly control by so many rules. Young people use hair in almost every generation to make an identity statement.

The dream may have indicated an opening of mind and spirit to new soul dimensions, but at the time of the dreaming I had little, if any, understanding of the notion of dimensions. The feelings of "lifting" and "leaving" my body produced serious fear and anxiety.

The symbol of the pregnant woman? Pregnancy is a time of new life, growing within. The earth is alive with new life at Easter; it is pregnant with the possibilities of new growth and the celebration of fecundity, generativity and creativity. This pregnant woman is "a colleague," meaning I am somewhat familiar with this fertile aspect of myself. The acidic, gossipy tongue I fear is my own self-censoring, abusive inner voice telling me that I am a fraud, and most surely deluded by thoughts of healing and miracles. Doubt. If I am healed, then why am I still feeling terrible and anxious? Why am I not ... why am I lacking? I can't even have a proper miracle. In Jungian terms, this is my acidic, hateful, negative inner feminine and an aspect of my shadow. But, I am pregnant with possibilities. The shadow work so often spoken of by Jung has only just begun. Within my shadow lie the many aspects of self hidden away, cut off so I can be socially acceptable to parents, church and community. Every single person lives with their shadow. Silenced from early childhood, I can only imagine the layers of feminine soul that lie festering in my basement, the personal unconscious. I can't even begin to imagine the state of the collective unconscious given millennia of repression of the feminine, of the woman and earth; surely the collective unconscious retains much shame and bitterness together with golden treasured gems.

The symbolism of sexual energy between two women brings intense shame. The rules around sexuality, learned by osmosis from 1945 to 1991, are many and buried deep. However, when I gather the nerve and the energy to research sexual imagery, an entirely new world opens up. Subsequent to the search of early January 1989, and the charismatic healing at St. Basil's Church a few weeks later, many so-called "female problems"— dysmenorrhea, scattered and missing menses, pain, bloating— completely disappeared. This *Fourth Dimension* dream opened a door to the beginning of understanding of the feminine principle that lives within every human person. It began my journey into understanding that the earth is feminine. The feminine face of God became faintly visible. I reread *When God Was a Woman*[33] and alternated between euphoria and darkness.

During early dreamwork, I read the Bible often. Simply opening it to a page and reading became a favoured strategy. I open the Bible to Deuteronomy 8:2–3. It speaks to wandering in the desert for 40 years. "Not by bread alone does man live, but by every word that comes forth from the mouth of the Lord." Jung suggested to his new patients to revisit their childhood religion. He also made clear that the soul does not live happily

---

[33] Merlin Stone, *When God Was a Woman* (NY: Harcourt Brace Jovanovich, 1976).

with the bleakness of rational thought. Dreams are the rich, deep language of symbolism. The Catholic Church is filled with symbolism but much of the richness, the depth, the artistry, the possibilities and the imaginative have been reduced to literal words. Through Protestantism, there has developed a fear of symbols. Listen to the rhetoric about the literality of the Bible. Truly ridiculous. Pretending to take the words chosen by male scholars as literal Truth after countless language translations and countless adaptations to the vernacular of many cultures? I don't think so.

The Bible includes deep symbolic wisdom when read with the god, Hermes (the winged messenger), in mind, that is, through the lens of hermeneutics. To take the Word as literal is to steal from your own soul. I don't pretend to understand; however, I reserve the right to search. I am sure She can handle my puny questioning. Any God not strong enough to prefer my doubts to certainty is a stunted anthropomorphic God made in the image of despots. Finally, I discover the root of the fight over the concept of sin. Pelagius, Irish Celtic monk, preached that love was written on the human heart by the hand of God, and that living like the Christ was more important than believing *in Christ*. Pelagius lost. Augustine and Jerome, backed by the Roman Empire and the Council of Nicea 325 CE, won. I guess I missed it in my rushed reading

The Inner Garden

God plants, she weeds, he prunes, she waters and hoes.

Always the garden grows.

I will remember the growing
on the mountain tops

when I am weeding in the
dark shadows of the valley.

I will remember the
growing when pruning

shears snip away the
falseness.

Love.

I stretch out my arms and fly

to the Garden of Love.

of *Original Blessing.* But it has and will continue to spiral back into my dreams.

I am reading Edgar Cayce, a controversial American mystic who spoke of reincarnation, healing and trance, as well as Eastern and European mystics. I am also reading approved books, such as Father George Maloney, *Uncreated Energy,*[34] *about* the physics of miracles, that is "seeing what has always been there."

I write poetry to honour the dream. Poor poetry perhaps, but dreams do not demand great poets. Writing helps me deepen my interpretations and try to overcome the fear that still remains my constant companion.

I return to the *To the Fourth Dimension* dream again on February 9, 2015. Through the wonders of technology, I find on YouTube *4th Dimension Explained.* It is absolutely astonishing. Ludwig Schläfli, a 19th century visionary Swiss geometer, understood that space has a high number of dimensions. There are at least a quadrillion things I do not understand. The video says simply, understanding the fourth dimension requires significant learning. What is the meaning of hypercube, tetrahedron, simplex, the 24-cell with no analogue in dimension three? Remember, this was explained by Schläfli in the 19th century. My dream is much more amazing than I originally considered. Twenty-five years later, I still have little to no understanding of what it would mean to me to move into the fourth dimension.

When asked about the Fourth Dimension, Carl Jung purportedly explained it as a realm of ideas, the world of imagination where we can make anything happen. It's a very big world, infinite; a world that is often referred to as higher consciousness, where one makes a leap in vibration of the human energy body. One thing is clear, that the possibility of imagination and change scared me. How do I move in space

---

[34] Father George Maloney, *Uncreated Energy: A Journey into the Authentic Sources of Christian Faith* (Rockport, MA: Element Books, 1987).

and time? Is there such a thing as space and time? And it may be that I am still afraid of my own imagination.

The Bridge, August 1, 1989

> *The dream that calls to us is also a bridge between*
> *worlds; uniting the inner realm with the outer world can't*
> *be easy or more would do it ... the bridge represents a turn*
> *to the inner life and a willingness to face the depths.*
>
> –Michael Meade, *Fate and Destiny:*
> *The Two Agreements of the Soul*

Rachel and I are going somewhere close to Grandpa Miller's homestead. The road is blocked by strange bridges. We cannot get the car across. Then, we are at an unknown house. A very beautiful young woman, is in the house. I can hear her talking to my mother about New Age and saving the young people from something or other. I am outside or in a closet but I can hear part of the conversation. Then I am on the other side of the bridge and a man comes and steals our dog, Rascal. The dream ends.

I was delighted when I discovered that Meade calls dreams the "bridge between worlds." I see my dream bridges as not only connecting the human and the divine world, but linking the child and the adult whose soul hungers for the imaginal, and perhaps even linking outer religion to inner spirituality.

How old am I in the dream? About 10 years old. So my younger self is visiting the past. Water is representative of the unconscious. The house is my inner world. My younger self is talking to the parent mother, the voice in me that represents beliefs rooted in the land of my ancestors. My grandparents lived on the homestead in the Cornwall Creek area in the 1930s and '40s as a result of the Great Depression. I think about the catechism of the Catholic Church of my grandparents' era. I could cross the bridge but am resisting moving myself, the car, across to "another world" where there is a beautiful feminine presence inside the "house." The homestead may be symbolic of ancient wisdom, the land of soul.

The young woman represents the beautiful and youthful inner feminine. I found this particular real-life person very intimidating though I only knew her at a distance. The young dream woman may be an aspect of my inner world and spirituality. Perhaps I am being shown the feminine beauty of following my intuition.

Sometime during these early years of dreamwork, I met an older woman at a meditation group who insisted on giving me a 1930s copy of the Baltimore Catechism. As I read it I realized that, despite the changes in the church during the reign of Pope John Paul XXIII and the Vatican Council of 1962, my personal unconscious retained the beliefs of my ancestors when Catholicism was even more rigid, particularly in its view of women, sexuality and discipline.

The dream brings to conscious awareness my fears of the institutional disparagement of the so-called evils of "New Age." *The Teachings of the Inner Christ*[35] would most definitely be judged heretical. So, the dream comes to show me that I am keeping my views in the closet and just beginning to recognize that I have an intellectual belief system and an unconscious one. Bringing the two together requires crossing over the bridge of consciousness, bringing ancestral beliefs out of the closet.

In dreamwork and mythology, dogs may indicate healing, as in The Porch of Asclepius or its precursor, Ba-ba, the goddess connected with healing and her sacred animal in the myth of

---

[35] Ann Porter Meyer and Peter Victor Meyer, *Being a Christ!: The Basic Course of the Teaching of the Inner Christ* (San Diego, CA: Dawning Publications, 1975).

Inanna.[36] Rascal is our border collie. I am in the borderlands. Some unknown aspect of me is trying to steal my ability to follow my instinct, intuitive right action (or inner intuition) as symbolized by my healing dog. So in the symbolic language of the soul I am reminded or warned not to allow the material world, conscious thought, the intellect, the ego to steal the blossoming new life, the growth of the inner child toward wholeness and individuation.

There is a good deal to this dream that eluded me years ago. It reminds me that writing and revisiting dreams leads to merging the multitude of layers and deepening understanding. Enfoldment continues.

According to Jungian theory, some dreams are compensatory (from the Latin *compensare*: "to equalize"), meaning that rather than the psyche being overwhelmed by fears, dreams bring the fear to the surface to dissipate. I intend to heal my confusion. I intend to accept new and deeper truth. I have no desire to divorce myself from Catholicism, neither do I intend to accept dogmatic tradition blindly. I claim deep understanding of my own oneness with the Father. The Father and I are one.

As I write and pray, I don't even notice the incongruence of my thoughts. How often do I pray to the Father out of pure habit?

I claim deep understanding as I lie down to sleep at 12:00 September 24, 1989 in my farm home I ask for deep inner healing. I awake from a big dream at 1:00 am in which the seeds are planted for the journey across the threshold and out of my "Father's" House toward the understanding that I seek.

---

[36] Florence Vanderdorpe, "When Myth Shows What the Mind Does not Reach. (*Storytelling, Self, Society: An Interdisciplinary Journal of Storytelling Studies*, Volume 7, Issue 2, 2011, Pages 91–109.

SECTION *III*

LEAVING MY FATHER'S HOUSE

Chapter Six

Inner World Learnings

Who looks outside, dreams. Who looks inside, awakens.

–C.G. Jung

Seeds of Truth–The Sprout, September 25, 1989

I am in my mother's house, which seems really to be our farm house. One brother and my parents are there. We have a meal of watery broth with old unpeeled potatoes with long, tangled sprouts and what looks like prunes or plums in it. The house is messy, dirty and chaotic. An unknown man, his wife, and child come to rent the house. The child and Rachel or some other child spill milk all over and throw it around. I don't notice. I go to the sink where the lady is getting a drink. She rinses the cup and throws the water on the floor and laughs. I yell at the children to come. I berate them and then go back to the table where I notice a pile of dirty old boots under a cupboard. I grab Rachel, shouting at her to clean up the mess. I twist her arm and sit on her. She yells back, "NO." The man comes by from somewhere and says, "We can have it. My brother made a phone call and we can have it." I say, "You will be very lonely here." My mom tells the woman she will stay with her for a couple of days until she is used to it. I insist, "Others have been lonely but they got used to it."

The house motif will repeat many times over the years. In this early dream, I don't seem to know if I am still in childhood or have grown up into my own home. Apparently, I am firmly in neither but both at the same time. I do not see but sense Dad's presence. Within me, transformation is creating mass turmoil and upheaval. The dream is filled with feminine symbols as well as symbols of transformation. We change raw vegetables into cooked. Milk and water are spilled. Change of ownership is happening in the hearth. Such inner chaos requires of me a good deal of energy to continue to function in the outer world. The dream tells me that I am still fearful, struggling and angry with the new ideas on the spiritual, emotional plane. There is substance—potatoes will be produced from the sprouts. I am beating up on myself, and trying desperately to sit on new ideas, to keep new young ideas under control but the inner young feminine is refusing to be held back. Perhaps my mother's voice speaks truth. Perhaps many women have lived lonely lives disconnected from their inner world. Maybe I will learn to "inhabit my aloneness" as John O'Donohue says in *Eternal Echoes*. He also says, "This is slow work; it takes years to bring your mind home."[37]

The old boots? Still reflecting. Most dream writers encourage sitting with the dream for some time before actively searching beyond the self for any explanation. I sit. Years. Nothing.

---

[37] John O'Donohue, *Eternal Echoes: Celtic Reflections on our Yearning to Belong* (New York: HarperCollins, 1999), 93–4.

Milk is a fascinating symbol that at the time of the dream had no meaning to me. I do find references to milk and the Cow Goddess. The milk of human kindness. The Milky Way. Apparently, I don't recognize the feminine nourishment as the milk is thrown around carelessly. After subsequent cow dreams, I realize that the ancient Cow Goddesses have different names in different centuries in different parts of the world. Hathor is the most famous of Upper Egypt and Bast of Lower. I find some of the current archaeological research literature instructive. Hathor was known as "the Great One of Many Names" in the predynastic period of Egypt, which is dated by various sources as circa 4000–3050 BCE. There are references to Hathor as the goddess of beauty and patron of the cosmetic arts. In fact, she is associated with many aspects of women's lives. She is referred to as the Mother of Mothers and the Mistress of Heaven. As a Catholic, I find it very simple to cross reference to Mother Mary, Virgin Mother, Mother of God, and the Litany recited over many years. Dreams open the way to cavernous learning.

Seeking to understand dream symbols and my experiences leads to major chaos. Eventually I find a descriptive term in learning theory, "the pedagogy of discomfort." It becomes clear that I know nothing of either modern or ancient women's history. I have no inner feminine symbol system. I am damn mad at yet another betrayal. This journey has led me to *The Creation of Feminist Consciousness, Why History Matters* and *The Creation of Patriarchy*. In *Why History Matters*, Lerner says: "Beginning in the Renaissance, state governments continually used history as a tool for legitimizing power and for creating a common cultural tradition based on that history."[38]

Curriculum as a tool of the patriarchy continues to this moment. As for my youth, it wasn't hard to locate my 1959 Grade

---

[38] Gerda Lerner, *The Creation of Feminist Consciousness* (NY: Oxford University Press, 1993); Gerda Lerner, *Why History Matters: Life and Thought* (NY: Oxford University Press, 1997), 202; Gerda Lerner, *The Creation of Patriarchy* (NY: Oxford University Press, 1986).

10 social studies text in the University of Alberta Archive. The cover image is permanently etched on my mind. According to the records, the text was provincially authorized.[39]

What did I "learn" from this text? New & Phillips say that the god Osiris preceded Jesus Christ. There is no mention of a goddess and Osiris is given the role of Persephone, goddess of the greening fields of springtime.[40] There is no mention of women in education or any other aspect of society except the influence of the feminine on body and on home fashion. The biblical stories of Abraham and Joseph are written as true historical accounts and the Hebrew people, while dismissed as relatively insignificant, are accorded the honour of "true greatness to be found in the contemplative life of those whose minds were opening to a new and truer conception of God. Yahweh, or Jehovah, was worshipped as an unseen or spiritual power, not a thing of brass or stone in human or animal form."[41] Historical events are often explained as the fulfillment of biblical prophecy. For example, with respect to the biblical siege of Nineveh, "And the Lord shall cause his glorious voice to be heard, and the descent of his arm to be seen, with the indignation of his anger."[42] "Thieves and honest businessmen alike sacrificed to Hermes to ensure the success of their ventures."[43] The authors explain that Zeus was god over all the gods and king over all. He is described as an avenging god who has great and terrible power. The text leaves no doubt that as a male God he has the intellectual power to create life. There is no mention of Hermes as the bringer of dreams, and Sappho is only mentioned as the best-known poetess in the world and credited with "The Hymn to Aphrodite." Athene is represented as springing living from

[39] Chester W. New and Charles E. Phillips, *Ancient and Mediaeval History* (Toronto: Clarke, Irwin & Company, 1941).

[40] New and Phillips, *Ancient and Mediaeval History*, 33.

[41] New and Phillips, *Ancient and Mediaeval History*, 49.

[42] New and Phillips, *Ancient and Mediaeval History*, 50.

[43] New and Phillips, *Ancient and Mediaeval History*, 107.

the head of Zeus, while it is noted that Sophia is Greek meaning knowledge.

I have found scant reference to the goddess in my nearly 50-year study of patriarchal religion. The Bible? Christian scholars have eradicated nearly every vestige of the presence of goddess religion. If there were references to the goddess, I wouldn't have recognized them anyway. It is impossible to see what you have never seen before. Any small tidbit of evidence about women's religious leadership within Christianity must be given deep attention since every effort has been made toward its removal. I read Starhawk, *Truth or Dare, Spiral Dance* and *Dreaming the Dark*.[44] My search brought me to some deeply unsettling historical evidence. It became glaringly apparent that goddesses have been dismissed as "mythology" and that in Western rational thought, mythology holds no significance. I have lost count of the times I have been yelled at when I question the Bible being the inspired, literal word of God. The evidence provided by the works of anthropologist Riane Eisler and archaeologist Marija Gimbutas must be taken into serious consideration. When goddesses are dismissed without careful consideration of evidence from prehistory, and scholars continue to spread an inexcusable ignorance without questioning simple old memorization of past history, then unawareness continues.

Working with dreams, which Freud referred to as the royal road to the unconscious, ensures that the history of the goddesses will not be denied. History as taught in the Alberta school system mentions little to nothing on dreams, goddesses, race, slavery, planned abolition or attempted forced assimilation of Aboriginal people and the oppressive constraints on women. Albertans and Canadians, until very recently, were held to be

---

[44] Starhawk, *Truth or Dare: Encounters with Power, Authority and Mystery* (San Francisco: Harper & Row, 1990); *The Spiral Dance* (NY: Harper, 1989); *Dreaming the Dark: Magic, Sex and Politics* (Boston, MA: Beacon Press, 1982).

somehow devoid of racism and certainly did not participate, like Americans, in the—gasp—slave trade. I realize, I must disrupt the patterns of my own complicity. I must acknowledge the ways in which I, as a mother, teacher, consultant and now writer, do the work of the patriarchy. That is not an easy admission of guilt. To this end, I work with dreams to contradict prevailing cultural myths with an account of my deep life experience. By noticing, writing down and working with dreams over time, one begins slowly to discern myths repeating in recorded history.

In 1935, the Social Credit party of Alberta, led by Baptist Minister and school principal, William Aberhart, came to power on the promise of monetary reform in Alberta. He neglected to notice that monetary policy was the responsibility of the federal government. The federal government declared his monetary legislation *ultra vires* (beyond legal power or authority) but Albertans, impoverished by the Great Depression, were too ravaged by drought and bankruptcy to see past the hope offered. Their anger was directed at the federal government. Superintendents of the schools worked directly for government. I have no way of knowing for certain but am somewhat suspicious of the influence of the Baptist religion on the social studies program in Alberta schools. The official text of my youth contained some deeply erroneous religion as part of the mandated social studies program in 1959. Was it ever questioned?

As a social studies consultant at Alberta Education, I generated ministerial responses to parent complaints about social studies curriculum. There were some complaints about the inclusion of Greek mythology in the Grade 6 curriculum and a few parents believed it would teach children to worship idols and false gods. One particular set of primary school readers filled with delightful images generated massive complaints from the religious right. The problem? Images. In particular the image of a red-haired girl brought wild accusations of witchcraft, evil and the work of the devil. I was stunned. Somehow the beliefs of *Malleus Maleficarum,* the witch hunter's manual (1486), a treatise on witchcraft, live on in the collective unconscious. These parents are not to be laughed at. They believe fully in the evil of witchcraft. How does society unlock the unconscious?

Alberta curriculum (2005) provides only cursory mention of women and their role in history. There is lip service, a kind of cursory mention, as in "add women and stir." In 2009, in a fourth year Education class I was teaching at the University of Alberta, we were deep in conversation about what big ideas needed to be included in a high school textbook. We had created huge clusters of the main ideas. I asked, "Anything else?" I repeated the question several times, leaving the space of the possible for emergence of thought, conversation and creation of new ideas among the six groups of students. Finally, I asked them to think of main themes that might be missing. Silence. This was a class of 23 with very close gender balance. Nary a mention of women's history. When I asked why this might be, one young man suggested, seriously, "Well, really, maybe it's because women have never done anything historically significant?" So, then. That's it for teacher education in 2009.

I think I might claim the following as an archetypal dream that is mythic, great, grand, since it occurred at a particularly significant time in my life. I feel as though I have learned a good deal from working with it and that it has much more to teach me. It surely has an element of impossibility, is extremely vivid and comes often to mind after many years. Archetypal dreams envisage endless possibilities, new forms arising out of old and ancient paradigms. Substantive new life, the real meat and potatoes of the issue; I have lived on thin broth. I am just learning about the power of the unconscious.

Tree of Life, September 28, 1989

I am in the kitchen of our farm home. Two beautiful, ethereal figures appear at the back entrance, one male and one female. They are wearing deep, royal blue suits such as astronauts wear. Their shoulders are dusted with white. They glow softly, within an orb of light. I think it is my eldest son and his girlfriend, home early for Christmas. I wonder why they are early and why they did not tell us they were coming. Behind them are beautiful, fluffy snowflakes falling gently. Christmas music fills the air. "I'm fine, Mom." Deep relief floods through me. As I stand in the kitchen, an evergreen tree appears as a Christmas tree but without the decorations. It falls gently over top of me. I am filled with a feeling of amazing peace.

I feel as though I have been visited by angels. It is mystical, magical, otherworldly. Beyond mere words. I am happy with the message from my son. Often, I feel as though I am able to "speak" to him over distances. The snow symbolizes clean and fresh, but also frozen inner feeling. The evergreen tree is symbolic of The Tree of Everlasting Life throughout years of goddess religion, often called pagan by those who have never checked the etymology of the word. Pagan simply means "people of the earth" and early beliefs, contrary to the patriarchal Enlightenment thinking of today, were centred on the earth. Today some people understand the earth as home. Others? Not so much. A commodity for consumption but not held in esteem. The evergreen tree brings the freedom of new birth, the melding of the Tree of Life with the life of spirit, the Christ within me. Christ energy lives in my kitchen, which is symbolic of sustenance, transformation, change, the heart of the home. Home is a metaphor for the soul. I often sit at the kitchen table to read, write or cry in my struggle to integrate the changes that are occurring within. Jung refers to the Self as the aspect of divinity within human beings. This dream brings further gifts. I have always had a love of trees, the forest, the earth and Her gardens. Gardening is my deepest delight. This dream brings the gift of everlasting life as have the trees throughout the history of earth peoples. Again, archetypal.

I am deeply aware of the gifts of the dream *Tree of Life*. To this very day I feel the vividly blue figures clearly embedded within. The images come to me often when I meditate or pray. If I were an artist, I would paint this scene. I have tried, without much success. I considered a collage of ethereal blues for my study. I searched the internet. No image captures the beauty of this dream. None. In the gardens of my imagination are early may cherry, apple, plum, lilac and flowering crabapple blossoms. My farm gardens support and sustain me always. The blue of the sky beyond apple blossoms is magnificent.

Cleansing, October 29, 1989

My car sits beside the road somewhere fairly close to home. I am walking toward it and as I come closer, I see greasy, black gunk oozing out from under the hood onto the fenders.

Later, two boys playing jokes are coming into a room where they do not belong. I go in as well and show the male guard the numbers on the boys' clothing. I only recall one number: 617. One lad is tall, well built, muscular like my eldest son. I place a large blue cloth shaped like a bandage over the boy's left forearm. He does not appear physically hurt. The blue cloth fits perfectly.

Though dreams may appear in fragments, they are like the scenes of a drama. The car is often a symbol of the self; the etymology of "auto" is "self-acting or moving on its own." My "self" is oozing gunk, or toxins. If this were my Jetta, I would immediately seek a mechanic. Body memories are not so easily exorcised. In meditations over the past few months, my left side has grotesquely beautiful black, brown, slimy, dark fluids; I both feel and "see" the gunk oozing out. The most significant aspect of the dream is the blue bandage, or healing, which I place on the young man's left forearm. I am loath to write about these things because I fear the judgment and ridicule of the ultra religious who seem to think they have a right to something they call Truth. Somehow Right is on their side. This dream seems to tell me that healing the left is important.

Trauma gets under the skin and the body remembers. Every experience in this lifetime is imprinted on my body. For years and years I have reiki, massage therapy, myofascial release, craniosacral therapy, hundreds of hours of fitness courses as I continually work to clear the years of repressed trauma, breathe properly and move. Even after all these years of work, I will be diagnosed in 2014 with erythromelalgia. I will learn that my body still holds vestigial remnants of repressed trauma. That is a story for another time. Now? I am learning to breath through yoga and meditation. Both practices come under fire as potentially evil in the *Western Catholic Reporter*. Strange, I don't think to cancel the subscription.

Jung was clear that the body is merely the visible soul, the psyche; and the soul is the psychological experience of the body. In my understanding of yoga, that too deals with self, Self and body. Indeed.

It seems that my left arm—symbolically the unconscious feminine creative aspect, the imaginal mind of intuition and closed off since childhood—is healing beneath the bandage. Earlier peoples, people of the earth, used and refined that imaginal aspect of the brain, which is now considered irrational. Our culture values linear, analytical, logical, sequential thinking as a result of the 17th century Enlightenment and also very early writers such as Thomas Aquinas, Augustine, and many more who were insistent upon Logos, the word, as divine truth. For centuries, even millennia, woman has traditionally been considered less than man due to her "irrational" emotional being.

The right, random abstract, imaginal, creative aspect of the brain is threatening to my left. I have long prided myself on being logical. I heard so often the derogatory remarks directed at women about "random abstract" or "being too emotional." Survival and indeed success in my profession and my mostly all male world, I thought, demanded clear logic. I complied. Now, survival of my soul requires images. My soul is coming home and she speaks in symbols.

I see blues and purples constantly as I meditate. Blessed Mother wears a blue mantle. When I was a child, my family prayed the rosary together most if not all evenings before bedtime. The image endures. My grandfather Miller gave a statue of the Blessed Mother to the Holy Rosary Church when my grandmother died in April, 1946. She still wears the blue mantle. Blues and purples are also chakra colours.

The number 617 is interesting although I know little of the metaphors of numbers. In dreamwork, to play is to learn. Playing with these numbers, I notice that six + one is seven thus indicating two sevens. Seven is a sacred number ... there are seven sacraments, seven story mountains to spirituality, seven days in the week, seven days of creation, Noah brings seven pairs of every animal onto the Ark, the Menorah of Jewish origin has seven branches, there are seven deadly sins, seven colours in the rainbow, seven seas, and seven wonders of the ancient world. There are seven brides for seven brothers, and the seven-year itch, and purportedly seven years between passages on the human journey. I seem to recall from the song that Jericho fell on the seventh day after seven priests with seven trumpets marched around the city seven times.... Need I go on. There are probably many more associations to the number seven. So, again, as in *The Landing* dream, this dream chooses to show me the number seven. Significance will unfold as I continue on this journey. One is usually considered as integration or unity of conscious and unconscious. Six can be divided to make groups of three. On further reading, I find that Jung says three may signify that something is nearly but not quite complete; or that what I am lacking can be supplied by some part of my unconscious that I find too frightening or too amazing to acknowledge and use.

Dreams do not arise from the logical sequential mind. Perhaps that is why so little has been learned in modern cultures about the work of dreams in our lives. This short dream has a good deal of potential. It is not yet one full year since I recorded my first dream. I am overwhelmed with the amount of learning and the depth of possibility.

My dreamwork is based largely on Jung's theories. While teaching at the University of Alberta as a sessional lecturer from 2005 until 2012, I discovered Jung's theories of transformation had deep applicability to education. It was exciting to try to integrate my new ways of learning into my teaching. Difficult work, but the inclusion and experience of these principles helped me show young teachers how to teach differently than *they* had been taught. Jung spent a lifetime learning and theorizing about the personal unconscious as well as the collective unconscious. It was and is deeply disturbing to become aware of how superficial my understanding of myself really is. Understanding that many of my most deeply held beliefs are just that—beliefs—is indeed disconcerting. I now try to ensure I notice. For as R.D. Laing famously said: "The range of what we think and do is limited by what we fail to notice. And because we fail to notice that we fail to notice, there is little we can do to change; until we notice how failing to notice shapes our thoughts and deeds."

The difficulty in becoming more conscious is that I had no idea I was unconscious to begin with. Coming to know and understand oneself is the work of a lifetime. I attest to the difficulty of coming to change my religious beliefs. I return often to the words of my dad, "Don't confuse God with the church." Indeed, the institution with its rules, rituals, procedures and hierarchy may often have little to do with God. For me, the exclusion of women from the priesthood became a huge issue. And just what or who is God anyway? Who gets to decide? Reading became a deeper obsession. *Beyond Patching: Faith and Feminism in the Catholic Church* helped me greatly.

I am not a Bible scholar. Neither do I believe in the literal interpretation of the Bible, or what Daniel Webster of dictionary fame called, "plain and obvious meaning." In my belief system, the Bible is filled with much wisdom for the ages, together with many man-made rules and laws. The idea that the RIGHT creation myth is in Genesis when Genesis has two different versions either makes me crazy or fills me with laughter. Many verses can be used by the ego to beat up on someone who is not living according to the personal dictates of a particular purveyor of truth. I listened recently to a KKK member explain his beliefs about Black people. "The Bible says we must not lie with the beasts of the field." Huh? I nearly drove my car into the ditch. But the man was serious in his belief; it explained why the KKK lynched Blacks who showed even a passing glance at a white woman.

This winter of 2016 I walk often and long. Today, along my way, a gentleman is evangelizing at Ogden Point, Victoria Harbour, British Columbia. He thrusts two small pieces of paper in my hand. Back home, I read Malachi 3–6 and Jeremiah 9:25 together with his interpretations. The Book of Malachi is the last Book of the Old Testament, written approximately 430 BCE. According to the gentleman, beardless men as well as those who trim their beards or are uncircumcised are destined for hell. I show the verses to my girlfriend who immediately asks, "Did he have a beard?" I can't remember! So a few days later, walking the same route, I take note. No, he does not have a beard. His face is clean-shaven and hair neatly trimmed. He wears blue jeans and a hoodie. He continues to thrust his words into the hands of passers-by. I walk by and slowly shake my head. Hmm. Who says beliefs have to be congruent? I begin to understand that beliefs have more power than I ever thought possible.

Is it possible that my collective unconscious holds much that originated in the days before the Christ, in the days of the Old Testament? There is no way I could have had this thought in 1989. I knew not that I was living in exile—that is after the end of my life's endurance run, or, symbolically, the captivity of the Egyptians in Babylon—during the days of my intense depressions. I am no longer a slave to the depressions. I am now in post-exile where there is much still to be learned, and where I can ponder and ponder. Noting dreams does that to the dreamer. I find myself still pondering them years later. Dreams are the gift from the psyche that keep on giving if I write them down.

The Shadow, November 11, 1989

A young child about Rachel's age, about 10 or smaller, is walking toward me. As she walks, the packsack on her back begins to burn. I take a step closer and we make eye contact. The child removes the burning bag. We merge into one person and watch peacefully as the bag and its contents burn without a trace into nothingness. I am deeply peaceful. I awaken.

In 1989, I understand the dream to mean that a burden of garbage, old beliefs, misunderstandings, pain, and grief has been burned away. I write a long poem honouring the dream, the Mysteries of God, silence and stillness. I begin to question what the word or concept "God" means. I decide that probably every single person has their own "image." No wonder the religious fight continues.

The collective unconscious holds universal archetypes identified by Jung as persona, shadow, anima/animus, Divine Child, the Wise Old Man or Woman, the Great Mother and the Trickster. I will come to know them all in the course of my dream life.

The dream child was numinous, the Divine Child, an archetypal image. The child symbolizes beginnings, possibilities, potentialities and potencies. Innocence, trust and naïveté abound.

The child's back-pack is an archetypal shadow symbol. Archetypal dreams are mythic, great or grand and often occur during significant times of change, transformation and transition.

The shadow contains my treasure trove; those rejected and possibly shameful aspects of self that I wish to hide from the world. Literality has no place in the symbolic and metaphorical world of dreams. Everyone has a shadow. Proof lies in corporate sales of the latest and greatest stuff to help us hide ourselves beneath the latest fashions, rid us of wrinkles, sweat, natural body smells, hairy legs, or crooked teeth, together with multiple self-help courses in self-confidence and assertiveness. I think a lot about the child in the dream.

I imagine the little ones in their complete abandonment. Lost in a task, tongue pursed, or joyously explaining their latest passion. What happens to that child by adolescence? The socialization is nearly complete. The shaming, the shh, and don't do this or that admonitions. If you want to know and acknowledge your shadow and begin shadow work, pay attention to a dream in which your dream ego thoroughly dislikes or likes or is afraid of another person in your family, your tribe or acquaintances. Then, write out what disturbs or delights you about that person. Then, softly and gently look at yourself and your shadow. I continue to watch my dreams for signs of shadow bags. What am I dragging around that does not serve me well? Turns out, there is a never-ending supply of "stuff." I will come to learn that much of the content is treasure. The psychic depth of the unconscious with its inclusionary policy of all of human history means I have within me what also feels like real evil.

The world also drags around its shadow. We call it pollution, garbage, war, mayhem, murder, violence and rage. That shadow includes Job, Cain and Abel, and the myths of human existence. The more we heal ourselves, the more we heal the planet.

Eye contact between my dream ego and the child brings to mind the eyes as windows to the soul. I have shoved my divinity into the shadows. This dream definitely feels like an encounter with divinity. Through fire we change wood to ashes, raw to cooked, cold to warmth. In this dream, the fire transforms the garbage I hold in my shadow bag. It changes the inner baggage to nothingness. Every time I work with or read this dream, a deep peacefulness returns. I am so glad I found dreamwork. I hope when I am 90 not to be stooped over, nose to the ground, weighed down by the burdens of life held in my shadow bag.

I meditate. In the silence, I recall experiences during the pilgrimage to Lac Ste. Anne, Alberta, in summer 1989. Two friends prayed with me that afternoon. One told me she had a vision of a stone rolling away from my heart and peacefulness remained with me for many hours and into the evening. I read Luke 16:19–31. I am discovering the symbolic inner world of the Bible. I am coming to discern the difference between outer consciousness, worldly mindedness and sensory physical expression. Materiality starves the soul, which becomes like a beggar awaiting scraps from the intellect and the senses. The soul is eternal yet in death there is no physical expression, thus the soul and inner consciousness will be free. I begin to know that my search is within myself; thus the dreams. There is no outer authority that will "fix" me. I am seriously on my own. As a midlife woman, I am looking for depth, not rules. Not external authority. I long for understanding. The intellect, the rich man in Luke, does not hear the still, small, inner voice. The heart and soul hear but the ego self formed in patriarchal fire refuses to give up control via the rational intellect. I am seeking integration, I guess. I begin to write. I AM. I contemplate the meaning of omnipresence, omnipotence and omniscience. Childhood words memorized and spoken back to the catechism teachers in summer and written in the correspondence lessons in winter. Understanding? I don't think so. As now, most learning in the 1950s was confused with simple regurgitation. Memorization. Now freed from the world of fill-in-the-blank tests, I am determined to develop my own deep synthesis of ideas from many sources. In a prayer of thanksgiving, I sing Glory Alleluia. I repeat my mantra. I am ready to take one more step. I move from birth of the inner life to maturity in the inner life. I am. I trust the process. I trust. I hope.

Gefilte Fish, November 19, 1989

There are two rooms. I move from one to the other. In the "other" room I eat some unfamiliar fish, "gefilte" fish. I think to myself, "This is the Bread of Life."

There was more to the dream but in the morning it had receded back into the unconscious. Again, I make the total rookie mistake of not getting up to write it down at 3:00 a.m.

I can't even figure out how to spell this fish word. I try every possible combination. And I wait. Word association is one of the few strategies I have learned so far. So, in the Catholic tradition, fish could easily symbolize the content of the sea of the unconscious. Church vestments, altar cloths, the Communion rail, Christ as fisher of men, feeding the 5,000 with five loaves and two fishes. Manifesting endless substance in the form of bread and fishes. Limitless oceans filled with fish, surviving the Flood. Fish are associated with the Christ in biblical times and water with new life. Even as a small child I believed that the so-called second coming had nothing to do with the person of "the Christ." I don't have much option but to research the qualification of this symbol as I can find nothing in my experiences nor my imagination related to gefilte fish. I come to realize it has a long tradition as a Jewish food. And of course, throughout my growing up years, fish was always served on Fridays in our home. There are several possible interpretations. One includes the idea that we ate fish on Fridays in a subtle nod to Venus. However, it was explained as a "sacrifice" or "penance." More and more I see the depth of concretization and literality that sucks the life and power out of the symbolic life. Dried up and desiccated. I must bring the symbolism to life within me. I simply can no longer even listen to dogmatism, rules, orders, authority. It is time for me to become more fully conscious. I wonder if there is just a really simple explanation. Fish is symbolic of the Great Piscean Age. And a song of '69,

"The Age of Aquarius." Jesus Christ was Middle Eastern. Fish in the seas. Not herds of cattle in the fields.

I grip this dream tightly as a sign that I am coming to some sort of new consciousness, centred in Life. I think about the saying that "A house divided against itself cannot stand," and I know that I have spent many years divided and that hearing voices in 1984–85 was an indication of a potential psychic split. I don't have the proper psychoanalytic terms for it. Does it really matter? What good have labels or diagnoses done for me up to now? None. Sadly, I have lost all trust in medical or psychological help. I am learning to trust my own inner world, my beginning understanding of my own Inner Christ. I have always believed in miracles. Now, I am experiencing my own. My inner voice: "Miracles are seeing that which has always been there: perfection." The dream movement from one room to another could symbolize straddling the threshold between the Piscean and the Aquarian Ages. Some authors will say that these Ages are like vast tectonic plates shifting deep within the collective unconscious. And further, that humanity has begun a transition and is now manifesting a series of seismic changes: quantum physics, channelling, the new mystics, emergence of studies of emotion and consciousness, complexity sciences. As the song says, "This is the Dawning of the Age of Aquarius."

In Mass on Sunday mornings, I experience the Eucharist in a new way. The Ultimate Presence and Unity with the Inner Christ. Over and over I pray, "In me, with me, through me." One morning in prayer, the two rooms in the dream become One.

On November 26, 1989, the Feast of Christ the King, late afternoon, I am overwhelmed by beyond-imaginable sadness, pain and fear. Unwilling to burden my husband or the kids, I go to our bedroom. I so badly want just one person in my birth family to show some bit of an expression of joy in this healing which has changed my life so deeply. I am met with inner admonitions: "Be careful," says a speaker. "Satan heals. You are dabbling in the occult." Sad.

Then, suddenly, I am so damn angry I could spit. I pray over and over: "Jesus make it safe." I claim peace. I remember Isaiah: "He has sent me to bind up the broken-hearted." My heart aches for some words of understanding from my family. I am too afraid to ask. I try to be understanding of the fears people have. I am furious with this great big Catholic family that professes belief but doesn't really believe unless it is by their own particular set of rules. Who makes all the rules anyway? Why is there so little understanding or interest in dreams? How come there has never been a Sunday morning sermon on the power of dreams? Why do I need an "expert" to tell me what it all means? Is there something wrong with me that no one else gets it? The loneliness sits inside like a ragged sore. Dammed up. Crystal tears sit behind the walls of my eyes, dry, dusty grit. I have been lonely my entire life. What a pity party. All those years of stiff upper lip? Well, guess what. Not real.

I see around me three stages to healing: first the "miracle," then preaching, and finally self-righteous zealotry where the healing isn't complete but suddenly God is telling that person all the answers for everyone. I keep encountering that know-it-all person who has the answer and the truth for everyone and it scares the hell out of me. I am projecting my own fears onto others. This process is far from complete. Do I have the stamina, the courage, the just plain guts to see it through? Maybe this healing is only a fantasy. I tell no one. I need unconditional love. Not advice. I have advice from my abusive inner voice, "You really are crazy, aren't you? You do know that, don't you?" I hope I stop crying soon. Soon, it must finish.

Somewhere during this month, I discover that within the unedited great long version of my journey to healing and the end of the endurance run, there is incredibly beautiful symbolism. Numinous names of people and places, the Bible of numinous symbols of God's Forgotten Language. The sadness shifts.

There is much more in my journal pages. Mundane mystery. I discover more about the gefilte fish symbol from the wall behind the lunch counter at Hello Deli, on 124th Street, Edmonton where my colleagues and I sometimes go for a quick lunch.

Union, December 11, 1989

> Two unknown figures come together in a seemingly sexual way. I am in a room where the door will not open. There is tension. Then, I am one of the figures and I am very afraid the door will open. I want it locked. I am afraid of something but cannot identify what. The door opens and "the dream" enters the room. The dream is hazy and at a distance. As the door opens, the room is filled with peace and a deeply pervasive sense of security.

Sexuality as Symbolism

In our hyper-sexualized, rational and deeply literal world, symbolism is difficult. This dream indicates to me both a deep desire for and a deep fear of integration. Who will I be if I change? What does it mean to integrate masculine and feminine aspects of self? Jung writes a good deal about the masculine and the feminine. He is not writing about gender. Nor is he writing about the societal beliefs surrounding the role of men and women in our world. He writes about soul language. This dream indicates a desire of soul, or psyche to integrate my inner masculine and feminine energies, that is to create new life, new ideas, new birth. The birth of harmony within me. *Hieros gamos*. Mystical sacred inner marriage; coniunctio. I learn later that the sacred marriage was first mentioned in Sumerian writings some 5,000 years ago. The coming together of human and divine, masculine and feminine. There is a great deal to be learned—and for me, possibly even more to be unlearned.

"As some alchemists had to admit,
that they never succeeded in producing
the gold or the Stone.
I cannot confess to have solved
the riddle of the coniunctio mystery.
On the contrary, I am darkly aware
of things lurking in the background
of the problem –
things too big for horizons."

C. G. Jung
Letter
October 15, 1957

Inner Sacred Marriage Mystery[45]

The Iron Woman

In what ways am I locked? The door is unlocked in the dream but only after an expression of fear. I begin to take note of the changes within me since January, 1989 and the major inner healing both January 2 and January 21. My menstrual cycle, always a source of pain, tension, with a diagnosis of dysmenorrhea and one surgery for a 'tipped uterus,' has become 100% free flowing, a 28-day cycle instead of anywhere from 10 to 45. The nagging aches, cramps, headaches, excruciating backaches and PMS symptoms have disappeared. Exaggerated fears of pregnancy have receded.

The dream tells me I need balance and shows me the creation of balance within. I begin to understand that in order to survive, I have unconsciously chosen to emulate my father who represents calm, control and invulnerability to hurt. I am chained to a Puritan work ethic, rigidly withhold my emotions. I am considered "tough" and have sadly overheard male colleagues

---

[45] www.jungcurrents.com

say, "She has balls." Today, I would correct that to, "That takes ovaries." Ha.

I was also inflexible with myself while I tried hard to be supportive and understanding of others. I was determined to meet all of life's issues in a full-on, "head first" frontal attack. I have worked and studied and honed my intellect to the best of my abilities.

Other details are too personal. However, I will say that prior to learning of the symbolism of sexuality in dreams, I was terrified whenever I experienced nightmares with a sexual connotation. I notice now in dream workshops that the participants are reluctant to speak of "sex" dreams and yet sexuality is both the height and depth, the joy and horror of living. I had not ever learned symbolization. I recall clearly, during a time of extreme stress and hearing voices, experiencing a series of very sensual dreams involving a wise, gentle, kind and loving co-worker. He was the one professional friend with whom I could share a tiny bit of my distress and anger, my terrifyingly overwhelming fears. The series of dreams, or rather my interpretation of them, caused me to withdraw from the one source of professional collegial support I had.

I have been mired in our culture's pathetic, outdated, fundamentalist, Old Testament consciousness with its emphasis on the body and sex as evil, dirty and sinful. The separation of body from soul and spirit, focus on sex in consumerism and corporate advertising, and the objectification of the female body have robbed me of the creativity and healing of dreams, the richness of my soul life. I find deep satisfaction in the freedom to become whole. I also find a source of deep inner friction and tension in trying to overcome my early-life learning, as I wrote earlier about Saint Maria Goretti. Dream imagery of sexual union contains a powerful energy. I have much yet to learn.

My balance problems have disappeared. Back when the depressions were deep and deepening I became afraid to walk on any kind of edge or height without holding onto Bill. For example, in the summer of 1981 on a trip that included parts of

Ontario, Michigan and Minnesota, I was often panic stricken that I might fall over the edge of a bridge, a trail, or going up stairs in the Minneapolis Baseball Stadium. I became panicked, unable to move until Bill came to rescue me. I covered these fears as best I could since the kids and Bill found it irritating. "You can't fall off nothing." My heart pounded out through my chest. I clung.

Reading metaphysics, I find that such irrational fears indicate possible fear of bondage, being trapped with no escape route. Now, after healing depression rooted in preverbal childhood molestation, I am free of motion sickness and fear of falling. Motion sickness is one of my earliest childhood memories. I am in the front of the truck. Dad has to stop because I need to vomit.

There is much written about balance and feeling trapped. Unfortunately, it took me 43 years to find the root of my problems and I know not how long it will take to heal the vestigial remnants of fear locked down into my very soul and manifest in my physical body.

Last, the dream supports my thoughts about non-rational being. In 1985, on my 40th birthday, a poem came to me. *Warning: When I am an Old Woman I Shall Wear Purple* by Jenny Joseph speaks of unconventionality. "When I am an old woman, I shall wear purple, with a red hat which doesn't go, and learn to spit in the street and do all manner of unseemly things."

I read the poem to my Grade 9 language class and announced I planned to be irrational, unconventional and do my own thing now that I was 40. They laughed. And with all the loving candour of junior high school students told me, "But you are already weird."

"Just you wait. You ain't seen nothing yet." Three years later, I was healed of depression and incited all manner of raised eyebrows among friends and colleagues who decided, laughingly and lovingly, that I was weird. When my children smile and say, "Mom, you're weird," I take it as a great compliment. Most of the time. Dreams love etymology. Weird was originally Wyrrd. Please tell me you know the Women of Wyrrd.

It's 1989. I am trying hard and practising. When I speak of dreams some people wonder. Turns out, in our society it is too personal, too emotional, too irrational, and just plain not scientific. By 2008, I will complete a dissertation using dreams as symbolism in the symbolic interpretation of a Carol Shields novel. But not at the University of Alberta. And that too is a story.

Quiet the mind, and the soul will speak.

–Ma Jaya Sati Bhagavati, *The 11 Karmic Spaces*

Gaining the Inner Authority to Learn from My Dreams and to Begin to Teach Others

I was 16 when Vatican II and Pope John Paul opened the windows and let the light shine in and many Catholics began to understand that blind obedience to authority was no longer the requirement of the church. It would take me a good long time, but I would come to a place where I could say, "I am my own authority."

As I write this, I remember the letter I sent to the *Western Catholic Reporter* sometime in the late 1990s in response to an editorial about the refusal of the Official Church to recognize and ordain women priests. I was mystified, saddened and furious. The editorial presented a pathetically ill-informed position. The tradition of male priests seemed to be the sole reason. Nothing, apparently, that Jesus ever said would justify women priests. I choked. I opened my computer and started rattling the keys. Who the hell wrote the Bible? Well, if my readings are anything to go by, St. Paul actually started the church. Then there was Constantine. And the Councils of Men who decided which Books should be included. Hmm. There are those pesky little details about Mary, the Samaritan woman at the well, and a whole lot of other details. Nothing born of a man. How did the earth get turned upside down?

January 13, 1999 Letter sent and published in *The Western Catholic Reporter*

I too have read the letters to the editor and the commentary directed toward those of us, Roman Catholic by birth and as adults by choice, who support the ordination of women (Benoiton letter January 11, 1999). "Who in hell do they think that they are?" Well, let me explain. Who do you think that I am? I am woman. Somewhat in excess of half the human beings on the planet. I am created in the image and likeness of God. I am among those who went to the tomb on that long ago Easter morning and those who proclaimed, "the Lord has been raised" even though the men present did not believe them. I am among those who walked with Christ to his Crucifixion. I am a radical feminist following in the best way I know in the footsteps of The Christ, who was first among radical feminists. I am following The Christ who healed Peter's mother-in-law, healed the woman with the hemorrhage, raised the daughter of Jairus and conversed with the Syrophoenician woman. Against all the Jewish laws of the day, he touched the woman, allowed himself to be served by the woman. He went against the righteous who were filled with their own self-importance. As a radical feminist, I seek to question the traditions of the Church to ordain only men. And to those who claim that I am not entitled to my own thoughts, I simply have a smile. I will take full responsibility for my own thoughts and words and deeds having been created by The Creator who is far more than male or female. I fear sometimes for the anthropomorphic nature of the argument. To reduce God, Mother or Father, to the attributes of humans is truly amazing. To reduce the decision to refuse to nurture the vocation of woman to the priesthood to one of tradition is also amazing. How can tradition be the source when women have been excluded from creating the tradition? And when that "tradition" is based on Scripture written during a time when Paul, so often quoted in a most superficial manner, admonished the Galatian community: "As many of you as were baptized into Christ have put on Christ. There is neither Jew nor Greek, there is neither slave nor free, neither male nor female; for you are all one in Christ, Jesus." My question is simple: When do we take up the model which Christ left us and live it out in all its fullness?

So, I say to the gentleman, I am neither slave nor free, neither male nor female, but one in Christ Jesus, together with many other Christian men and women. And so, I will speak out even in the face of the anger of those who seek power over rather than power with and through.

The letter was published. I received phone calls from across Alberta and beyond in support of my stand. The following Sunday morning as we left Mass, Father Brabant shook my hand and leaned over to whisper, "Loved your letter. If I wrote it, I'd be excommunicated." I smiled. I often think of the difficulty of priests and nuns in their journey through life. Difficult work leaving your beliefs. But, here I am. Travelling.

Revisiting My Inner Living Room

Two years after the *Living Room* dream, I am rereading my journal. I am learning that meditation, perhaps akin to Jung's active imagination, is another way to honour my dreams. Tonight as I move into meditation, I imagine the *Living Room* dream images. I am filled with love, light and peace. A luminous vision of Mother Mary appears. Words begin to pour through me.

"I am indeed the wise Mother. I come to bring you comfort, wisdom and guidance."

She sits close by me on the arm of my chair. Just sits and gazes lovingly at me. I am deeply relaxed and drifting. Warmth spreads through me right down to my always very cold feet. The image of Mary is replaced by the Christ. A deep sense of unity pervades my being. Time is suspended. I have absolutely no idea how long I meditate.

"Mom. Did you buy any fruit?" It's my elder son.

I open my eyes. I say thank you for the injection of peace and the energy to re-enter the physical world and focus once more on healing the closed-off and painful aspects of my being.

In January 1989 I began a long restoration project to return my soul to my body. I felt literally broken, fragile in the extreme. The recognition of the divine essence of being is an ongoing process. I was moving through serious physical issues. I breathed with difficulty; there were iron bands around my chest. "Your central nervous system is shutting down, Pearl. I don't know why." The nervous system controls and coordinates the organs and structures of the human body. Years of depression had built misalignments of spinal vertebrae and discs. I was plagued by insomnia and dizziness. The kinesiologist said the blood supply to the head, pituitary gland, scalp bones, brain and sympathetic nervous system had been affected by the very early childhood trauma. The psychotherapist said similar things. The medical doctor, unfortunately, had no understanding of the effects of depression over years. He simply thought pills were the answer.

Depression is physical. The hurting had begun so many years before, even before I went to school. I wore garters and ugly long brown stockings …to keep the cold out. The doctors prescribed little red pills for childhood rheumatism. I have no idea if that was a real diagnosis or something to get me out of his office.

The little red rheumatism pills are mentioned in a letter home to my parents in September, 1961, "Mom, can you send me my little red pills. I can't stand this constant aching and I forgot to pack them." Thanks goodness for Mom. She kept every letter. I know I am not "just imagining" the little red pills.

The reiki practitioner, kinesiologist, and a bit later, the psychotherapist and the yoga teacher all said, "Stay in your body, Pearl." I had no idea how to do that. My friend, Verna, worked with me to "stay." Stay with the pain, let it move through you. Feel it. Stay in your body.

Healing Shame is Not Popular

I was molested as a small, preverbal child. There. I said it. Again. Our culture, and indeed almost the entire society we live in, prefers to believe that this kind of molestation does not happen. A baby? Children forget. A huge lie. Shortly after my healing, I read *Slayer of the Soul: Child Sexual Abuse and the Catholic Church*.[46] Nothing is ever lost in the universe. The preverbal child has no way to tell anyone what has happened. Had my parents known perhaps they would not have put my childhood silence down to quiet personality, shyness. My body pain, the doctors said, was childhood rheumatism. The depressions that began as I entered womanhood via menses were labelled "teenage angst" and then "nervous breakdown." Today, I hope, medical doctors are wiser. Good psychotherapists certainly are much wiser. However, society has not caught up. Given the stories I have heard from other women of my generation, sexual assault is common. Since I told my story, many, many friends and family members have come to me with their own stories. They told no one. Even if they were older and had language when the assault happened. We are not an honest culture. The good old days weren't ever so good for many girls and women. And now across the world it isn't much better. I was lucky that when I did tell my parents, not long before my dad died in December, 1990, they were supportive. Among my papers, I have the letter of validation, love and concern my mom sent after she and Dad

---

[46] Stephen J. Rossetti, *Slayer of the Soul: Child Sexual Abuse and the Catholic Church* (Mystic, Conn.: Twenty-third Publications, October 1990).

returned home from our house—after I had told them what happened. That letter is among my most prized possessions. Mom shared my story far and wide. Until one day, an extended family member with Catholic credentials said, "Tell Pearl to be careful."

The Play, December 18, 1989

There is a large room like a theatre. I am in the audience. It feels like the Performing Arts Centre in the school where I worked in the 1987–88 term. The director is a kind, very skilled English and drama teacher, a man loved and respected by students and colleagues alike. Black hair grows out of my nostrils. The director gives a speech about someone I do not know. Her name is Pearl. I have strong negative feelings in the dream but no fear. Most of the audience leaves.

Seemingly, I block understanding of this dream for years. By 2016 I have some soul perspective on it. If my eyes could see soul instead of body, I would have a very different idea of who I am. I know now that over many centuries, the feminine soul principle has been beaten, burned at the stake, imprisoned, colonized by the patriarchy, and overruled by rigid institutions, including religions that to this day either actively or passively resist the full inclusion of the Divine Feminine. And I am not just speaking of women. Men too are in search of their feminine soul. Feminine and masculine energies are not gender based. But women in particular have been girdled, subjected to patriarchal control with impunity. I begin to ask myself in a million ways, how did I decide what it meant to be woman? I don't like my answers. I learned from outside sources. I was colonized by foreign sources.

Dreams are the key to decolonization. They are the language of the soul. The symbol meanings are both collective and personal. Archetypal images in dreams hold meaning for a lifetime. I have only to think for a second about the construction of dreams as dramatic theatre and *The Play* dream comes alive in my imagination.

All the world's a theatre. The inner world is filled with millions of actions over millions of years. My own unconscious has many actors and actresses. My inner director has the attributes I so admired in the English drama teacher at that school. According to Jung, all these attributes are really parts of me. Using a common dreamwork technique, I draw two columns to list what I like and what I dislike about the director in *The Play* dream. I admire his kindness, patience, teaching skill, and knowledge of literature. I admire the attention and love he lavishes on his students and his kindness toward me. There is nothing in the dislike column.

Not all my inner school staff are kind. They are indeed truthful! Although the director is filled with praise toward "Pearl," she is someone I do not recognize. His speech produces deep inner anxiety. He is telling me I have a lot to learn about myself.

Dreams come to bring new knowledge. When I think of the stage I have walked on every day of my life, I know I did my best to hide behind the many masks of my persona. I stayed, or so I thought, out of notice.

Dreams often emerge as three-act plays. I have learned to think of these long, seemingly unrelated scenes in my dreams as moments in a play. Like a good play, this dream asks many questions: What is the theme of my life that I have hidden away? What is stopping me from seeing myself as I am? Where in my life am I hiding from myself? Why am I so afraid to take my place in the world? What is so dreadfully embarrassing about my feminine self that the black hair grows out of my nose? How am I tyrannized, immobilized by anxiety? What is the symbolism of Pearl?

The black ugly nostril hair is rather self-explanatory ... or so I thought in 1989. Over years, I realize it is an inner self-image. This morning I draw the dream image following Jung's concept of active imagination to facilitate communication between the conscious and unconscious aspects of my self.

The dream shows clearly my shame at being seen naked, metaphorically, in public. Once again there is hair, a symbol of the feminine. Long, flowing tresses the mark of the goddess. But nose hair? Not so much. In my imagination I see myself cowering before the crowd in the theatre. Disgusted. Also, the nose is masculine when I draw it. The hair like a nose moustache. Like Hitler. Is this my Inner Tyrant? The enemy in my own household refocusing my thoughts on how irrational I will seem if I continue this path of dreams?

Public acknowledgement. Never mind. What about me acknowledging me? Pearl. When my inner voice spoke lovingly of *Faith and Old Treasures* as my soul name I was embarrassed to even write it down. I tell myself the dream director has spoken kindly. In dreamwork, research is always the last thing I do. So. I have had these pretentious thoughts. I really do know that my Inner Tyrant, Inner Censor, Inner Editor is part of my self-protection. I finish the drawing, thank him for coming and remind myself my real purpose in these days of healing is self-exploration. The truth shall set you free. I must seek the truth, even if painful.

Biblically, and in healing workshops, the pearl of great price is created through irritation, through grinding and torment. A grain of sand or a bit of strange organic matter enters the shell of the oyster and can't get out. The oyster can't expel it. Calcium carbonate rings begin to build up around the grain of sand until it is covered and the irritant becomes a pearl. Whatever is most valued, most beloved, most beautiful, from a child to the Kingdom of Heaven, we have called "pearl."

What if the dream has come to point me toward the beauty of my own soul, as created in the image and likeness of the divine? I have heard this said among religious people. Created in the image of the divine. Do I believe it? The dream tells me I absolutely do not.

I read years later, in *The Book of Symbols: Reflections on Archetypal Images*,[47]

In the Gnostic Hymn of the Pearl, the pearl is the gnosis or "self-acquaintance" that reunites the soul forgetful of itself with its divine origin (Layton, 367). Pearls have been likened to drops of rain that bring moisture and renewal to the sere[48] land, and to teardrops that are the priceless emollients of bitter sadness.

Tears of bitter sadness, a drop of rain. I am a woman in search of my soul.

Shoes, December 1989

A shoe appears cracked in two places—at the heel and also split in the front. The heel actually has two cracks at angles to each other.

Shoes are normally worn whenever we walk from place to place. An old cliché: The bigger the feet the bigger the

O wretched despair

lost again in intellect.

Light

Fleeting there

Through the tunnel of darkness

Again.

Wholeness

Longing

Always gnawing

Yearning

Seeking

Almost finding

Falling backward

Ritual leaning

Ceremony talking

Despair.

Presence of light within

Shine.

I am willing to be made willing.

-personal journal, 1990

---

[47] Ami Ronnberg and Kathleen Martin, *The Book of Symbols: Reflections on Archetypal Images* (London: Taschen, 2010), 784.

[48] dry and withered, Merriam-Webster Dictionary.

understanding. It would seem that my understanding is cracked. Also, shoes are symbolic of "lowly" or "base" nature. Shoes are also status symbols in our society. Perhaps cracks are appearing in my understanding of sexuality. Not surprisingly, I hold unconscious ideas of evil and unclean feminine sexuality from the patristic society and churches of my culture and inheritance. Also, I recall that Mary Magdalene washed the feet of the Christ with ointment and dried them with her hair—once again, that very feminine symbol. The disciples were scandalized. Later, the Christ, at the Last Supper, washed the feet of His disciples to show the necessity of cleansing the understanding. There will be much more to learn from this very simple dream image.

The Life Within, January 31, 1990

Four beautiful and shiny black cats are catching and playing with four beautiful yellow baby chicks in the kitchen of my home. One cat sits quietly, his paws cradling the chick. Another swallows a chick whole while the chick appears content within the cat. The chick is visible to me. There is no fear. Serenity prevails within the whole scene.

The scene changes to a very hazy place where a very overweight person, familiar to me, a male superintendent of schools, is asking me about my plans to return to school.

I argued constantly with myself regarding the depth of faith, the totally ridiculous stupidity of the belief in the presence of Jesus that pervaded my being. I struggled to maintain an attitude of love and openness. My journals are filled with pages of questions and Jesus kept feeding me answers in incredible ways. Still from somewhere came doubt. I remained venomously angry somewhere deep within. I prayed silently. I smiled a lot in public.

The Life Within was a beautiful healing message. Somewhere I have read that cats are archetypal anima images of the spiritual forces beyond the personal. The dream shows that all emotion, whether it is dark (anger) or light (love), is a field of energy. So the dark emotion is nurturing, is consuming, but consumes without need for fear. The dark emotions of the ego such as pride, fear and doubt are indeed present within me. The light (love) represented by the chicks can move into the fear, represented by the black cats and yet love is not afraid. The darkness can nurture the light, can be gentle, can be protective, and in so doing is tamed by the light. The doubt hovers in the background and is not called forward except in the very darkest of moments. The ego, doubt, is anxious and wonders when I will return to "school." School represents, for me, the intellectual aspect of being. It may be that I give too much weight and control to the inner superintendent. The suggestion of further learning comes from the intellect as well.

During the weeks preceding the next dream, I read the Catholic classics about the lives of the saints and mystics such as Dame Julian of Norwich, Jan Van Ruysbroeck, Thomas Merton, Sister Faustina and many more.

I begin to see the paradox in my pathetic attempts to understand and analyze mystical experiences with Cartesian logic. Mysticism cannot be structured, cannot be contained in a system of man-made constructs. Dogmatized Christianity attempts to keep God and His creation in a steel box. Whenever God appears outside the box, He is accused of heresy, blasphemy and all manner of evil atrocities. I am amazed. Can I place life carefully within a structured conceptual framework? Can I compartmentalize joy? Capture joy in a box and sell it? Western logic uses this as advertising. Joy is a perfume. A commodity. Experience the joy. From a bottle. Speak of joy in the living experience of unity with the living God and suddenly the shutters of my intellectual, logical and rational system close around me. I doubt that the joyous experiences really occur. I am obsessed, compulsively eaten away by my clinging to rational logic. I read Scripture. John, the disciple of love, says I am to experience eternal life, not death. What does that even mean? Hope, love. Consummated in union, now, with the invisible God. I am to share in the divine nature. Not past, not future. Not *have shared* or *will share* but *to share*.

March 3, 1990

At the healing service in St. Joseph's Basilica last night, those laying hands on me received the following prophecy:

Prompting

> I have not given you a spirit of fear but a spirit of wisdom and great knowledge. Do not try so hard. Rest. I will do the work. Not you.

The Parkade, March 5, 1990

> My heart pounds with deep thudding tremors; then a sexually explicit scene arises, the details of which I cannot remember in the morning. Then I'm in my office building underground parkade. There are no lights and I am afraid. I put my briefcase down and then can't find it. I am on an elevator in the dark still feeling all over to find my briefcase. Verna and several unidentified people in the elevator. I am also searching for something else but can't remember what. Verna says something. What? I find the briefcase and am pleased.

I awake. As I fall asleep again, I repeat over and over: I am one with the Father. The Father and I are One. In the morning, only glimmers from the dream remain but there are several definite symbols.

The briefcase may represent the storehouse of real knowledge locked in. And missing? The darkness of the underground parkade seems to represent my personal unconscious within which I search for ideas. Forgetting most of the dream details simply shows me the level of fear I have of changing old comfortable ideas in my religion and being lost in darkness. In religious tradition, darkness often represents evil. Unknown feminine aspects share the journey. The elevator, as in past dreams, represents moving within the darkness/descent to the unconscious. I am surrounded by light; I am protected. I find the briefcase, the real knowledge, even in the darkness. The elevator is available to lift my consciousness out of the pull of conformity, group mind, worldly knowledge, sometimes called collective groupthink.

Several days of peacefulness, gentleness, stillness, and trust follow *The Parkade* dream. I reflect on the experiences of the last two weeks. I affirm the ability within to capture the essence of thought and transmit this energy into words that speak of my longing. I continue to meditate and a few days later in my imagination I walk in giant steps all around planet Earth. I felt like Neil Armstrong. Jesus, lift and heal this beautiful planet.

Van, March 22, 1990

My husband is in the driver's seat Corrine is behind him. They are talking. I am not sure where I am but I am there. Two men appear at the back of the van. They are there a long time. As one pulls a wiper loose, Bill jumps out and rushes to knock the men away. They wrestle. A white car appears on the right side at an angle to the van. It has a light-coloured licence plate. Two men are inside the white car. They wear light-coloured uniforms. The dream ends peacefully.

It seems I am willing to let my masculine drive me. Behind him, a long-time friend who is a fun-loving person, joyful and spontaneous, feminine. Unknown aspects of the masculine are there and make some attempt to pull away, wipe away the wall covering the glass. If I allowed the wipers to do their job, I would be able to see behind (the past?). But the driver, the one who controls my life direction, refuses to let go and surrender to seeing the authorization for freedom as symbolized by the white car and its white licence plate. Even the conformity as shown by the uniformed men is light. I could change. I continuously give my inner self permission to change peacefully.

I am reading Thomas Merton, *The New Man*,[49] for the second or third time. Merton is both intelligent and compelling with questions of spiritual identity. He could have been sitting in my living room chatting with me. How can I recover my true self? Why is outward identity so significant when my entire being craves knowing the God within? Merton is my search for Catholic "authority" and social acceptance on which to rest. I first encountered Merton as a teenager, stumbling across his 1948 autobiography, *The Seven Storey Mountain*,[50] on Mom's living room book shelf. I was probably 15 or 16 and I don't suppose I understood much but perhaps that book planted seeds. After the *Library* dream, I write down this quote from *The New Man*:

---

[49] Thomas Merton, *The New Man* (NY: Farrar, Straus and Giroux, 1961).
[50] Thomas Merton, *The Seven Storey Mountain* (San Diego, California: Harcourt and Brace, 1948).

Man is fully alive only when he experiences, at
least to some extent, that he is really spontaneously
dedicating himself, in all truth, to the real purpose of
his own personal existence.... And this realization does
not come into being until his freedom is actually devoted
to its right purpose ... a life that transcends individual
limitations and needs, and subsists outside the individual
self in the Absolute—in Christ, in God.... Man is truly
alive when he is aware of himself as the master of his
own destiny to life or to death, aware of the fact that his
ultimate fulfillment or destruction depend on his own
free choice and aware of his ability to decide for himself.
This is the beginning of true life (p. 4).

I will return to this quote many times but I will only begin
vaguely to understand it years and years in the future. In 2018,
I can summarize it as: I am my own authority.

The Library, May 30, 1990

Everything is very hazy. There are several people, mostly men
and all superintendents of schools. It is a rather large room
filled with shelving and books. I am presenting some kind
of material.

When I awaken I ask to remember the dream. Over
several days the image becomes clearer, more focused. The
superintendents represent a cluster of thoughts within me which
resist my writing and my own knowledge. The books on the
shelves represent my own inner knowledge, inner knowing. The
healing energy in the dream pushes me forward. On March 3,
1990 when I heard, *Write Dreams Along the Way*, "The Way"
had a deep spiritual significance for me. My dreams are a series

of clearly linked messages that ever deepen and widen the spiral of understanding within me. Stray thoughts are not "stray" at all.

Housecleaning, June 10, 1990

Someone, The Bully, comes to the back door and is sweeping the back entrance, and the hallway to the bathroom of our home. I have no clear picture of this, only a feeling of discomfort that others will "see" my dirty, dusty back entrance.

The Bully has been dead for many years. When I was little, he and several other boys teased me about being Catholic. I remember how easily intimidated and afraid I was even though he wasn't much older than I. Now, he represents my fears of ridicule, scorn and persecution for my deepening beliefs in a Real God Who Dwells Within and provides a Source of Incredible Energy. I haven't thought of this teasing in many years. Daily it becomes clearer to me that the unconscious forgets nothing. The dusty, dirty back entrance symbolizes the clearing of old beliefs and misunderstandings from the intellect and unconscious mind—beliefs I thought I had put behind me. My intellect, embarrassed at cleaning out the mud, the old ideas, will cling to those ideas rather than face change. The male figure represents that resistance, and the childhood teasing comes back not because of the teasing but as the ammunition of fear to resist inner change. I have been concerned because the dreams are unclear, but the misty haze clouds my knowing. There is much healing wisdom within the cloud.

July 13, 1990

I am troubled by every sound that reverberates INTO my being. I feel "looked through," vulnerable, opaque. What is this? My body hurts in a tinny, strange way like a gong on the tattered aluminum garden shed. This is palpable, living, longing. Reaching out but never feeling secure. Today I am filled also with vivid, deep rose. Deep purple. Squares and doors of rose. Circles of purple. A sense of knowing something just outside my being. A sense of expansion into nothing, with scattered shafts of light emanating from a centre within me.

The Spirit of God is within me.

Will the real me please stand up?

Chaos, July 2, 1990

There is an anniversary. Of what I do not know. Corrine's four-storey motor home is to take us to the church. I park our car out of the way. The car turns out to be my old antique sewing machine and I have trouble unplugging it because a bull is tied up nearby. I know he is halter broken but have trouble getting the halter on/off. One bull has jumped over the fence but I let him go as there are three more.

I decide I need a groom or best man. The ceremony is set for 2:15 p.m. and I am now late. Yelling and screaming, I convince a young red-headed man whom I seem to know but whose name I can't remember to take me to the church. He has crooked teeth. He reminds me of a lad who always hangs around the arena looking lost and forlorn.

We never do take the four-storey motor home anywhere. My hair is a mess. When I take the rollers out my hair is all big lumps and doesn't brush out. Makeup is a mess. People keep coming to the door, all with a problem. Corrine, a next-door neighbour in Leduc, seems to live next door to where I am now. Somebody is jealous of somebody else. I try to pacify everybody but Bill. I yell at him. I never do get into the driver's seat of the motor home. There are too many stairs to the fourth floor where the driver's seat is. Sometime in the midst of all this I sew a wedding garment—a blouse, I think—but when I put it on I find the machine has automatically sewn a thin silk ribbon inside the lapel. I am somehow pleased with the ribbon. I never see clearly what I am wearing.

The silk ribbon is the most meaningful symbol in the dream. The thread of life connecting me to Spirit sewn in by the Creator on the wedding garment of every dweller of planet Earth. In Matthew 22:1–15 many are invited to the banquet but they are "busy." The words of a song come back to me from many Sunday mornings: *"I cannot come to the banquet. Don't trouble me now. I have married a wife; I have bought me a cow. I have fields and commitments that cost a pretty sum. Please hold me excused; I cannot come."* And so the dream tells me to come to the banquet; to unify the external and internal aspects of myself. It calls me to harmony with the inner revelations. The thin ribbon within links me, begins the preparations for future integration. Not now. It's not yet time.

The four-storey motor home may refer to a previous dream journey *To the Fourth Dimension* or the fourth time span mentioned in the Bible. The four bulls are reflective of the four powers—intellectual, spiritual, physical and emotional. The one that I know is halter broken and the ones over the fence hold less significance and I continue to work to make meaning. The halter-broken bull may be my intellect, which I may in fact have unified with the rest of me more than I am consciously aware of. The anniversary is a call for celebration. Should I be celebrating the Spirit of God within instead of thrashing around trying to understand? The flaming red hair of the young man may indicate the passionate feminine energy within me that waits to assist in creativity. The crooked teeth, messy hair and makeup are all external and may represent my fear of being unacceptable. Hair, symbol of the feminine, yet again. In this dream, my inner feminine energy is "a mess."

People with problems and the jealousy of neighbours may simply be my inner tribes warring with one another. There are too many stairs to climb to the fourth floor. Do I think I have to do it all on my own? By my own power?

Count on the Inner Christ, July 9, 1990

I sleep lightly and fitfully. Three people, two feminine figures and myself come upon the man in a large room with several adjoining cubicles. Only this man is totally clear: a huge man in a muscle shirt. He rushes, grabs and body slams first one then

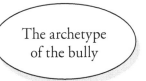

The archetype of the bully

the other of the women. As he starts threateningly toward me I repeat, calmly it seems: Jesus. Jesus. Jesus. Jesus. Jesus. Five times. The man disappears. I stand perfectly calm.

Later during the same night as this dream, a voice tells me they have seen my son Colin playing hockey and he had an excellent game. I am very pleased since he wants to play well with his new team. This is the second clear voice in the night. Mid July, as I ask daily about the haying weather, a voice speaks clearly and unequivocally as I sleep: "There will be 10 days of dry haying weather." Strangely enough, exactly 10 days later it rains. Bill is delighted in my forecast. I do not speak aloud of the voices.

In the dream, the feminine in the form of three women is threatened by the tyrant. Again, as in *The Landing,* my call to the Inner Christ results in healing.

This Is a Crooked Story

There are no heroes or heroines. It is my life. It circles, stops, turns back upon itself. Its patterns, if you can see them, are a beautifully woven, stitched and curved tapestry. Sometimes it just stops and refuses to move. Transformation through destruction. A black and shitty mess.

Section *IV*

The Search for the Mother:
Becoming Conscious

Chapter Seven

Breaking Through Stone

The Statue, August 5, 1990

A statue of the Blessed Mother falls forward face first from a pedestal on a church altar. I am there in the sanctuary with two people but I cannot remember their faces. We pick up the shattered statue and lay it on the altar. From within the middle of the shattered statue arises a young, very beautiful child of two or three years. Three times I am told to do something but I cannot remember what. Three times, Zealot, who appears from somewhere, walks away angrily declaring her annoyance, anger and disbelief. God does not deliver on His promises.

The child is genderless as are feminine and masculine energies. I am coming to know my childhood and indeed lifelong devotion to Mother Mary as a one-dimensional expression of the Great Mother. Over the next many years, dreams and experiences of the Divine Child and the Divine Feminine and healing of my own feminine energy and that of my ancestral family will become more and more apparent. This is the first of many dreams that will lead me to a deeper understanding and eventual acceptance of feminine energy as part of who I am. I will remember what I knew as a child. The Divine Feminine has been expressed throughout history in various forms as the Virgin, Mother, Crone. The Triple Goddess usurped by the Holy Trinity. The goddess reduced, dismembered and born smaller living on a pedestal in Catholic churches as Mother Mary. Blasphemy.

Later, September 1990, reading *Women Who Run With the Wolves* I begin to see that the dream statue represents the atrophied inner child: the child encased in the stone statue. The beauty and radiance of the inner child is startling. I must recognize the divine inner child, and learn to listen.[51]

The church, through Mary, has kept a bit of the feminine alive but placing Mary on a cold, stone pedestal

Shadow Sister
Deceptive painted face
chinless
Haughty, alien
remote, dead eyes.
Walks through
reflected glass
stains above black bubbles.
Out of her and through invisible
doors.
Angry, swirling flounces
intricate steps
in childhood patterns
like wind in tall willows.
Encased in raging walls.
Out of her and
through invisible windows.
Plastered, broken shatter pieces
Thawing, growing life within

has frozen the goddess, the feminine, and woman into a one-dimensional image of deadened societal expectations. The nice, good, pure, gentle, patient, long suffering, desexualized-unless-controlled-by-society, sweet, pious, ever-smiling woman. From her pedestal of stone, woman must fulfill the role placed on her by the patriarchy, which entombs her energies in unfeeling, untouchable, white, cold, sepulchral stone. The statue in the dream broke. I release the Ancient Woman Spirit to live again. I come from within a society

---

51   Estes, *Women Who Run With the Wolves*, 88.

where "that long river of women [...] has been damned."[52] But, says Estes, "One creative act can cause a torrent to break through stone."[53]

Estes speaks of intuition as, "the instinctive psyche, of the soul, and it appears to be innate, having a maturation process, a perceiving, conceptualizing, and symbolizing ability. It is a function belonging to all women, perhaps imaged differently through culture. This intuition is not that of the Jungian typology that includes feeling, thinking and sensation."

The Inuit story of *The Stone Child* tells us that hot tears cause a cold stone to break open. Perhaps my tears have broken the grip of the plaster-statue feminine. C.S. Lewis said that a bottle of child's tears heals any wound with one drop. In ancient women's religion, the young sapling is pruned with an axe in order that it grow fully. I cringe with the word "pruning" and feel its bite.

How many selves in the psyche? Many in the One. One is usually dominant. I am threes—the old fallen down part, the part I live in, and the part under construction. Self in Jung means the vast soul force; self means the more personal, limitable person I am. I need to remember these things.

The Two Faces of Eve, September 16, 1990

Everything seems hazy. I am in a large hall, like a dance hall of my teenage years. I go to the ladies' room and as I stand in the doorway a young woman turns from the mirror over the sink to leave. Her face is arresting. Very stark white, costume-drama makeup covers her face to somewhere at chin level. The open neckline reveals normal skin colouring below the chin. She wears gold jewellery, which appears very real. The face is a startling contrast to her black, very fashionable dress. The

---

52   Estes, *Women Who Run With the Wolves*, 90.
53   Estes, *Women Who Run With the Wolves*, 299.

dress is close fitting and made of filmy, bubble-like material. She sweeps past me, remote, haughty and cold. There is no emotion in her eyes. She does not make eye contact with me. I do not speak. Nor does she.

Later in the night a voice explains to me that Isaac in our office is a good Mennonite father planning to have seven children. I am surprised as he is late 40s and only recently married to a woman of similar age. He is a gentle, loving man who does not "threaten" me.

In the morning I am extremely irritable and snappy with everyone including myself.

Keeping a dream journal enables deeper insight and a record of changing and accumulating ideas. I have learned to add to rather than replace my interpretations to remind myself of how little I knew when I began this process. I also understand that I read unsystematically and yet ideas that seem erratic aren't. They simply illustrate that it is futile to think that one interpretation is better than the one already recorded. With each idea a new layer or field of understanding arises through my crazy-quilt reading habits and decades-long searching.

The bathroom is symbolic of elimination of toxicity, dirt, a place for cleansing. The gold jewels may represent the light of wisdom. The pure rage, anger and resentment that have surfaced from within me during the past summer are essentially represented by the black dress covering the woman—the other me which still requires much inner healing. The dress could also be symbolic of the healing in the darkness so appropriate to women. Eyes mirror the inner condition of the soul. Eve's eyes are blank, emotionless, dead. There is no doubt I have spent many years feeling just like that—empty, cold, dead—while covering up this emptiness with business-like cold remoteness.

Seven in sacred mythology represents wholeness. If seven children are born within me from the masculine aspect of my being, indeed, I will be opening up to newness and wondrous potential. The gentleness and peace of the voice are very powerful. I write poetry to honour the dream.

Other possibilities include seeing the mirror as a way to "see" myself. I know that mirror has symbolic value but at the moment I cannot think what it is. The white makeup is thick, the colour of bones, the colour of death. The *white* makeup covers the *face* (what is visible to others, the head, the intellect) and may symbolize the persona (rational, reductive, analytical, cover, armour) I have been unable to take off. It covers the face and stops at the *throat* (voice) so it may be once again the one-sided persona that coldly refuses to allow intuition and feminine energies to speak or to manifest comfortably in my life. The *line* between the mask and normal skin may show that I have been able to move the mask partially away. It may also show two "me," split between what is authentic and what is not. The *bathroom* is an inner/outer cleansing. Inner shit. Rot. Unconscious archetypal forces that devour and destroy but also incubate and birth the sacred.

The *mask* may be covering my toxic shame surrounding the patriarchal imperative of sex as sinful and the feminine as limiting/molested instead of as a source of physical, emotional and spiritual creativity. Certainly, the face I show the world is inauthentic. When is it safe to be feminine? When I had this dream, I was coming into midlife; perhaps this is a ritual death mask, white clay, symbolic of the skeleton or corpse.

The gold jewellery might point to the "pagans" who used their jewellery to make the Golden Calf (Exodus 32: 1–35), under Aaron's tutelage. When Moses returned he ensured it was destroyed. He railed against the evil of the people.

Giving dreams a title is important and, in the case of this dream, *The Two Faces of Eve* was the first idea that popped into my head. It may have come in the dream to show me potential links to the destruction/demonizing of early goddess-based religion. Or the demonization of Eve, and the serpent. Also, the calf may symbolize the ancient Cow Goddess and the golden light of wisdom. The Catholic version of the Bible retains the

Book of Wisdom, which briefly refers to Sophia, Lady Wisdom, whereas the King James version does not.

The tight-fighting black dress could be indicative of *nigredo,* the process of rotting, or putrefaction so necessary to the transformative process. The process of alchemy includes elements of Christian mysticism and for Jung is an early formulation. Alchemy is defined in the literature as essentially a symbolic process endeavouring to make gold. Gold is symbolic of illumination and salvation. In 1990, Rachel and I visited Old Quebec City and the spectacular old Roman Catholic Churches laden with gold. I have also visited the great cathedrals of Quito, Ecuador and Lima, Peru and wondered about the amazing amount of gold. I know little and understand less about the alchemical processes. This dream seems to have all the alchemically symbolic colours that signify various aspects of soul: black, white, red and gold. It is clear that I have much to learn before I try to apply the alchemical framework. For now? Transformation is my goal.

Then as I'm writing this another strange coincidence occurs. It's January 2015. I am packing for a winter of writing and dreamwork. I am taking a few books I am sure I will need. At the last moment, I go back into my study, and take a slim, black volume, *Descent to the Goddess.* Looking for bibliographic detail I open the book and there I find a treasure trove of personal literary anthropology, marginal notes complete with dates and dream references. So much of what was, is and will happen is there. It is a moment of decision that will inform the unfolding of this life. Finally, I notice the second half of the title, *The Way of Initiation for Women.* The author, Sylvia Brinton Perera, is a Jungian analyst. Perera writes of Ereshkigal, the Dark Goddess and Inanna, the Queen of Heaven, who lives unconsciously in women under patriarchal repression.

Perera provides deep and radical hope for me in this personal journey, which becomes a journey for all women. "Lived consciously, the goddess Inanna in her role as suffering, exiled feminine provides an image of the deity who can, perhaps, carry the suffering and redemption of modern women."[54]

I had no knowledge whatsoever of this Great Goddess of Heaven, Inanna-Ishtar. Now, constricted, repressed and denigrated by patriarchal institutions, I can begin to accept my boundless rage as not sin. Ereshkigal is the "dark sister" of the Underworld symbolic of the Great Round of nature: of birth, life, death, continuous growing, seeding and dying. First, the dying of ego. I accept my rage and allow room for its death and transformation into fierceness. This process of transformation is suffering. It is an aspect of being woman.

"Suffering is also a major part of the underworld feminine. It may be unconscious until the advent of the goddess of light awakens it to awareness, stirs the silent numbness to pain. On the magic level of consciousness, it is numbly endured. There is no awareness of suffering."[55]

How I wish I had known a whole lot more in 1990. How is it that I read, made notes and then forgot completely about Inanna for some 25 years? Something about the depths to which dreams will penetrate the soul. Something about the "eyes of death" embodied in this dream and something about my reverence for change. For the eyes that stare back at me in the mirror are the eyes which see and which must look coldly, objectively at the false beliefs I am entangled within. Instead, I go unconscious with fear. Too many years later, I read the dream again and look through the cold eyes of the Medusa. I look inside and outside. Finally.

I look in my own mirror where I see reflected back yet another image: the image of the older woman. I understand the imperative to invent, create, write myself and reclaim the past when healing and the wise arts were associated with old wise woman rather than the decaying, disgusting, rolling flesh and

---

[54] Sylvia Brinton Perera, *Descent to the Goddess: A Way of Initiation for Women* (Toronto: Inner City Books, 1981), 20.

[55] Perera, 1990, 35.

ugly, wrinkled, evil, demonic witches. I find the mirror alchemy in the words of Virginia Woolf in the mouth of younger women saying, "Women have served all these centuries as looking-glasses possessing the magic and delicious power of reflecting the figure of man at twice its natural size."[56] "The mirror is the ultimate image of enclosure; instead of looking outward through a window, a woman is driven inward, obsessively studying self-images as if seeking a viable self."[57] It seems that as far back as Petrarch's Laura, the mirror was seen as the image of the idealized woman, the pedestal woman who could never live up to the cultural idealizations. I am complicit in the deification of the masculine.

Faces of Eve is an archetypal dream of a lifetime. It provokes, disrupts, calls and incites. It points me toward the myriad ways the feminine and dreams have been silenced or misrepresented, ridiculed or condemned in academic and popular discourses. In 1990, I had been in school or university for 18 years. Where and how do dreams fit in Western scholarship? My dreams have stories to tell me about myself, my early life, my past lives, consciousness and unconsciousness. Dreams question accepted beliefs and practices. In her book, *Leaving My Father's House*,[58] Jungian analyst and author, Marion Woodman, provides insight into the process required to bring feminine wisdom to consciousness in a patriarchal culture. Where in education have I ever found the voice of a dream? Where is the dream in the Western theory of knowledge? Where is the dream as a method of acquiring or discovering knowledge and knowing what is "real"? Questions. Questions. Open.

---

[56] Virginia Woolf, *A Room of One's Own* (London: Hogarth Press, 1929).

[57] M.A. Paludi and G.A. Steuernagel, eds., *Foundations for a Feminist Restructuring of the Academic Disciplines* (New York: Haworth Press, 1990), 94.

[58] Marion Woodman, *Leaving My Father's House* (Boston, Mass.: Shambhala, 1992).

The Father God of the patriarchy is the colonizer and yet the dream says I am birthing aspects of wholeness through gentleness and peace. The dream continues to dream me. When the dream ceases, so do I. The dream shows me the space of the possible as a probable resistance point.

Over the years I will have many dreams filled with aspects of the goddess, relegated to realms far outside patriarchal consciousness. There is such an incredible depth to the feminine. I am only touching Her cloak. My complicity in patriarchal consciousness is deeply unconscious and a father complex has powerful defences. Thus the weeks and months become years of work.

I have inner guides if I listen, a supportive husband and one damn good friend who travels with me in so many ways even when she has no idea where or why I am going.

The White Heifer Returns, September 18, 1990

I see neither myself nor my husband but we are both present as the white heifer returns from the bush with three white heifer calves. We are astonished to see her since we thought she had perished.

The dream seems so strange I do not record it right away, but the thought that it holds great meaning and potential healing will not recede. On September 23 I write down all I'm able to recall.

In reality, in 1987, a beautiful white heifer, the first and only ever, was born amidst celebration after we returned to the farm from six long years of city living. Jason was sure she would be the basis of a wonderful herd of purebred cattle. However, her first calf, a heifer, was stillborn. The next winter yet another calf died in a spontaneous abortion. We sold the white heifer. No wonder in the dream Bill and I were so surprised to see her "return" home with three healthy heifer calves.

The white heifer dream image symbolizes abundance, wholeness, fecundity, providence of creativity. The milk of human kindness. White is made up of all the colours thus the white heifer is a reminder of the totality of the universe. White is symbolic of pure love energy. In Catholic tradition, white is the symbol of purity. In my childhood I was fascinated with stories of saints and virgins. White holds incredible promise, energy and love. In October, 2016, on a pilgrimage to learn more about Celtic spirituality, I visit the Isle of the White Goddess in Ireland often referred to in poetic mythology.

There is much written in mythology of sacred animals as portents of peace. I am aware of the Aboriginal myth of the White Buffalo, the many stories surrounding its return. The dream is comforting.

For several weeks after the *White Heifer* dream, I resist every urge to write. Only sporadically do I read or meditate. I am tired. Joyless. Another valley. I continually, silently affirm that I am willing to be lifted. I am willing to look deeply into the self. I believe the resistance comes from egoic consciousness that says: "Enough, already." But it is not enough. The longing for integration of self is stronger than the desire to quit. Today after meditation I find myself repeating, *Jesus, gentle, Jesus* over and over as I do the housework. A slow gentleness is growing deep inside and should be nourished with outward gentleness. I am a screeching rollercoaster. Sounds, harsh voices, chatter, the smallest things irritate. What if, maybe, just maybe, the original healing in February, 1989 was fantasy. What if I really am an idiot? And yet the series of dreams, the presence of the Christ in meditation, all reassure me.

This is my own resistance. I would like to blame it on the world. But I am the world in a cell. I must be the change. What a cliché that is!

God in a Box. I recognize that eventually I will have to give over, surrender and write how I feel about the concretization of Ultimate Reality into rules, rituals and traditions; into theology, institutions, a hierarchy with doctrines and structure that holds humans fast in our own limited self structure. First I must blow up my own box.

I begin to see a glimmer of self-understanding. I am love. I am filled with grace. My healing work has brought deep theological questions that will take many years and much pain to resolve. I am beginning to recognize Mary as whole unto herself. Not the literality of physical virginity. Even writing the words makes the belief seem amazingly contradictory to so many other Catholic teachings. For one steeped in unquestioned Catholic tradition and teaching, this is an extremely difficult change. It also lies at the heart of the issue of Catholic women's lives.

There was not ever the stain of original sin. I am not flawed because of the decisions of Adam and Eve. That myth was created slowly over many centuries to replace earlier myths such as that of the Triple Goddess; the Great Goddess *was* replaced by the Holy Trinity.

Writing this puts me in the company of heretics and sinners who, according to Catholic doctrine, deny God. I have a very strong desire to acknowledge that I am one cell in a perfect evolving universe. Nothing in that statement contradicts theologians like George A. Maloney, author of *Uncreated Energy*, or Teilhard de Chardin, physicist and priest. These shifts in thinking are an aspect of my descent to the Goddess, the initiation into the underworld where ego identity is shattered. There will be many more aspects of my identity as Catholic that may be demolished, stripped away.

I had many questions before the *Two Faces of Eve* dream. Now dozens more arise. The question of the origins of the concept of original sin. In my questing I find Matthew Fox's *Original Blessing* and, many years later, Dara Molloy's *The Globalization of God*.[59] I feel whole when I look out my window at the original blessings of earth, and read archaeology,

---

[59] Dara Molloy and Tess Harper, *The Globalization of God: Celtic Christianity's Nemesis* (Aran Islands, Ireland: Aisling ArannTeoranta, 2009).

anthropology and the lives of early peoples, the so-called pagans. Their gods and goddess were everywhere. What happened to drive the monotheistic god so far away skyward?

Years later, I have a different, related question. How much do pew Catholics know about the debates between Pelagius and Augustine? I knew totally nothing till 2016. On my two-week pilgrimage in Ireland I toured goddess sites, prayed, meditated, dreamed and met Dara Molloy, a former Roman Catholic priest, now Celtic priest. I read *The Globalization of God: Celtic Christianity's Nemesis*. I returned home wanting every single person I knew to read it. I am very afraid. I think I am heretical. There is no doubt left in me, intellectually, that the pagan heretic, believer in the perfection of God's creation, Pelagius, had it closer to my heart. My task is not to believe in the Christ but to be *like the Christ*. To be *a Christ*.

In my life, denial of the inherent goodness of God manifested itself in fear of God expiated by rigid, personal rules of moral conduct that resulted in very near real spiritual and physical death through depression. Depression resulting in suicide is the ultimate self-hatred. Irony? There must be a stronger word. How could the child of a loving God misunderstand that God to such a degree as to attempt to kill God by killing the self? I am forever thankful for the grace of God, which leads out of self-hatred into real self-love. Is the inner urge to suicide then really the psyche's archetypal urge to transformation? I wonder.

The white heifer has returned and with three calves. Wholeness indeed. Strange. I await the manifestation of that wholeness in my life.

The transformation process deepens. This is seriously the first step. I am awake. There is a great deal written of the alchemical processes of the *nigredo,* the blackening, dissolving stage at the beginning of psychological maturation. Perhaps that is in keeping with the ancient ways of woman. What will I sacrifice in the *rubedo* (final) stage and when will I arise to new life, rest awhile and begin again? I am an earth woman. How is it that it took me this long to see the manifestation of nature in my life as woman, the cycles of birth, death and rebirth? What are the links between *The White Heifer* and *The Two Faces of Eve*?

The Sacrifice

August, 1990, Mom calls to say, "Your dad has asked if you kids can come for Thanksgiving." This is a first-time Dad request. We all go except Michael and family who live in England.

It is a good weekend albeit one of anxiety for me. I am overwhelmed by the need to write. I do chat with Mom, and Bill does his best to speak with Tony and Mom about the healing and my intense need for family validation. I do not know if they "hear" him. I do not even think to question why I need Bill as intervener. Hmm.

The Wise Old Man, October 11, 1990

I am walking into a school, down a hallway and into a classroom. I am surprised and delighted to see a man who comes smiling, arms outstretched, toward me from the right side of the room. He takes my hand and twirls me around in a joyous dance step. It is P.E. Trudeau wearing a bright green elf hat with a small bell at the tip. I wonder why he is in the classroom. There are other aspects of the dream that are less clear when I write this down. PET is directing four children—two boys, two girls—in some kind of play or skit. We are in a different room. At first I think these are his children but then recall he has three sons. Some other people come, unclear, and are not very pleased with what PET is doing but I sit at a small kindergarten table, at the right-hand corner, and watch and listen carefully as I would in a school or teacher evaluation.

I was 23 in 1968 when Pierre Elliott Trudeau slid down the banister at the Château Laurier Hotel. The '60s was an energetic, nonconformist decade in Canada. In the dream, the unknown aspects of myself are not pleased. So, I return to the kindergarten to find my playful, joyous and childlike self. The court jester upsets the order of things by absurdity. The number four is often that of wholeness and balance. Creativity. I must return to kinder (child) garden. Delight in joy. Dance.

The archetypes of the Child, The Clown and Wise Old Man all appear to support my feminine journey. I am amused by the prime minister's ways. In fact, I was and still am the only sibling, and one of very few Albertans, who share the amusement. Now, the dream sends an image of dancing as taught by the "fuddle duddle" prime minister. The serious intellectual person who did not really take himself seriously. I am that very serious person. I was a very serious child. Where is my joy? Where can I slide down banisters? In wisdom there is joy. It is religiosity, false sanctity, pietistic pathology that says I must be serious. My dreams over the next few months are a mosaic of healing my inner child. Cribs, kindergarten tables, feces, a prehistoric animal, teenage years, and a deep prophetic look at my future.

In December 1989, my yearly family Christmas letter spoke briefly of my healing. I received a response I treasure greatly from a childhood next-door neighbour we called Auntie Jean. In her letter she shared her memory of me as a "deeply sad and serious child." She wrote, "Now I guess I understand why." I have that letter saved carefully among the memorabilia of my life.

Our mythology is changing as evolution continues. Beliefs are changing about the Father God who intervenes in human problems choosing who to help and who not to by their supposed holiness. Last week, a young man told me seriously not to be concerned with the drought. "God will provide," he said piously. "Tell that to the climate refugees in Sudan," I said. It slipped right past my tonsils. I didn't pursue the conversation. He does missionary work. His next posting is Engineers Without Borders. He walks a different path but I am trying to learn to honour the paths of all others. Once my inner voice explained that all paths lead to the same place. Some people go in Volkswagens and others in a Cadillac. Somewhat prosaic? It makes perfect sense to me as I look around the world. Different paths on the journey home.

And when I write things like this, my heart hammers. I hear the priest far back in the mists of childhood and yet again yesterday. Christ is The Way. And I have prayed and meditated on that until I figured out that Christ or *Christos* is not really a name but an appellative, or even a title. In the time of Jesus, Christ was used as a word to describe an appointment, a role in the religious structure of the times. Jesus was known as Jesus of Nazareth. Today you would be hard pressed to find someone who actually knew that Christ is not a surname. Etymologically, the noun χριστος (*christos*), meaning anointed, comes from the Greek verb χριω (*chrio*), meaning to smear or anoint.

Consciousness is not an artefact of brain consciousness. Consciousness is. How to understand there is no material world? Who understands quantum physics without understanding consciousness? What is reality? Physical? What I see? Or, experiencing my own consciousness. Experience in-forms. The brain affects what appears in our consciousness. How easy to get tangled in my own entanglements. Back to 1990.

As a teenager I had never heard of virtual reality. Nor did I even know the word consciousness although it is obvious my unconscious did. Huh? No-thing-ness. And in my journal notes, with no attribution, I find ideas that may come from Teilhard de Chardin, the great Jesuit priest, scientist and mystic who voiced the law of complexity-consciousness. Teilhard viewed consciousness as the ground-of-all-being. Not too surprisingly, the Vatican suppressed his views. His writings were published posthumously. I think about attribution and realize this too is an attempt to control. Ideas are available. Unless I use someone's exact words, I am giving up trying to attribute every idea.

Global Brain

I am walking along a road headed to Debolt. I have a jacket over my arm and a book, the *Global Brain*, with me. I arrive at the Debolt Hotel. On my way into the village, I am surprised at all the new buildings that have been built since my teenage years. I walk up to the door and up several steps. Bill is there and I ask him if it is open. "No, the game is on television but not till midnight." "Is there anywhere to get a chocolate bar?" I ask.

I go into a larger room walking in behind two people seated at a semicircular counter in what seems like a newly decorated room. One of them is Farmer. He speaks and I answer. I notice he is wearing a new grey-black tweed jacket. A female companion is on his left. I do not recognize her nor does she speak. She seems to be in the shadow. I go outside and I realize I do not have the *Global Brain* book. I retrace my steps carefully, looking on counters and tables. A young woman, a former student in a school where I taught and who I only recall as disdainful of books and school, sees me. I pick up a different book, a high school psychology textbook, see it isn't mine. The young woman snickers and goes laughing to join a male figure. I do not see but rather feel his presence. I think they must be laughing at me. I do not find my book.

If you want to stride into the Infinite, move but within the Finite in all directions.

–Goethe

The *Global Brain* dream suggests I need to look into my teenage years. Myss speaks to the Artist archetype revealed as my "passion to express a dimension of life just beyond the five senses."[60] I completely lost any sense of the world as my inner magical child fell asleep, the sleep of the unaware. My reading and research shows that many young people lose contact with the deep inner meaning and purpose of their life as they "adapt" to the outside world. It's patriarchal culture from the outside in. Parents, teachers and the world tell them where Truth Lies. I surely conformed within millimetres. Young women are particularly vulnerable to domestication of their inner ground of being and their instinctive lives. Sleeping Beauty sleeps till awakened by the prince. Cinderella is poisoned by the patriarchal Queen who must die and be reborn as the young feminine. Many of us, like the stepsisters in the Grimm brothers' version, chisel off parts of our feet, the ground on which we stand, in an attempt to fit the glass slipper. Only when the dwarfs trip over the root of the Tree of Life, the feminine, does Cinderella fly from her coffin, the poison is dislodged and she wakes up! Somehow, symbolically, I abandoned my understanding of the wholeness of the earth, the energetic synapses holding the cosmos, the earth and me.

I chiselled. I lost consciousness. Went to sleep in my glass coffin. Fainted. In the grotto and at morning Mass in Midnapore, and on the dance floor in Crooked Creek.

Farmer was Bill's best man. He is one of my favourite people. A well-educated farmer, eldest of a large family and respected community leader. For me, he represents a deeply rooted security on earth, the masculine aspect of self. I welcome his presence as an aspect of myself.

There is no doubt I have known the global brain since childhood. I just misplaced the connection. My intuition and imagination were replaced by the intellect as symbolized by the book of psychology, or the psyche, soul. The dream may be

---

[60] Caroline Myss, *Sacred Contracts: Awakening your Divine Potential* (New York: Three Rivers Press, 2001), 368.

telling me I need to connect heart, mind and soul. Everything is One. We are all One.

Years after the dream, in a class on complexity science in doctoral studies, I will be handed *The Global Brain* by Peter Russell,[61] a British physicist interested in Eastern religions. He coined the expression "global brain" as a basic analogy to organizational emergence via the internet. Russell's book has the same cover as the book in the dream. Obviously studying complexity science, the science of emergence, gives me a far deeper understanding of the metaphor of the global brain as consciousness. It seems rather literal, but I guess I went to sleep about the time I lost my global brain book in Debolt as a teenager.

Of course, there is the never-ending fear of ridicule. This fear of not being loved, the pure existential fear of non-being, lives on shame. That shame includes the sin of being born female. It requires a great deal of self-awareness. I have deep fears of rejection in even the smallest relationship. I am not even involved with the young student. Yet I think she is laughing at me. This general fear of failure is pathological. It could be an aspect of the Victim archetype. I recognize that I am ashamed of this constant pathetic need. The chocolate bar could represent the sweetness of life. Life lived in joy would indeed be sweet, not chocolate-bar sweet but the strong sweetness that comes from ripe, luscious pears at the harvest. As dreams often do, this one propels my thoughts in many directions.

Losing Ground

For centuries, Western society has attempted to categorize women as intellectually inferior because we are too emotional and irrational. Hysterical women. The Inquisition and the persecution of witches, the Wise Women of many peasant villages. Today,

---

61   Peter Russell, *The Global Brain: The Awakening Earth in a New Century* (Edinburgh, Scotland: Floris Books, 2007).

witches are cast as women in black with broomsticks doing evil. Holy Evening, the night before the feast of All Soul's day when we honour the dead, has been recreated as Hallowe'en. Perhaps by the Trickster. Feminism is the new myth of witchcraft. Patriarchal mythologies of the evil seductress luring men to their doom are difficult to bring to consciousness. And whereas many women may believe that they will find equality through competition with men rather than in inner healing, the seed of truth is contained within the misunderstanding. Where can women learn our own history?

The patriarchal understanding of the myth of Eden is strongly entrenched. Interpretations, false readings, misuse and abuse created horrors such as the burning of nine million (some sources say as many as 12 million) women. The feminine went to ground. I see possibilities of resurgence in my lifetime as many people work to excavate their personal myth. It is difficult work. In order for the hierarchy (patriarchy) to maintain total control, it instituted educational standards and then refused to allow women to attend the institutions because of their supposed inferiority, vulnerability, weakness and a propensity to hysteria.

Jesus physically touched many women in healing. He took the hand of the young girl, age 12, of marriageable age. No rabbi in Jewish tradition did this for fear of becoming unclean. Jesus surrounded himself with women. He healed them, taught them, lived with them, walked with them, ate with them and accepted them as equals. He was crucified.

The doorway, so briefly open, closed. Soon after his death and Crucifixion the culture quickly deepened its traditions of exclusion. Keeping a journal in the late '80s and early '90s, I watched and sought help from the medical establishment, which continued the fight against women in discriminatory research practices, hospital births, unnecessary caesareans, hysterectomies, and the diagnosis of menstruation as a disease. I find the following entry in my 1990 journal:

The historic decision to include women in the legal definition of "persons" was handed down by Canada's highest court of appeal—the Judicial Committee of the Privy Council of Great Britain—on October 18, 1929. My mother was 21. My grandmother, 55. Is it any wonder then that I deny my e-motional self when the attitudes of the collective unconscious denigrate women and given my own childhood experience of assault? So I heal not only the personal feminine but the ancestral and the cultural feminine as well. No, this is not about blame although blame appears to be one of the more important of our cultural commandments. I want only to explain for myself how to know my Divine Self. How to find that which I have lost but which can never be lost because it is a part of myself. There is fear in me that my family of men will find the concept too threatening, too intimidating. Yet I realize that they too have been infected with the pathetic strong man myths of the cultural collective unconscious. I am born into a family of six brothers.

By 2013 I would have six grandsons. Coincidence? I think not.

It may be that I am to bring out the emotional energy from within my feminine soul to assist in healing. For as I heal myself I heal those around me. I am safe. In terms of Myers-Briggs personality types, my inferior feeling function is inexpressible. My father did have a feminine soul expressed in his life through his banjo. I learned early on to simply watch Dad's eyes. I was afraid to hurt his feelings by talking about this. Afraid he would then take responsibility for my hurt. It is not responsibility I am seeking. I seek unconditional acceptance that my feelings are valid. I began to think this fear of vulnerability was rooted in fear of intimacy, rooted in pain which includes a fear of too much success.

The newly decorated room is a small detail that escaped my thoughts when I pondered the dream in 1990. Now, I see I have been redecorating my living space with many new ideas. I can only assume I am still working toward more awareness.

The Wise Old Man and *Global Brain* dreams led me to understand the tears and why I told brother David at my kitchen table in 1990 that I would scream and cry until someone in my family listened. Why I told another brother, Tony, I wouldn't talk about my feelings on the phone since I would only cry. Why my quietly desperate bids for emotional support from my family were never made explicit. When Mom made time available to talk that Thanksgiving, I intellectualized everything so I wouldn't cry. I was astonished with myself for leaving the dream manuscript with Mom and anguished that reading it would cause pain for both her and Dad. Apparently, Mom read the beginning since on Monday morning, as we were saying goodbye, she mentioned the nightmares I had as a child—how she had had no idea. She did put a curtain over the opening in my closet. I had associated the curtains with the nightmares. Now I wonder, did she make the curtain coincidentally? Of course. How could she have known about the nightmares? I don't remember telling her. Perhaps I did. Memory is confusing.

Dad commented that he was glad he didn't worry like us women because it would probably kill him. I should have told him that he was being hopelessly patriarchal and it wasn't simply women's worry. Instead, I took the easy way and followed the tradition like a good patriarchal daughter. I grinned and said, "Well Dad, it damn near did kill me." The Patriarchy's Daughter. Always be nice. Ingrained in me in my baby carriage. Dressed in pink, frills and ribbons. Or handed down through the ancestors in the collective DNA.

I clearly remember any comments I made to Dad that disagreed with him in even the slightest, most remote way. Pretty strong need for approval all the way to the advanced age of 45. That goodbye on the back steps of my childhood home at Thanksgiving, 1990, was the last time I saw Dad alive. His eyes told me he loved me and sparkled blue as always. He would come in dreams over many years, but I wouldn't recognize the father complex for a long time.

Today I come to two inescapable conclusions. First, religion, in its original meaning, "that which ties us to our common source," has been lost for many centuries. Second, physics and other hard sciences are penetrating theology and vice versa. The early scientists were often religious mystics in the fullest sense of the term. Who else had access to writing, to reading, to time and conversation? Certainly not the peasants. The organized church, fearing loss of dominion and authority, decried science as evil for several hundred years. It is hardly more than 300 years since the Official Church, together with university professors, insisted that Copernicus and later Galileo recant the ridiculous heresy that the Earth moves around the sun. Copernicus, out of fear of reprisal, did not publish his works until late in his life. Some of his supporters were severely punished, some even burned at the stake. And when his work was published, it was placed on the Papal Index of forbidden books. It seems that the hierarchy of science then moved away from religion and religion from science with the advent of Sir Isaac Newton's *Principia*, written in 1687. Three hundred plus years for a "new truth" to become accepted.

Can society afford to wait another 300 years for acceptance of the idea that there is a level of order not perceivable by the senses or any physical apparatus wherein every part of the universe contains the whole universe enfolded within it? When will the ideas of implicate order,[62] well known in quantum physics, and also in complexity sciences, become common knowledge? Can we wait while science and religion feud over territorial rights to the human psyche? Or will religion produce a scientist-religious or science a religious-physicist who will do for religion what Carl Jung has done for religious psychology? A person with a deep

---

[62] "The theory of the Implicate Order contains an ultra-holistic cosmic view; it connects everything with everything else. In principle, any individual element could reveal 'detailed information about every other element in the universe.' The central underlying theme of [physicist David] Bohm's theory is the 'unbroken wholeness of the totality of existence as an undivided flowing movement without borders.'" From David Storoy, "David Bohm, Implicate Order and Holomovement," https://www.scienceandnonduality.com/david-bohm-implicate-order-and-holomovement/

spiritual commitment who is courageous enough to integrate rather than separate?

In high school and through university, I read and studied relatively little about Albert Einstein. Now I find that I missed the whole point. Perhaps others did as well. The point of his Theory of Special Relativity debunks the myth of space and time. There is no time-construct nor any space-construct in consciousness or God. These are simply human-made symbols, experiences that enable Western man to understand our world. God is time-less, space-less, form-less, structure-less. God has no beginning and no end. The alpha and omega. Eternal life, everlasting life, is not something that begins with physical death. Following the trajectory of Copernicus-Galileo-Newton, it will be about 2200 AD before all the peoples of planet Earth become faithful to connection among all. Surely Mother Earth cannot withstand the broken relationships with the divine, self, neighbour and nature for another 200 years while we come to an agonizingly slow understanding of the quantum physics that shows oneness of all creation with Infinite Source of all Life. How many today are treated as Copernicus and Galileo were before them? Matthew Fox, excommunicated for his refusal to recant his writings about rejecting original sin. Teilhard de Chardin, Jesuit priest, exiled by the Vatican in 1920 to China where he worked as a palaeontologist.

In the late '80s and early '90s, Jean Houston's books presented themselves to me at conferences, in the psychotherapist's office and in the Chapters book stores. I especially love *The Search for the Beloved: Journeys in Mythology & Sacred Psychology.*[63] She had read and written extensively about Teilhard's theories. A combination mystic, Jesuit priest and scientist, Teilhard argued in his early writings that creation is evolving toward the Christ as the Omega Point pulling the

---

[63] Jean Houston, *The Search for the Beloved: Journeys in Mythology & Sacred Psychology* (New York: Tarcher/Putnam, 1987).

whole cosmos inexorably to itself. That's what got him exiled. Apparently, in 1962, the Vatican warned about the dangers of Teilhard's works and of his followers. Just yesterday, in casual conversation, I was told his writings are still not accepted by the church. Turns out that is not the whole truth. In a recent *Huffington Post* article, I read that Joseph Ratzinger, as a young theologian, warned against Teilhard; but now he is Pope Emeritus Benedict XVI and he is praising Teilhard's great vision for seeing the cosmos as a "living host." "That raised a few eyebrows and prompted Benedict's spokesman to clarify that 'by now, no one would dream of saying that (Teilhard) is a heterodox author who shouldn't be studied,'" says the *Post*. Further, "… Vatican observers say it would not be surprising if Teilhard made an appearance in an encyclical on the environment that Francis is currently writing.… The growing global ecological crisis is prompting demands for the kind of holistic scientific and moral response Teilhard would have endorsed, and the internet is itself a digital 'noosphere' of universal interconnectivity."[64]

At the time of the *Global Brain*, I was wondering if I had the courage to withstand the criticism that accompanies a personal paradigm shift. Am I courageous enough to continue to work to heal the false, induced self so fearful of losing control? I wonder a good deal about the *Global Brain* and *To the Fourth Dimension*.

All this comes from working with these two dreams. I cling to Dionysus, who reportedly received confirmation in a dream that he was to study both heretical Christian and pagan writings. A voice in a dream assured him his faith was secure. How secure is my faith? I have dreams that help me face my fears. I will

---

[64] David Gibson, "Jesuit Pierre Teilhard De Chardin's 'Conscious Evolution' Plays Role In American Nuns vs Vatican Debate" *Huffington Post*, 1 June 2014 http://www.huffingtonpost.com/2014/06/01/teilhard-american-nuns_n_5374368.html#comments.

eventually learn to hold the eternal tension between doubt and faith. I will remember often my inner voice: "I would rather that you doubt than be blinded by your certainty." Might have to make a poster!

Chapter Eight

Learning to Dance

Every interpretation is an hypothesis, an attempt to read an unknown text.

–C.G. Jung

Pushed and Pulled: Joining the Dance

At 12:05 I look at the clock. It is lunch time. There is a lot of food in the staff room but the hot food is not ready. I go somewhere. I am not sure where. I think it is in the same room. I return. I am surprised it is already 12:45. The clock is round and seems significant. There are a lot of staff in the room. A secretary is eating beside one table where I stop to put salad on my plate. I ask her about the food in the oven. Is it ready? She sort of smirks and says, "Yes" in a tone which indicates I should have noticed for myself that it has been ready for some time. As I move toward the oven, one of the other secretaries comes in to say I am wanted at the front desk. I mutter, "Who the hell needs me now?"

I am annoyed but leave my food and go. The scene shifts from the office to a hall. As I walk to the back of the hall, Dancing Crone, a gentle, smiling woman from the community we live in, now grown older, and with a cane, is there. I greet her gladly. "Why are you here?" I ask. She gestures to the front to indicate I should take her there. Once there she joins in a circle dance. I see only another woman who comes down the centre of the circle and begins to sing. She is a good singer. I think, "I used to do that; I could sing like that." Soon a lot of people are there. I recognize them but not by name. They are practising their circle dance. I stand out of the way but inside the circle because somehow I feel I am responsible to help Mrs. I., because of her cane, I guess. More people join the dancers. I am beginning to feel in the way.

A tall, thin man in a brownish suit seems annoyed and as he shifts aside to avoid dancing over me, he asks someone, "What the hell is she doing in the way?" He does not address me. There is a bulge in the circle of dancers as they go around me. I am very hurt and start to explain why I am there and try to get out of the way. I stumble out of the circle.

I wake up and as I lie thinking and reflecting, feelings of deep rejection well up and I start to cry. Then, strangely, I feel relieved. I am reminded of a favourite song from Mass, The Lord of the Dance. "Dance, dance, wherever you may be / I am the lord of the dance, said he. / And I lead you all, wherever you may be. / And I lead you all in the dance, said he."

It is March, 1991 before I sit down to reflect on the dreams from the previous October. As I read again the *Pushed and Pulled: Joining the Dance* dream, I slip easily into active imagination. A deep rose colour fills my mind. The numbers are significant in that there is 40 minutes difference between the two numbers. I am

45 years old. The Bible refers to 40 years in the desert wandering. It seems the dream is telling me that I could move out of the desert. Time to nourish the feminine soul. My spiritual assistant, the secretary, tells my dream ego that I have been too stupid to recognize the available nourishment. Then, instead of feeding my soul, I rush off, muttering, to help someone else. How often do I interrupt my own needs to meet the needs of others? And worse still, resent it. The secretaries, friends and helpers in the dream, are the aspects of myself that recognize the beginning awareness of my purpose in life. What is my purpose? What am I here for?

I have been wanting to go for a weekend to a writers' workshop but have put it off, telling myself my family is more important. Another reason I have given myself for not going is that the cost is more than the family budget can absorb. My job keeps me busy during the week and how can I be away on weekends? I have been resentful when women who do not or have not worked outside the home suggest that I am somehow selfish because I do not remain at home with the family. Why does the seeming criticism of others have such an effect on me? As a very young teenager, my elder son had some issues around my inability to be normal. It was 1984. He was 14. "Are you ever going to be a normal mother?" We discussed his version of normal, which included Mom making his bed, lunch, and all manner of other things. I thought a moment, and told him the truth. "If that's normal, then no, never." We talked about my need for learning and concluded that he was doing fine and learning a lot about independence.

At the time of that conversation, I was studying for a master's degree. Bill was home with the kids due to the massive downturn in the oil economy of Alberta. Bill's home presence and completion of the daily household chores had a balancing impact on my sons. Rachel? Well, I felt cheated. It was her dad who took her skating. Her dad who picked her up from skating. It was her dad who spent the time with her. Somehow, I always felt less than adequate as a mother. Who would teach her to sew, to do the crafts she liked to do but in which I had absolutely no interest? Somehow, I was still caught in the patriarchal exterior feminine. Do sewing and crafts make a woman a woman? "Not bloody likely," says my inner self. "Oh, yah, rationalizing your selfishness," says the Accuser. I don't yet recognize the goddess of the hearth.

I am reminded of the problem of opposites presented in Bible characters. For example, Cain and Abel. Or Esau and Jacob. Seemingly I carry within me the opposite sides of myself. Is it possible to reconcile the differences or will the struggle within end in alienation or disaster? I am reminded there is no either/ or. The story of Jacob and Esau or Mary and Martha are too long to tell here but a clear look at them will explain what I mean. Or the prodigal son and his elder brother. In every case we have the introverted/intuitive versus the extroverted/sensate personality. We have Martha and Esau who could represent the world's collective moral righteousness. They have the law on their side but their hearts are not really into loving, deep personal relationship. They all do the "proper" things. In actual fact, they are self-righteous prigs. Conscientious, responsible, organized, with a sense of social morality on their side. The inward-looking versus the outward. The biblical characters appear as two people. The two sides of one personality must be integrated in order to inherit the kingdom of wholeness and holiness. When Scripture is viewed from the perspective of the individual human journey, two figures could represent the public side and the shadow side of the same personality, as in Matthew 5:25–26:

> Lose no time; settle with your opponent while on your way to court with him. Otherwise your opponent may hand you over to the judge, who will hand you over to the guard, who will throw you into prison. I warn you, you will not be released until you have paid the last penny.

From a Jungian perspective, or a layperson's perspective of Jung, indeed, the thwarted animus extracts the last penny. Our whole world can attest to that. Everywhere, except in small tribal societies untouched by the rational thinkers of our time, our world is in chaos. The more energy I spend trying to repress, deny or eradicate the problem, the larger and more overwhelming it becomes.

Perfection everywhere now. I repeat the words of 14th century mystic Julian of Norwich endlessly since I read her works in early healing days: "All shall be well, and all shall be well and all manner of thing shall be well."

How will I honour the dream? I'll write. I'll forget the closets and the ovens that need cleaning and the bread that needs baking. I will affirm that the writer within needs love and affirmation. For it is the Infinite Source of Love who placed within my being the need to write. Somewhere, the purpose of my life, the gifts and talents of words and creativity, were placed within my soul at the moment of conception. Also, I have learned from reading von Franz that I must continue this dream work for if I stand still the Self moves on without me. I must follow the dance. I am the dance.

I will honour the creativity within. I will write. I will dream. I will be a healer. I will be a guide. I will honour my family, who indeed has given me incredible support in time and assistance with my need to write. The unhealed feminine is within me. I will not project the negative onto Bill and the kids. I will give free rein to the spontaneous, creative child within. In my *Pushed and Pulled: Joining the Dance* dream, the man in the brown suit represents the negative animus figure, which threatens me and does not want me to join in the inner circle, the sacred circle of dancing and singing. The negative animus within is in need of healing. The brown-suited man is me: a gift I give myself when I recognize that I am being pushed into the real purpose of my life. For dreams, writing and dream workshops are a service of love. Shimmers of possibility.

Although it feels totally ridiculous, I have more and more active imagination conversations. Thank you for coming, brown, Mother Earth, feminine, creative, nurturance. If you will come again, we can talk. What would you like from me? How can I help you? What do you have for me? You and I are really me, so let's be friends. You must be kind of tired of being ignored all the time.

And the Mrs. I. symbol. My wise, dancing older self. I awaken to the dance. The clock tells me the afternoon of my life has begun. It is five minutes after midday. Indeed, a new cycle has begun.

Sometime in winter, 2016 as I write and ponder, I realize this work is probably the best thing I have ever done for my feminine self. In fact, I could say, since this is the best energy winter I have had in my life, that I am truly finding my soul journey. I am becoming aware, putting into words the pre-birth covenant I signed. There is a good deal of theoretical work in revealing the animus. I notice now that he appears when I am feeling particularly successful, or given credit for some writing, like my dissertation or whenever I receive recognition for my work. This Tyrant holds sway far too often and I find myself sometimes yielding the most enriching and delightful aspects of my life. In the 1990s, every time I really enjoyed a holiday—days at the lake in summer 1988, a weekend of writing or dreamwork—the bloody damn negative animus screamed. I am my own authority. Now, he wants me out of the dance when I am just waking up.

Now, back to 1990 where that as yet unknown, unrecognized negative animus Inner Tyrant rants long and often. Once more, I descend. Deeper this time. Facing more fears, I am slowly crushed.

Holy Shit

I awake to go to the bathroom. An enormous gob of white guck comes from within into my mouth. As I'm not in the bathroom yet and can't keep this "stuff" in my mouth, I spit it all in my hand. I wonder where it came from. As I rush into the bathroom, I see there is no toilet bowl. I put the guck in the sink and it disappears. Some voices come from another room. One says something like, "How can you go to the loo when there isn't one? On the floor?" And there is laughter. I awake.

The Gold of Transformation

I am hurrying to the bathroom. I eliminate a large pile of feces in the toilet bowl but one large, round lump is on the floor. I am appalled.

These two dreams, just days apart, contain common symbols of transformation. I have passed through perhaps another of the gates of the unconscious. Unconventional methods of healing bring a lot of fear. I am reluctant to share these dreams as dreams are supposed to be beautiful. Instead I am brought down to earth as a human being with a body. I bow before the porcelain throne. How often have I heard, "I am going to sit on the throne." A subtle and more acceptable reference to what it might mean to eliminate waste from the body. My superego is dethroned, brought low, as is Inanna as she passes through the seven gates. Becoming conscious requires elimination and change.

The psyche, I am learning, is relentless when we are moving to consciousness. I am symbolically being cleansed and my "shit really can smell like a rose."[65] I wonder often about the descent to the unconscious foretold in *The Landing*, in 1988. I just thought it was a lovely dream that left me feeling very safe. I now know that I have a calm, serene inner healer who prayed all the way down. This is true. I just didn't know the meaning of safe.

---

[65] Ami Ronnberg and Kathleen Martin, Archive for Research in Archetypal Symbols, *The Book of Symbols: Reflections on Archetypal Images* (Kokn, Germany: Taschen, 2010), 428, quoting Jung.

Inner Revelation—Learning to Love My Inner Child

This morning as I wash my face and start to put on my makeup, I "see" my dream in the mirror. In the dream I carefully and lovingly remove all the makeup from Rachel's face. We have a warm, loving time doing this.

Knitting My Soul

There's a sweater of Mom's that needs some changes—to be made bigger is the notion I have. Anyway, the place I take it to says they need $12.00. I bring it back to Mom. She is very surprised at the request for $12.00 since no more materials are necessary. She says she will take it to them herself and see what the real problem is.

Again, the theme of completion cycles and new beginnings; the number 12 has appeared in three recent dreams. Moving into midlife, I will create a wider and deeper understanding of the feminine. Knitting is symbolic of creation. The real problem? Striving to live according to old conceptions of the feminine while disintegrating. The patriarchy will not honour a woman's time. The feminine is only seen in terms of materiality, physicality.

Today, I am sick and tired of this constant introspection. I am confused, restless and unclear. Friday was filled with both good and different times. Jason's hockey game was awful. By the time I came home, had some soup and read an article in *Sacred Heart Messenger*, I was crying. I worked several hours at my computer creating a record of all my journal entries over the past three years. I am thankful for the quiet time.

Jesus said, "Where I am, there you are also." I long to walk and talk with you. I have so many questions that no one can answer. And, seriously? This is all pathetic, constant snivelling.

I find comfort in reading and reflecting on the *Meditation Newsletter* from the Benedictine Monastery. "Every shadow depends on light for existence…. And every light source produces a shadow except for the Light itself 'where there is no darkness at all.' Each of us is a light source and therefore, each of us casts a shadow. Our commitment to the deep process of the spirit within us, the stream of light that flows and energizes our being, is our liberation from the shadow." Deeper within the newsletter, I read that, "Pure self-knowledge (which is God's) cannot produce evil. It is from our ignorance of our whole self that the inability or refusal to forgive derives and out of this is bred all the evil of the world." This is an explanation that I can consider. But how? It is beyond my thinking capacity to reason out evil.

November 1, 1990

Tonight I open a letter from my mother. Deep sobs arise. I am so thankful for her words of love, support and encouragement. Healing the inner child seems slow and laborious. I wonder how much pain is necessary. Jesus, my inner wisdom, says pain is unnecessary but that I have learned to experience pain and have convinced myself it is good for me. Actually, this is the church teaching. Pain and suffering are The Way to heaven. I am learning this is so very deeply wrong not to mention confusing. I yearn for the felt Presence. It feels now like
anthropomorphizing the divine. Then, I discover the descent of Inanna in which Perera considers suffering a positive aspect of the journey to consciousness.

I am thawing out and as my emotions melt I drip water freely from the soul. The eyes shed rivers of flowing pain. Glacial melt waters my soul. Volcanoes boil and seethe beneath the glacier and love burns the jagged crystals. Will there be anybody inside me when the glacier thaws? Rage is indeed fuel for my creative journey.

I have a million more questions.

Why don't I tell my dad I love him? What stops me from running, flinging myself crying in his arms? The memory of silent communication runs strong. Dad is always there. His eyes shine with joy and pride in his children and grandchildren. I watch silently as Alexia greets her grandfather at the restaurant Sunday morning after Mass. Dad's eyes absolutely shine as she hugs him and holds tightly to his hand. I watch Rachel run and almost knock him over in her effort to hug him. And silent ice grips me. My guts hurt. The children are not afraid. I descend again into the pain of repressed emotion. Free the icy grip that holds my heart jagged and sore in its teeth.

All the inner screaming asks only, "What's wrong with me? I probably did it wrong. Everyone thinks I'm an idiot." Even when they never say it, my ego reads it in their eyes. Ego lies.

I am in a continuous search for myself. My journal is filled with pages and pages of prayers, mantras, and questions. I can't seem to quit. I am filled with loathing about my own neediness.

I have long conversations with my Inner Christ figure. I ask a thousand questions I can't ask anyone else. For a long time, I have wondered why prayer groups eventually dissolve into infighting. I wonder why they demand conformity. If Christians are to be known for love, somehow there must be a way for the group to be love. How do I resolve this apparent contradiction between love and prayer and fighting and splitting? No, I am not nuts. It is active imagination that helps me to make sense of what is happening. This journey I am on is not something you find in a travel guide.

Be real. No simplistic attempts to heal, to sidetrack from the real inner pain. No fear. Don't try to "fix" people. No hostility. Don't try to change others. Change yourself. Doubt in prayer groups is unacceptable. In fact, viewed as heretical. Fear is unacceptable. Brokenness, vulnerability, individuality, intimacy, honesty allowing for open, healthy, conflict—not allowed. I found a lot of smugness, as in "God tells me truth; therefore you must be wrong." No one person has Ultimate Truth. Saccharine, sweet falsity results in conformity on the outside and hatred on the inside. I am confused. The most beautiful gardens are wildly multicoloured, riotous, and glorious. It seems the Christ broke all the laws of the Pharisaic community except one. He didn't even keep the Sabbath. He did however love God and loved his neighbour as himself. How do I heal this confusion so I do not self-destruct?

A dream comes to shatter my very rational approach. It is almost two years since *The Landing* dream.

Reclaiming the Inner Child

It begins with the little man with the big grin and the green elfin hat. I think it is the Wise Old Man and I am pleased.

Then, I am in a crib with a beautiful child. I do not "see" myself but the joyous child appears to be in the crib in my childhood bedroom. I have a "feeling" of another child, smaller, less joyous. The joyful child and I play and talk. We touch each other's faces tenderly and gently. As the child leaves he/she tells me I will receive a great gift of energy. I feel myself lifted.

Later, or so it seems, I am in a farmyard. I come around the right side of a pile of hay. I glimpse four men in black suits sitting at a table. I do not want them to see me, so I retreat behind the haystack. Someone is there and beckons to me. He (I am unsure if it is male or female but male seems right) is facing a fairly large, white-looking animal, a kind of prehistoric animal. I pick up something, sort of menacing, and take one or two steps toward the animal. It looks at me very gently and passively but does not move. It is not an animal I have ever seen anywhere in my life.

When I awake, my first thought is the dream. I get up and rush to the shower. It's gone. I panic. That dream made me feel so much better. A song comes and stays with me. When I am halfway to my office, laughter breaks through. The inner Spirit is so wonderful. One word in the line of the song is … baby … and I remember the dream clearly.

The child in the crib seems self-explanatory and I choose not to analyze or intellectualize this dream. It seems that I am reclaiming lost aspects of self, soul and childhood—trustfulness, joy, exploration. It seems of special significance that the child in the crib is androgynous and thus really does signify the integration, the restoration of what has been broken and shattered within me—the relationship between the left/right, the feminine/masculine within. I should write a song. I should shout from the rooftops.

The farmyard aspect of the dream is less understandable and I go looking for understanding.

O'Connor[66] suggests that dreams demand little but *humility* and *time* wherein a *friendship* can be fruitfully cultivated. When the ego-conscious, rational mind grabs hold of the dream, it negates these attitudes, because part of us wants to impose meaning and cannot abide letting the dream reveal its own meaning, which takes time.

The farmyard dream setting suggests an organic process. I should not be asking: "What then?" "Why are you there?" "Why now?" "What do you want?" "What is it like?" "What is this scene like?" The dream dreams me. I will be patient and befriend the beautiful white, peaceful, prehistoric animal within.

Hope, encouragement and energy flow through me. I am filled with wonder at the ways of the Inner Christ. When I "sleep" in a straw pile, I feel one with myself. I clearly remember sleeping in the straw stack on a sunny day in May 1962, the year I spent

---

[66] Peter O'Connor, *Dreams and the Search for Meaning* (Mahwah, NY: Paulist Press, 1987), 89.

out of school at 16. Even though I was ill, that event stands out clearly as peaceful. Warmth. Security. The childhood bedroom and the farmyard are connected in the dream. The loss of the child in teenage years when I buckled under the weight of inner anxiety. The dream seems to tell me that the inner child is joyous, is free, and that the past anxiety is indeed past. I should let it go. The healing is complete. The child is free to explore feelings, be warm and tender, be gentle and joyous. That is the message the dream holds, now, for me. "The Willow," a little, nonsensical poem, creeps onto the page.

I am joyful. *Deus absconditus.* Hidden. Unknowable. The felt absence of God. So many days I have waited restless, impatient, yearning, sad, rejected. But the inner presence is always there. Wondrous. Beyond understanding.

The prehistoric archaic, ancient, unknowable animal eludes me to this very day.

Freedom

I come around a corner to find a team of horses standing placidly while another pair of horses is apparently being encouraged to mate. A stud is on one side of a fence. There is a small opening in the fence. A mare is just outside the opening. There seems to be a lot of activity, not much result. A male figure is holding the mare's halter.

The Willow

A willow does not become
an oak.

But an oak grows deeper
roots, higher branches.

I live within the myth and
symbolism of Catholicism.

It is part of me.

It grows deeper, wider,
higher and

bursts the iron pot.

The scene changes. I am at a rodeo barn somewhere close to the earlier scene. A lot of animals want freedom and feeding. I walk through a tunnel to a long bus. It is moving. The people are unhappy with the animals' lack of freedom and food. As I pass by I remark nonchalantly to a couple of the figures something like, "It wasn't always this way."

I am reclaiming a bit of my power as I wander through this journey. When I explore my feminine instinct lost as a molested preverbal child, the dream points to possible integration, feminine/masculine instinct coming together. There is an opening in the fence. Freedom beckons.

The summer of 1990, I hardly rode horseback. When I was a child and teenager horses were inescapably bound up in my feelings of freedom. Then after my own children were born I developed a fear of my own horses and sometimes resorted to taking Valium in order to stop shaking enough to ride at the local gymkhana on Sunday afternoons. Certainly, that was kept secret. I was very angry and ashamed. In 1984, the psychiatrist dismissed it.

"It's normal," he said. "Riding isn't that important. Why worry about it?"

But it was important. Once again I allowed myself to be silenced. The dream reminded me that I must find my instinctive feminine power. It is critical to my well-being as a woman to go through that hole in the fence. Horses represent beauty, wisdom and intelligence; in other words, my inner feminine soul. How many books are written on various aspects of knowledge and support horses share with humans?

In Grade 12, assigned to write a short story in English, I wrote all about horses. On the recent pilgrimage to West Ireland in search of Celtic lore, I learned that horses were sacred to the goddesses Epona and Rhiannon. They symbolize fertility, freedom and power. Horses are often associated with lunar energies through the powers of the ocean and the crescent-shaped marks from their hooves.

In dreamwork, and in writing, I sometimes use stream of consciousness to get underneath the intellect. So, when this memoir wanders, remember: wandering is important in the journey to find out who you really are. Even though the expert tells me to forget about my fear of riding—pats me, figuratively speaking, on my hysterical fuzzy little head and dismisses me— my inner world tells me otherwise.

Go Through the Fence and Fly with Your Beautiful Feminine Soul

I am small and I am furious with my three older brothers who are too busy to come and hold our old horse, Dais, so I can climb on. I jockey her close enough that I can leap off the fence onto her back. It's clearly a metaphor for my life. When there is no one willing to help, I go it alone. In a fury.

Off we go. Fast. Sixty-five years later, I imagine myself a child astride my beautiful white, winged horse Pegasus, flying through the forest trails, across the fields, to visit my cousin, Larry. He gets his black horse and off we go! We race our horses, fast. A clear memory comes of riding down the road, west of my childhood home.[67]

I am 15. I get the best birthday gift of my entire life, an actual riding horse. Not a clodhopper, or farm work horse.

---

[67] In *The Woman's Encyclopedia of Myths of Secrets* (Edison, NJ: Castle Books, 1983), Barbara G. Walker writes that Pegasus is the "winged horse of Greek myth, symbol of the sacred king's or hero's journey to heaven; an image of death and apotheosis, like the mythic death-hordes of northern Europe. Pegasus had archaic, matriarchal origins. He sprang from the 'wise blood' of the Moon-goddess Medusa, who embodied the principle of *medha,* the Indo-European root word for female wisdom. Or, alternately, he was the magic horse Arion, 'the moon creature on high,' born of the Goddess Demeter and ridden by Heracles in his role of sacred king in Elis. There was an earlier female Pegasus named Aganipe, 'the Mare who destroys mercifully,' actually a title of Demeter herself as the destroying lunar Night-Mare."

Astride my bay gelding, riding bareback late in a warm fall evening, reining easily around the grain stooks. A full moon gleams from an open sky of stars. I can feel the horse beneath my legs. Now, as an old woman, late of a fall evening, I remember this scene vividly.

I'm 20. I return home from Calgary to take a job with General Motors Acceptance Corporation (GMAC) in Grande Prairie. I have a new three-year-old black Standardbred mare that I board at stables just outside town. (Strangely, I cannot remember her name.) She is only green broke, not well trained. I get tossed off often enough that my boss, Jim Hansen, asks quizzically, "Just what do you get out of this?" when I show up at the office with black eyes and bruised knees. A three-point landing. Truth be told, the day before, as I swung into the saddle, I grazed her rump with the heel of my boot. She went berserk and bucked me off, finally stopping only when the saddle came loose enough to slide beneath her belly.

I am leaving for university in Edmonton and Eugene buys the mare. He can tell you stories. She ended up dead, hung in a forked willow bush. She always was a bit spooky.

I am 29. I purchase a grey mare, with a palomino half-Arab colt at side, and my first good saddle. I train Sinroy, the colt, to ride. We fly through the fields of an evening on our farm at New Sarepta, Alberta. The story continues through seven more foals and a Welsh pony for the boys. Not important?

I rode Grey Lady, dam of Sinroy, in gymkhana and trail rides while Colin rode another gelding. Soon he preferred hockey and then we moved to Leduc. When we returned to the farm in 1986, I still had my horses, still bred a few colts, but the fears were greater than the love of freedom; excuses were easier. I was busy as a career mother, wife, constant student, a farmer and community volunteer.

"It wasn't always like this," I say in the dream. Clearly it wasn't. The dream tells me I have turned the corner. Gone through the deeply feminine labyrinth or birth canal in the movements of the unconscious toward individuation. In the direction of freedom. I need to feed my instincts.

This week, I am reading Kelsey, *Discernment: A Study in Ecstasy and Evil.*[68] Again, my search for someone who said it first. I am learning. I find answers to many of the strange inconsistencies I see around me in the several charismatic group events I attend. I am not moved to return to any of them. In Kelsey, I find some answers to the most pressing questions I have about the domineering authoritarianism I found in those groups. Certainty. I am deathly afraid of too much certainty. Kelsey nails it for me.

Rigid beliefs are most often a defence mechanism used as protection from having to face one's own uncertainties. I am too full of uncertainties to try to even mount a defence. Fanaticism seems to result from what looks like emotional conversion, in times of extreme stress such as sudden death, unexpected divorce or abandonment, perhaps even transition from an abusive environment. Perhaps an overdetermined archetype explains much of what happens in prayer groups when an unbeliever suddenly finds a healing miracle. He/she instantly decides this is THE WAY. Sometimes this early zealotry remains for many years. When I cannot see beyond the archetype's confines, and I begin to interpret more and more of my experience only in those specific terms, I become single-minded. An archetypal idea per se is an overvalued idea that must be 'seen through' and placed in perspective. If I come to think I know the Truth of the universe, I will know I am gripped by an archetype.

And I admit it scares the hell out of me. I run. Over these years, I have been told by Certainty folks, that I am Evil. Dreams are Evil. My daughter wears Black so she is Evil. I have been called a Feminist Nazi Bitch in relation to my dissertation. I admit. Certainty scares me. But then so does Uncertainty. But the dreams have brought me deep healing and I continue to cling to the Bible verse that says, "And ye shall know them by their

---

[68] Morton T. Kelsey, *Discernment: A Study in Ecstasy and Evil* (Mahwah, New Jersey: Paulist Press, 1978).

fruits." I work very hard to refrain from judgment. Sometimes I am even successful. For a minute or two.

I can clearly understand the desire not to look inside. What am I afraid to know? To look inside myself and assume responsibility for all the hidden worms is not an easy task. Jung calls inner healing the task of Hercules—to clean up in one day the Augean Stables, in which hundreds of cattle have dropped decades of dung. This is the task of the committed spiritual person. To clean up the dung of the ages deposited in the collective unconscious. This is a task so daunting that I as an ordinary mortal become discouraged by the mere thought.

The shadow. The phrase suddenly leads me into quiet inner laughter. "He is afraid of his own shadow." Even clichés seem true. The shadow aspect of personality holds those parts of me I don't much like—fear, anger, resentment, false pride, blame, and all negativity. I too am afraid of my own shadow. But I will have to befriend the shadow in order to be whole. Jung refers to the shadow as the dark side of our personality. I do resist the shadow side of my archetypal Child. For hidden therein is an absence of belief in the wondrous side of life, especially in the crisis of depression. I lived in that shadow for a long time. Now, I am finding the goodness within, the inspiring, magical Child. The archetypal Child who believes in miracles, goodness, transformation and the sacred beauty of all things. The artist Child, the laughing, dancing Child. Green elfin hats, circle dancing, barnyards and the transformation gold to be found in shit.

I am struck by the fact that this dream sequence began October 11 with *The Wise Old Man* dream. These few weeks of the journey have been arduous. I wonder again why I must do this on my own. And it comes to me that I can get on the horse by myself. Years ago, I often said, "All I need is a room full of books, a good chair and good music." Well, I have that. I am surrounded by natural beauty on the farm. I spend any available hours spring, summer and fall creating my garden. This is truly a family affair as Bill and the kids are often with me. My inner world provides the mystery.

More Gates

Despite the dream's healing energy, I am very tense this week. I long to experience life in its very deepest meaning and depth. At the same time, I have much to be thankful for. Tonight, I have just come out of meditation and feel very peaceful. Also, I can sleep like a child and I feel like I am beginning to live life more deeply. It is a feeling, not yet a conceptual understanding. I claim my deep willingness to understand.

Timidity—Afraid of a Mouse

I am in a large auditorium or horse-racing track. I am dressed in a ball gown. Several people sit behind a semicircular counter in a VIP room. The counter has hinged glass windows that I am cleaning and polishing. I have the outside clean and pull the windows into a position to clean the inside.

The inside of the glass is thick with green specks like bits of leaves or mown grass. I start to wipe this away. I am surprised at the amount of stuff on the inside since I hadn't seen it when I was cleaning the outside of the windows.

As I wipe the dirt away, a woman seated at the counter points to me and says, "Do you not see the mouse? He's right there." Fearfully, I try to look down to the heart area where she is pointing. I can't see the mouse. But I feel something there. I sense a nesting mouse under the bodice of my gown. I want to pull the dress off over my head or shrink away into nothing. The lady just continues to point. The others are staring. I feel sobs start from my very guts. Big rolling, tearing sobs. No one helps. Jagged pain. Inner gut pain. Hot flooding tears. I awake with streams of tears running down my face.

I face another wall of fear. I am in a ball gown in a large room with no companions. In daily life that would never happen. I would simply not go to the ball. The dream suggests facing yet more of my inside life. Clean the glass. Watch for details that may escape your notice because they are small. This is the second animal in my recent dreams. I hope this means I am reclaiming more parts of my instinctive self.

The mouse is a timid, fearful animal and represents my fear of the unknown, the unseen, of what might be hidden, sneaking through myriad tunnels. Perhaps the mouse represents a primitive and negative manifestation of the animus. Since the archetypal cats appeared in my dream *The Life Within*, maybe I can call on the cat. Not.

The mouse may be calling me to pay attention to small details. Or to be resourceful by finding the bits and pieces of life, like my missing or injured feminine instinct. Perhaps also a phallic symbol in that it is in and out of my dress. Are masculine attitudes obstructing the softness of femininity? Apparently, my prayers for courage have not resulted in lion power.

The action of cleansing is clear. I don't like the idea that I am probably living with many bits of hidden stuff—yesterday's outdated ideas, attitudes, prejudices, thoughts and garbage—which I keep hidden where neither my cultural tribe, my family nor I can see it. Perhaps the lady who is pointing at my breasts is trying to help. Green bits seem fresh, new, living. I am on a journey to find my inner feminine and the Divine Mother. The glass could be like a clogged inner eye. The green specks represent knowledge, inner knowing for me, which I do not "see" from the outside while cleansing the glass. Glass is a mirror held up in front of me so I can recognize the inner knowing hidden in the depths of my being. I affirm over and over, "I can see."

Of course, I am surprised at the "stuff" on the inside even after all this healing prayer, meditation, pain and tears. Creativity, inspiration, new life, new learning is symbolized by the green; the spring colour of new life. An image of the green vestments worn by the priest at Mass after Easter rises in my mind. The first bits of tulips that poke forth in the snow of early spring create a clear picture for me.

Besides words on a page, what does the unconscious mean to me? The deepest parts of myself, hidden aspect of being. Here I have stored all the experiences of lifetimes. I am beginning to think that it is true that I have been here before. Not as I am now but here. This is the realm of soul, of light and darkness. The realm of real living and of being, which lives everlasting moments. This is psyche, from wherein arises joy and pain. And it is the paradoxical realm, which I can choose to experience as both enlightened and endarkened. God breathed soul into my being and soul is me. I try to be. In truth? I have very little understanding.

I begin slowly to recognize the archetype of the Artist manifest as wannabe writer. I have always wanted to understand and to go beyond the five senses to the deeper dimensions of life. Perhaps that's becoming clear in the earlier dreams of *To the Fourth Dimension* and *The Global Brain*. A writer? It feels pretentious and ridiculous. How much do I risk? My soul? Family? Security? Love of family? Who in my life will support this craziness? Why am I still afraid? The inner war rages on. Seriously, this can only be my own fears. If I am pretending to actually believe, I must follow my soul journey.

I am still reading Morton Kelsey with amazement and delight. He summarizes my last three years with one statement, "These talks with the 'Other' were my profoundest experiences; on the one hand a bloody struggle, on the other, supreme ecstasy. They were an annihilating fire and an indescribable grace."

I couldn't possible explain any better. In my next dream, my outer house is rendered invisible.

Annihilating Fire

When I drive in our yard, the house is gone. The garage is still standing but without siding or shingles; it is a brown shell. Later the "house" is there because I am "inside" however there is no exterior, only the feeling of being inside. I feel strongly there is a need for an insurance claim. I meet with an unknown someone who is experienced with insurance claims. The essence of the dream remains very strong but the details are unclear.

I understand only that my outer house or appearance to the world, my "outer" shell, is gone. The essence of me is there. It is a strange dream and I want insurance coverage against wrongful belief.

For several nights, I am aware only of unclear dreams. Something I am not ready to remember lies just below the surface. I am vaguely disturbed by free-floating anxiety.

We have the flower shop deliver one red and one white rose to my parents as they celebrate their 54th wedding anniversary with a trip to Grande Prairie. They dress up for a photo. Mom is the best family historian we will ever have. Life is about to change dramatically. We will be glad for the photos.

November 19, 1990

In my need to protect my ego, the meditation tonight was most unsatisfactory. Our friend, Sally, is a reiki practitioner. She often sits behind me during our meditations, her healing hands on my shoulders. Reiki is an ancient form of healing energy with its roots in Japan. I find it deeply healing and soothing. There are articles in Catholic papers warning of the potential evils of such practice. Apparently, it isn't Christian. I am definitely aware of the condemnation and very aware of my promise to myself. I will be healed. I will dance with the devil if need be. Given what I am learning, the devil (as in "the devils made me do it") is fear.

Tonight, my issue is vulnerability. Sally tells me my back is freezing cold and wonders at the lump of negative energy she feels there. She places her hands on my back, feet and neck while I cry the whole time. Tears of pure utter anger, rage.

Why the constant inner restlessness? Constant irritation with people who ask me about next year. I get it. The irritation is the unconscious projection of my own fears. I have no idea if I will be deemed competent enough to be offered a permanent contract with Alberta Education. I love the work. It also provides me with time for all of this inner work.

November 26, 1990

I pray into the depth of the silence. Lift and burn in the fire of God's pure love all fear, all misunderstanding.

Last night a voice spoke over and over in my dreams. I was certain the message held deep significance. I awoke hot, headachy and could not remember.

I have no idea how to write poetry. Hated it in school. Teachers always asked, "What did the poet mean...?" I had no idea! I still don't. Now, I think, "Isn't that the whole point of poetry? To make meaning?" Hermes is the god of poetry; hermeneutics the art of interpretation. Now, poetry,

Listen child. Listen

As surely as a seed planted in the earth

springs forth and carries within it the

momentum of the flower or the tree

so it is that in you are the seeds of

the full potential of your soul expression.

Tend the seeds. Meditate. Affirm.

I am the expression of my fullest potential.

or what might pass as poetry, has begun slipping onto the page. When I started to write my memoir, I didn't include it. I am no longer afraid. Sure, it won't win any contests. Healing work isn't meant to compete.

I have just reread the hundreds of pages written between April 1988 and February 1989. I reflect silently for a very long time. I am on a very deep soul journey. Ever so slowly I learn that I receive what I ask for. It's just that I forget what I ask. This soul journey has only just begun. I even asked for amazement.

For the last several months, one thought returns and nags over and over. Read the Book of Wisdom. Finally, I read the Book of Wisdom. No wonder the thought has nagged. This seems to be one of the few Books in the Bible with feminine connotation. She is Wisdom. Wisdom is She. Last night I dreamed of strange events.

Returning Feminine Soul

Somewhere Bill rides off on my horse, Pauncho. I let him go thinking the horse is well enough trained. Bill is seriously hurt but not severely, not disabled. "All I want is to be able to pay the mortgage," I say to a figure that I am unable to identify.

The dream sits just outside my awareness. It is set in adolescence when the depressions became serious and I got Pauncho for a birthday gift. Paying the mortgage may be an inner reference to my constant insecurity. Or it may have more to do with the French verb—*morte*. My feminine instinct, Pauncho, has supposedly been fully domesticated. Trained. Under control. The dream says differently. The negative, patriarchal, masculine is no longer in control of my feminine soul. Literature on dreams tells me animus is Latin feminine for "soul" appearing in the dreams of women as a male figure. So the feminine aspects of soul within me are not crippled permanently, only injured. My attempts to pay the mortgage are my attempts at using my masculine to provide safety and security in our rational, hypermasculinized culture. It began with my unconscious attempts to control menstruation. I am in recovery.

There are two different times represented. Now, Bill is hurt; then, early teenage years. My dream ego still assumes that my feminine instincts are well trained and will continue to carry the external ego. This is no longer true. Horses symbolize feminine instinctive body in archetype, mythology and folklore. It may be that I am afraid that if I follow my instincts, I will be hurt or disabled. The ass or donkey in biblical mythology is similar to the horse in Western Europe. Horses are also closely related to Mother. Horses may also represent animal impulses. In Christianity we have clearly established that our animal nature is base and low. It isn't. Again, my inner knowledge is fully in opposition to authority. Recall my *Broken Church* dream. I am in recovery.

Dreams have as many interpretations as the eyeballs on a dragon. Perhaps this one is bringing to consciousness my denial of the flesh in my rigid attempt to please an avenging, angry God who hates women due to the actions of Eve. I was always fascinated, mesmerized, traumatized by early childhood interpretations of purity and impurity. I still live with several addictions expressed as fear of not being good enough, of being laughed at or ridiculed. I was addicted to the Virgin archetype, to rules, to work. The list is long. Recovering my instinctive self is indeed dangerous to the beliefs of the rational trained conscious mind. The unconscious assures me my ego is only hurt, not disabled. I am in recovery.

What do we mean when we talk about the process of individuation? I read the word often in Jungian studies. Practical examples are elusive. I consider that I am living with elusive glimmerings of awareness of what it means to individuate. I am healing, leaving out, annihilating, changing, reclaiming. I am on a midlife journey to become a whole woman. A virgin. Whole unto myself. Is this possible? If so, this may go on forever. I am in recovery.

The intuitive function does not care about security as in paid mortgages (morte-death) but rather in freedom. I am willing to affirm the creativity, the wellspring of intuition within. I am willing to honour the feminine/masculine. I will be my authentic self. I am a pilgrim; I have an image with me often these days: I am an old woman with my walking stick, my worldly goods tied in a tattered blue handkerchief bundle tied to the handle of my walking stick. I wander. I sing a lot. I can't hear the song yet. But I know I am singing. I carry a battered copy of *The Way of the Pilgrim*.[69] I am in recovery.

I have learned from dream workshop participants and my reading not to discount even one image no matter how seemingly insignificant. One group spent several hours working with the simple image of a screen. The dreamer was insistent, "It can't mean anything." Sometimes the leader has to lead. We began with each participant's association. The process unfolded. Turns out, the dream probably only needed one image to ask the question, "Where and what is the fear you are screening out of your consciousness?" We are in recovery.

December 8, 1990

The Feast of the Immaculate Conception is a day to commemorate the Mother. Mary, clothe me in pure love energy, the beautiful transcendent blue mantle of deep spiritual consciousness.

I open my Bible and randomly pick on Colossians. Epaphras is a Greek word meaning beloved, covered with foam. He was a faithful minister of the Christ to the Colossian church and a prisoner with Paul at Rome. Rome symbolizes the prison of the intellect. It would seem that I am definitely

---

69   Helen Bacovcin, *The Way of a Pilgrim* (NY: Doubleday, 1978).

imprisoned. I am tired of being a prisoner to anything. The *Solitude* dream takes on deeper meaning. I desire freedom. I am willing to search a little longer since I retreated into depression as a young person. I have no desire for that kind of retreat. Where shall I go to ponder, to reflect, to integrate all this learning? A full, deep day life and a full, deep dream life. Hmmm, *The Way of the Pilgrim* beckons but is impossible. I cannot face leaving my family to fend for themselves, nor face fending without them.

The world devalues the feminine through culturally conditioned expectations of the woman's role as compliant, submissive, seductress, sexual object, caregiver, recipient of male largesse, scheming, manipulative, and/or weak. This devalues not just women. It devalues all "Other" who may exhibit traits seen as feminine. These are the unconscious projections onto wo(man) of a society built on centuries of orientation to rational-masculine. Feminine energy has been relegated to inferior status. I am slowly becoming aware of the feminine. I work to heal the idealized masculine while learning what feminine energy might look, feel and be like. How is it we can imprison and torture the inherent principle of our own life-giving force? I am learning through dreams at a level deeper than ever I thought possible.

As I pray tonight I am again restless, unfocussed, irritated. A kind of vague, nameless, anxiety. Once, twice, three times, I meditate. On the third book, *The Life and Teachings of the Masters of the Far East*, volume III, I settle. Peace, not deep, not endless, but peace, steals over me.

"I know I would know this man, Jesus, were I to see him" brings washes of tears from a place of deep longing. I feel abandoned, tricked by my own intellect into somehow losing the connection while knowing that is impossible.

For most of December, the mists of illusion hang over my consciousness. I have read often about the need for patience in healing times. It seems I want to live on the peak of the mountain and yet the darkness of the valleys, the depths, are equally important. Solitude below.

Role Play

> I see Miss Perfect is running up the stairs, breathing hard; she is playing a role of some kind, trying out for a play. Someone asks me if I will play the part if it is too difficult for her. Somewhere I have a feeling of being laughed at. The scene changes.

By morning many details of the dream have receded. Miss Perfect's impeccable dress overwhelms me. She is very petite. My feelings of feminine inadequacy surface quickly and I become clumsy, ugly and uncomfortable alongside her perfect image. She was on staff in the high school where I was vice-principal for a year in the late '80s. There was a great deal of staff and district turbulence that year. Between staff turmoil, my own life circumstances, my outsider status and utter audacity of being—*gasp*—a female high school administrator, my stress was through the roof. I was transgressing every boundary of the patriarchy. One day, I found a small anonymous pink note in my staff mail box. "Why don't you go back to the elementary school where you belong? We don't want you here." I had been offered a couple of elementary principalships … and refused. I had never ever applied. I taught Grade 5 for three months … once. "We" was not speaking for a staff of 58 or "we" wouldn't have been anonymous.

Where am I role playing? This dream points to the thread of ridicule and laughter. A shadow figure brings to the surface my feelings of inadequacy as a woman who made hard, sometimes very unpopular decisions as an administrator in a large high school. Not feminine! I hesitate to tell the truth. I remember these same feelings from early childhood. Never pretty. Never sparkly. Never what the beautiful aunts in my life were. Strange what is tucked deep into the personal unconscious.

My understanding of feminine energy is woefully lacking in 1990.

December 29, 1990

Outwardly this is the best Christmas I can remember in many years; and I am having difficulty writing, meditating, or even reading. I am restless, hazy, vague and unfocussed. This morning I open my Bible for comfort. One verse stays with me:

"In a short time you will no longer see me, and then a short time later you will see me again."

–John 16

In the evening, I call home and speak to Mom, "Are you and Dad coming for New Year's?"

"Just a minute, you can talk to your dad."

Dad is not a phone conversationalist. We chat about the weather. It's cold. The snow. It's deep. "Are you coming for New Year's?"

"No, I don't really feel like making that drive, Blink. I am feeling pretty tired these days. I think we'll just stay here. You have a good New Year." He hands the phone back to Mom. We chat about family stuff. The fun we had at Christmas.

December 30, 1990

In the morning, I went early to visit a friend in Leduc some 25 miles from home. I had just sat down in her kitchen, when Jason phoned. "Mom, you need to come home."

"Jay, I just got here."

"Just come home, Mom." His voice caught. In that split second, I knew.

"It's Dad, isn't it," I said.

He sighed. "Just come home, Mom. OK?"

All the anxiousness, the hazy dreams that weren't really dreams and John 16. All manner of hints that tried to come but didn't get through my screens. Dad died this morning.

He just pitched forward through the back door, shouting, "Mom!" He had gone out to start the car and brush the snow off. He and Mother were going to Mass as they did every Sunday of their lives for 54 years. It was something like -38 C. Dad is never sick. Well, that's the lore. He hates hospitals. That too.

A few months later, brother David tells me this story. He had gone to the house to tell Mom and Dad he was leaving to work in the north and would be home after New Year's.

"I won't be here," Dad told him as they stood out on the back porch, smoking. Dad had quit years before, but every once in a while, he still said, "Give me one of those, will you?"

David asked where he was going. "Just won't be here," he said laconically. David repeated the question adding, "I thought you said you and Mom weren't going to Phoenix this winter?"

"We're not. I am having a little trouble with my heart. Don't tell your mother." He went back in the house.

True to his word, he wasn't there for New Year's.

I did not have a chance to say goodbye and the tears still flow with every thought of him. Many days later angry fury rises. I can hear Mom from deep in childhood. Only dogs are mad. Well, Mom, I am damn mad. I will write whether it scares me or not. I am livid. Raging mad. At God and pretty much everybody including myself. I don't give a sweet damn if it is a pity party. I am entitled to be mad. Mad at Dad for not saying goodbye when he knew he was planning to leave. I was not ready. So it goes for several days. The greatest, deepest fear of my childhood, young adulthood and indeed my life. The death of my father. Grief. This grief will last forever.

Chapter Nine

Iron Woman Tears

The stars are not wanted now: put out every one;
Pack up the moon and dismantle the sun;
Pour away the ocean and sweep up the wood;
For nothing now can ever come to any good.

–W. H. Auden

New Year's Day, 1991

After Mass, Shirley gives me *We, The Bride* by Sister Francis Clare.[70] It means nothing today. But it will.

The family home and brothers' houses nearby spill over with the generations. We are all home, including Michael and family from England, grandkids from cities and jobs far away. I am surrounded with love and the chains that bind.

---

[70] Sister Francis Clare, *We, The Bride* (Green Forest, AR: New Leaf Press, 1991).

January 4, 1991

We bury Dad in the Holy Rosary Cemetery. I am calm behind the masks. No one speaks about grief. We are all polite. I refuse to hear any clichés. I walk away from anything remotely patronizing. "Well, at least he was never sick. At least he didn't suffer. He lived a good long life." I hear myself saying … unprintable things. No one else hears.

I pray. A lot. Silently. Ceaselessly. Jesus, Jesus, Jesus. "And Jesus wept" repeats. My constant endless inner prayer. Survival.

"A mystic is someone open to intimate knowledge of God," says Sister Francis Clare. What does it mean? Intimate knowledge of God? I have no idea. I am compelled to pray, to meditate and to ask questions. I know this seems completely crazy to the rational world. I decide I don't really care what "other" people think. Of course I do. It is really my own fear. I understand that. It doesn't mean it goes away. In Jungian psychology/religion, these breakthrough thoughts are the wisdom of the unconscious. A function of my introverted intuitive self. I hear that. I have these conversations with myself.

Tears flow incessantly. Once I'm back home, family stays away, overwhelmed by the depth of my grief and loss. Over and over, I lost my dad. I lost my dad. I am 45. I am thankful that dad lived until I was healed of depression. I was a little bit ready to stand on my own. Surely, the past two years have strengthened me. I know.

Years later, at a small gathering of 13 women in a conference, *Seeing Red: The emerging feminine in turbulent times*, in Stonington, Connecticut, Muriel McMahon, Jungian analyst, mentions our culture's loss of keening rituals. In that moment, I am thrown back against the wall. I retreat to solitude. I remember my mom's curt demands to "stop crying" and come meet with the nun who was there from the parish to plan the Mass. I remember the first response of my colleagues at work, "How old was your dad?" I scream inside. Does it matter?

"82."

"Oh, well, he lived a long life."

Molten silent rage. Bottled. He lived a long life? Seriously? That's the response our culture gives to the death of a beloved parent? Or, come help plan the funeral? Whatever happened to the wake? To the keening, weeping, tearing of hair? Oh, yes. Far and away too irrational. He's in heaven. Blah blah. Compost.

January 7, 1991

I am reading, skimming, *Healing the Child Within* by Whitfield.[71] Go through the pain is the message that comes. Feel the pain. Thaw the ice.

I pray, Our Father, and open the Bible to Luke 24. It speaks of death and resurrection. The appearances of Jesus after the resurrection, the women at the tomb. Emmaus, and the appearance of Jesus to the 11. The women. The 11. Beautiful symbolism.

I am comforted by Bill who gives me the gift of space to grieve openly; and Rachel who says to imagine Grandpa is fine, sitting in his chair because we are here and really Grandpa is not gone. I come to deeply regret that my child comforts me rather than the other way around. Rachel's grief turns inward.

She is 11. She was born to a depressed mother with all the masks in place. Now two years with a mother in deep process of ... something. I remember Dad telling everyone about their conversation a few years back. She was perhaps eight. She and Dad were watching television downstairs. She, ever curious, touched the wrinkles on his neck and said, "How come you are all wrinkled, Grandpa?"

"I'm old," he said, "I will die soon."

"Don't be silly, Grandpa. Moses lived to be 900. I'm not ready for you to die."

---

[71] Charles L. Whitfield, *Healing the Child Within* (Deerfield Beach, Florida: Health Communications Inc., 1989).

Dad laughed and told that story often. I wasn't ready either. I have been dreaming unfocussed and fuzzy dreams every night since Dad's death. Looking back through December's dreams, the theme was confusion, lack of focus, haziness. I had come so far on this journey. Now, I wanted to retreat into nothingness. I couldn't go back. I couldn't go forward.

Speaking with God

I am semi-awake all night as I search through my journal for healing. Throughout the night, I read many books and speak with God.

I read. I reflect. For me, heaven is no longer a place to go. It is a process of yielding to the inner, transforming power of God's love, living within love consciousness. Why the Scripture about Emmaus? Emmaus symbolizes a place in consciousness where healing restores love and life. The truth of Spirit springs up and flows freely through man's being. Emmaus is a Greek word meaning *mineral springs, medicinal springs.* I will bathe in Emmaus. I am willing to flow in and with the river of life. The worst wound any human person can suffer is to be cut off from the tears that would flow out in healing waters. In our masculine, patriarchal society, we are estranged from our own woundedness; our source of healing water from within. I give myself permission to cry. I am sick and tired of crying.

What am I? Divine spark, God-centred nature, divine nature, Kingdom of God within, nirvana, awakened soul, Inner Light, Christ-in-you, Christ Consciousness, Indwelling Spirit, Inner Christ.

January 12, 1991

Write? Why? Of what use? I am so ready to quit. I don't ever. It is stamped on my soul. Write. I continue the seeking and searching.

> *Wherever there is a reaching down into innermost experience, into the nucleus of personality, most people are overcome by fright, and many run away.... The risk of inner experience, the adventure of the spirit, is in any case, alien to most human beings.*
>
> —Carl Jung, *Memories, Dreams, Reflections*

I am panicky. As I reflect on Jung's words, I can hear people asking, "When will this be finished?"

"I have absolutely no clue. Probably never?"

I am reminded of the poem studied with my Grade 9 language arts students, "The Road Not Taken" by Robert Frost. What does the other road look like? Where is the road to the essence of pure love in the ground of my being? How is it that I so easily hit the ditch?

January 15, 1991

Apparently, the inner world of all people is the outer world we all experience. Currently there is a massive, ugly, war in Iraq. In meditation tonight, we ask about our role in this war. The answers are fascinating. I experience my own personal Iraq. How can this be? This is the Jungian explanation for the collective unconscious manifest in the outer. I am very much intrigued. In 1991, with the Iraqi crisis, I try desperately to maintain my balance. My son, Jason, flirts with the idea of joining the

American military. I am yelled at by male colleagues furious with my stance that the USA does not belong in Iraq. I rejoice when Canada refuses to participate with the madness of weapons of mass destruction. The metaphor of the dangers of the Other surround me. As within so without.

In meditative active imagination, I ask to know how my inner world is akin to the Iraqi crisis. During the meditation, I sometimes see, sometimes hear, and sometimes simply intuit the words, images and ideas.

What is my personal Iraq?

Split sides of self

Family healing

Fear of persecution—being a misfit

Hussein symbolizes for me anger held deep within my physical/intellectual being. In meditation the left eye, left shoulder, neck are split away. My heart pounds wildly.

Bush symbolizes fear of loss of pride/dignity.

The United Nations symbolizes my desire for unity without self-involvement.

How Do I Resolve My Inner Crisis?

This is a crisis of the repressed feminine. Heal the dark feminine.

Continue to meditate

Continue to speak out in love.

Move forward in writing.

Heal pride by risking rejection for indeed this is false pride. Risk all.

Continue to focus in love.

Have patience.

Be gentle with yourself.

Continue to reach out to others.

Guns symbolize self-protective armour. Armaments of resistance. You have armed yourself with the words of the intellect to preserve the gentle spirit within. Risk being gentle and you will not require the arms. Be soft and vulnerable. There is no need for armament when you are surrounded by the presence of God. Yield. Surrender to Love and that will be your protection. For truly, child, your desire to see love is strong within.

Then I move deeply into a peaceful meditation. An "intuitive" crystal vase with lines of strength appears. A beautiful softly glowing white/pink orchid, or what I imagine is an orchid, appears. As I bring the vase and orchid into me, the peace deepens. As I reach out to put Iraq into the vase of love, the meditation goes into darkness. My heart begins to pound with well-remembered palpitations of anxiety. I begin sending love. Jesus, Jesus, Jesus. The darkness is pervasive. Then the feeling of a line of separation in the centre of my being from the chest up through the head. Left eye, left shoulder, left chest are pounded, pushed, prodded and "bumped" out. The left eye feels bulged out of its socket.

I put my hand out to hold the goop oozing from the left eye. The feeling lightens and lifts somewhat.

The group takes a few minutes to focus back into the room. I am a jumble. Quickly, I leave and head home. I am disoriented. My inner Censor is going crazy.

Once home I listen to Bette Midler's song, "From a Distance," several times over. I am determined to let go of the crystallized hardness in my heart. I dance around the house. I help Rachel get ready for bed, wash her face. She hugs me and I cry. She places her hands on my heart. I massage her feet to release negativity. She sleeps. My daughter.

I pick up my Bible. The Book of Tobit. The Archangel Raphael. I ask for inner understanding of the messages here. As I lie down, I pray my childhood Guardian Angel prayer. I am surrounded by the love and care of the universal God. I slip easily and peacefully into meditation.

Encounters with Silence

Sometime in the night I am aware of several words emblazoned within. SILENCE—THE OTHER. Peace gently pervades.

It is impossible to pray for peace with war in my heart. The so-called Wrath of God is really Love's severity or Love encountering mind to purify it. Supreme perfection of Love has no wrath, as shown by the Christ who prayed, "Father forgive them." Estes says, "grace to embrace." I write her words on a sticky note and stick it on the edge of my laptop screen.

I come across many questions about the truth of the Gospels. I wonder, what is truth anyway? At the end of the day, what does it matter? Mythology rules everywhere. The messages of love, forgiveness and compassion sustain whether or not words are meant or taken literally. I am puzzled by the constant argument. Is it the intellect or perhaps the tiny superego embedded in family and tribe that remains completely unaware of the deep layers of the psyche? It took a trauma to send me hurtling down, diving deep, as symbolized by the elevator fall from the intellect to lamb's wool in *The Landing* of December 1988. How many times have I taken that dive down since then? Pearl Diving, Father John Rich will tell me in New York in July.

As I read more Jung, I realize our culture is in constant contradiction. We claim to prize individuality; we allow for no difference. When Jung was writing and spoke out about the rise of Nazism in the 1930s, he was laughed at, ridiculed, called a fascist. A mystical fool? History has shown the dark side of the human psyche. The controversy about his views remains today. I reflect on these statements in the face of the 1990s presidential crisis of leadership. Is it fair to say that the moral high ground claimed by some parts of the secularist public is as warlike as all the wars of religion?

> The mass crushes out the insight and reflection that are still possible with the individual and this leads to doctrinaire and authoritarian tyranny if ever the constitutional state should succumb to a fit of weakness.

> –C.G. Jung, *The Undiscovered Self,* 14.

> Most people confuse "self-knowledge" with knowledge of their conscious ego personalities ... but the ego knows only its own contents. People measure their self-knowledge by what the average person in their social environment knows of himself, but not by the real psychic facts which are for the most part hidden from them.

> –C.G. Jung, *The Undiscovered Self,* 15.

This is as sensible as it gets. How can I be conscious of my unconscious through consciousness? Dreams are indeed the royal road to the unconscious. This path of woman healing is not the hero's journey. It is instead the cycling, spiralling of the feminine in search of itself. I endure constant symbolic death and rebirth. I will admit sometimes the pain of dismemberment of false beliefs is so intense that it feels like physical death.

Searching the uncharted depths of the unconscious, I am hauled through the petty power struggles of my ego-life. This search for the Feminine Christ Self cannot be undertaken by wimps and weaklings. Yes, my wisdom figure, Jesus, is male. However, that is the rendering of the patriarchy. Study the scriptures. The Christ was both masculine and feminine. And so I should listen when Jesus says, "Be Gentle," for I am in uncharted waters. No bloody wonder I wonder. I am so far out of my depth it is shocking when I stop to think. What happens next?

My all-too-human inner growth experiences sometimes involve a red-hot coal stuck in the throat. In summer, 1991, I take our truck and small travel trailer to Lethbridge with two friends for a week to participate in Four Directions Healing. During that time, I have some very strong red-alert experiences. I panic. I can't swallow the huge lump stuck somewhere between mouth and stomach. I can't cough it up, I can't swallow it. It sits burning, painful and searing. I can't seem to make this next incredible leap in inner growth by myself. How to remove and integrate the lump? The first step is to name the goop. It is death with potential birth. Something must die before something new is born. Basic science. The potential is amazing. I reflect on two earlier dreams: *Release of Inner Garbage* and *More Inner Garbage*.

> No aspect of the human psyche can live in a healthy state unless it is balanced by its complementary opposite. If the masculine mind tries to live without its "other half," the feminine soul, then the masculine becomes unbalanced, sick and finally monstrous. Power without love becomes brutality. Feeling without masculine strength becomes woolly sentimentality.[72]

---

[72] Robert A. Johnson, *We: Understanding the Psychology of Romantic Love* (Harper & Row 1983), 23.

I am awakened to an emerging truth.

Religuere, January 27, 1991

> A powerful, peaceful presence is seeking to show me that humanity, myself, is moving to an understanding of consciousness linked to all. I am filled with a deep sense of Catholicism moving through old doctrines and beliefs, to a new age of thought whereby the unique individuality of persons expressed in many ways is yet linked to One Divine Source. As I sleep, someone speaks, and I feel intuitively the underlying, invisible energy which brings each person mysteriously to sense a need for newness in thought. New thoughts that focus on the God image imprinted on the psyche of every individual on planet Earth. New thoughts that struggle to come to the surface of consciousness. Because these thoughts are still inexpressible, I feel both a struggle and a deep peacefulness. I awake with an inner smile.

This is sacred space; One Divine Source.

Section V

Chopping Open the Frozen Sea

Chapter Ten

Shrugging Off the Shroud of the Dead Good Girl

I have fallen deeply into the abyss, faced into the dark images of the repressed preverbal assault, survived convulsing paroxysms of emotional grieving, been ego humiliated and shaken to the core of my being. I have asked for and been granted the privilege of sacrifice to the Dark Goddess. Fire has annihilated many upper-world ego-identity beliefs. I am no longer prepared to live unconsciously as a daughter of the patriarchy. I have lovingly and gently washed the mask from the inner child. Together we have explored with great love and tenderness the image we give the world outside. I am not sure how many gates I have passed through on my journey through the underworld of Ereshkigal, but I've begun, tentatively, to shrug off the shroud of the dead good girl. I have gone through the hole in the fence shown in the *Freedom* dream. I am midwife to my instinctive feminine self.

I am peaceful with the word religion: to re-connect to the one Divine Source for all. The ground deep within my consciousness is shifting. A new age of thought is evolving in many ways. Peace pervades. Today Alberta's howling energetic January winds blow misunderstanding out and away from the landscape of my soul.

I circle. Tangle in the web. Move through one more coil on the journey to wholeness. I am young to these new realms of consciousness. I reflect on the image of the beautiful child in the crib. I am awakened and the world looks very new.

Once begun, the journey never ends. These dreams show expansive possibilities.

> *The dream is the small hidden door in the deepest and most intimate sanctum of the soul,*
> *which opens to that primeval cosmic night that was soul long before there was*
> *conscious ego and will be soul far beyond what a conscious ego could ever reach.*

–C.G. Jung

My Soul Moved: Rebirth in a Gradual Instant

There is a lot of inner movement. There are three figures but none are visible. I am in a bed with two male figures: The Director, and what seems to be the Other in the dream's hazy vagueness. The Director does not enter into the dialogue in the beginning. The Other is in the middle. He and I discuss things in mute wordless thoughts. We then get up and go down through a hallway or tunnel all the while engrossed in mute conversation. We return and I lie down. The Other disappears. The Director then speaks to me. Thoughts are present but very elusive. The Other returns and leaps in the middle between us. The Director seems to reach through and make grabbing motions but the Other prevents him from grasping on to me. There is a lamp on the bed stand. The room is unfamiliar.

http://lessons4living.com/labyrinth.htm

"A labyrinth is an ancient symbol that relates to wholeness. It combines the imagery of the circle and the spiral into a meandering but purposeful path. The Labyrinth represents a journey to our own center and back again out into the world. Labyrinths have long been used as meditation and prayer tools.

"A labyrinth is an archetype with which we can have a direct experience. We can walk it. It is a metaphor for life's journey. It is a symbol that creates a sacred space and place and takes us out of our ego to 'That Which Is Within.'

"Labyrinths and mazes have often been confused. When most people hear of a labyrinth they think of a maze. A labyrinth is not a maze. A maze is like a puzzle to be solved. It has twists, turns, and blind alleys. It is a left-brain task that requires logical, sequential, analytical activity to find the correct path into the maze and out.

"A labyrinth has only one path. It is unicursal. The way in is the way out. There are no blind alleys. The path leads you on a circuitous path to the center and out again.

"A labyrinth is a right brain task. It involves intuition, creativity, and imagery. With a maze many choices must be made and an active mind is needed to solve the problem of finding the center. With a labyrinth there is only one choice to be made. The choice is to enter or not. A more passive, receptive mindset is needed. The choice is whether or not to walk a spiritual path."

The labyrinth IS the feminine story structure.

image3.jpg: Labyrinth

Labyrinth

I seem to dream a very long time, then to sit with it for a long time. The dream is as confused as I am. The Other is critical in dreamwork as it signifies an unknown aspect of self and this Other figure is a known and respected masculine colleague. For many months, we have had long discussions about healing. The Director figure also has some authority and significance in my work life so may represent a positive inner masculine authority. The dream woke me up but I went back into and through it again. I was in a meditative state most of the night.

The *Gradual Instant* dream has deep inner meaning. I am intrigued with the total lack of sexual connotation. The bed symbol holds transformative possibilities with its place of birth, death, regeneration, creation and re-creation. The lamp is a symbol of learning, wisdom and light. I do not notice if it is lit or the room is dark. Together the bed and the lamp are strong healing symbols. The dream as a whole could symbolize integration, and soul balancing. It might be masculine authority and feminine healing, both aspects of soul. Three figures moving positions might signify soul movement. The walk through the tunnel signifies agreement to re-enter the labyrinth path of the soul back to the centre of itself. There is possibility, hope for the inner marriage—oneness with love meeting wisdom and power.

This dream is, in Jungian terms, a metaphorical statement *from* the dreamer *to* the dreamer. When I move too far in any one direction, off balance as it were, a dream comes to equalize a particular conscious viewpoint with its opposite. Just when I congratulate myself for becoming "better," "more healed," a dream comes along to remind me to seek inner balance given this new awareness. A compensatory dream, according to Jung.

It isn't very many days before the deep peacefulness is replaced by new fears and bigger doubts, all locked in an imaginary antique trunk. I know I need to look for the next tiny crack. That little opening into the world of my imagination, behind the worn, scarred façade. What will I find still hidden? I invite creativity into my life to bring warmth, hope, and new possibility. The key to the trunk is bound in concrete. I contemplate cracking. I imagine cracks opening so I can find and heal brokenness and imperfections. I may yet find my rotting corpse in Bluebeard's vault, that patriarchal mythical Pandora's box.

What fear is it? I must know what else is in there. My curiosity will not loose all the evils of the world, nor am I a scheming seductress bent on luring men to doom! Open the damn box. What else will I find besides assault, abandonment, rage and anger?

After three years of this, I fear for my sanity. Not the earlier years-ago fear. But a fear that I am too weak, lacking inner courage and conviction to descend deeper. The Accuser. The Judge. Spewing vitriol. Nothing new for sure. I have heard it all for years and years. What a hypocrite! Yesterday you were flying high on some imaginary dream. You're too dumb. Too stupid. No one likes you. You'll alienate your children, husband, family, friends. You'll lose your job if anyone knows how crazy you are. You think you can live like a hermit. You can't. Go ahead. Be an outcast. You already are. You read too much. You whine too much. You think you can write? Ha. You write all this crap. Who is ever gonna read it. No one wants this. And on and on and …

Tears and blood. Is that what the inner journey is all about? One long trail of blood? Then blood splattered on all those who come near me?

I learned something new during those days between Dad dying and the funeral. When the Sister from St. Rita's Catholic Church arrived to help with funeral plans, I was in my childhood bedroom looking at the newly arrived set of pictures taken in early December of Dad and Mom on their 54th wedding anniversary together with some taken at brother Bob and his wife, Cherry's anniversary celebration. I was crying.

"There is no point crying," Mom said. "You need to pull yourself together and come meet with Sister now."

I swallowed my rage and went. A full year later, Mom told me that crying was an affront to God. Disrespect for God's decision. God "needed" Dad. I could see that this belief was painful to her. "No. Mom. No. I choose to follow the story of Lazarus. And Jesus wept over his friend." I didn't hear more from her about crying as a sign of lack of faith.

My thoughts are interspersed with constant mocking. I know somewhere there is good in all this. You're kidding, right? I am blessed in the raw wound of pain. You don't really believe that. I am nearly done. That's delusional. But yes, pain does drive me deeper in this search for healing and wholeness. It is the ego that mocks. I have surrendered much this past three years.

And so I weep some more. Then I open Morton Kelsey, *Prophetic Ministry:*[73]

> I often wonder that some hardboiled and orthodox clinician does not describe emotional weeping as a "new disease," calling it paroxysmal lachrymation and suggesting treatment by belladonna, astringent local applications, avoidance of sexual excess, tea, tobacco and alcohol and a salt-free diet with the restriction of

---

[73] Morton Kelsey, *Prophetic Ministry: Psychology and Spirituality of Pastoral Care* (Rockport, MA: Element Books, 1991), 40.

fluid intake, proceeding in the event of failure, to early removal of the tear glands.

Laughter, too, is good for you.

Healing Feminine Instinct: Dancing Dog

Here is a teenage boyfriend now grown up. Rachel is with me. I want to go to a dance with him but he seemingly has to do something else. He leaves. I feel lost, forlorn, abandoned. There are no images.

> The Artist Archetype expresses the theme of joy, and manifests in the passion to express a dimension of life just beyond the five senses.

The scene changes to healing animals. One image appears late in the dream: a small, lumpish object—a puppy. I carry the puppy and lay it on what seems to be a church pew. The dream seems a mute discussion of the possible healing of puppies. Some say "No" you cannot operate to heal. Some say "Yes." I seem to insist that a simple operation would help.

Dance is an ongoing symbol in my journey to full feminine expression. I love dancing. Have always loved dancing. I loved the music of the dance that was present in our home throughout my life. Dancing is in intimate expression of the self requiring intricate steps and balance. It is an expressive art requiring the perfect partnership of masculine-feminine body, soul and emotion. The dream indicates my desire is to dance with the young masculine of many years ago.

The dream is both past and present. In the past, the inner child was lost. Now, the feminine instinct is symbolized by a very young puppy, animal instinct in need of healing. Women have been domesticated in civil society. The body shamed, claimed and maimed to reach the standards set by the institutions where our bodies live. I laid the puppy in the church pew. It may be time to come to terms with my inner church. It too is birthed. Something has to die. I am pointed back toward the *Broken Church*, 1989.

I am not nor ever have been a Gut Girl, that is, a slaughterhouse worker in Victorian England. I was born into a proper-lady religious culture that domesticates the feminine body, which clearly carries the shape of the devil. Not too loud. Not too proud. Not too intuitive. Not too emotional. Not too alive. Not too big. Not too real. Not too sensual. Not too sexual. No primal noises and screams may erupt from my Victorian mists. Religious experience is irrelevant, hysterical, and possibly devil-oriented in our culture. Since it does not fit the ordinary scientific paradigm, the rational Western fundamentalist religious mind deems it satanic. Such dogmatism insists most certainly that all experience, to be acceptable, must be reduced to material reality and fit within doctrinal formats created by hierarchical male authority. The Blessed Mother's appearances are viewed with suspicion by supposed rational theologians. No wonder she must stay in the stone and stand silently on the plaster pedestal where she was placed. She sometimes appears in tears.

There is no blame or condemnation of self attached to these comments. Only sadness that my soul has been so colonized by patriarchal beliefs that I have spent over half my life in confusion and fear. Dance is universal! What is the archetypal significance of the relationship of dancing, the feminine and the body? There are parallels unspoken, as yet unknown in my journey.

February 1, 1991

Snail-like, I begin to understand my childish dependence on Dad for approval and strength. This understanding feels like a traitorous betrayal; but I must accept my own power. I open the trunk. How much more is stuffed in there? I slam it shut. What if this is Pandora's Box?

For many days I have been unable to feel much of anything. Sometime in November the sense of being securely connected to Self, to God, to the Inner Christ began to elude me. Then, the lost child lost her Dad. Over and over I have cried silently, "I lost my Dad." Cold, remote, disconnected, I have flung myself back into work. Angry that I seemingly have no friends who care. No one. I feel ugly and fat and horrible. I have put on the masks again so I will be acceptable—for pain is above all a private affair. Clearly, the patriarchy lives me.

I have said and done all the appropriate things. If I told the truth about how I feel, the world would split in two and I am the world.

I am a raging, angry, bloodthirsty child turned to stone. I am a raging child whose thirst for love, peace, joy, once begun, once experienced, goes unslaked.

Anger. What is that? An emotion. An expression of futility in the face of permanent gaping scar tissue. A festering hatred brought to the surface. Damn it, why is it so difficult to express pain? Sorrow. What is that? Fear of being left to fend for myself. This is the rage of creativity, the rage of existential despair.

Once more the storm recedes. The body temperature, burning searing hot, subsides. The convulsive sobs become muffled. I am willing to try again. What is the highest wisdom for me in this moment?

Prompting

> *Wisdom comes from the Father's house and waits for your permission to infuse the cells of your heart with healing love. Within the chambers of your being is love that longs to be free. Free your heart to soar like the eagle with the sun. And I am the sun.*

Jesus, in the dream this summer when the large muscular man in *Count on the Inner Christ* threatened to destroy me, I called your name five times and the Tyrant disappeared—poof. I call you now, in this very instant: Come, heal my resistance.

It isn't long before I begin to question why all the prompting refers to the Father. Truly, I am in search of the dark feminine. When does my inner world shift at least to neutral? Asking the questions is paramount.

Integrating Energies

> There are two figures, myself and The Director. I join the male figure in the bed, and am very surprised and rather guilty to be attracted to making love. I cuddle close, feeling his face and hair in caressing movements. I long for closeness and intimacy. There seem to be some figures watching. I sense disapproval. The male figure is the same as in an earlier dream but this time he feels much more like control and authority. The male figure is disengaged, remote. He gets up and leaves.
>
> New scene. I sense an argument about what is right/wrong. Healing animals? I cannot remember more.

I have to smile when I reread the dream. Indeed, a very long two-part dream with the connection between the segments missing. The connection is missing. Healing the instinctive, the animal-emotion self follows immediately on the *Healing Feminine Instinct: Dancing Dog* dream. I was often told as a child, "Only dogs get mad." The connection is missing between the feminine/masculine aspects of my being. There is affection, sexual attraction, and nurturing emotion—but no connection to the inner animal, instinctive feminine. The inner patriarch remains aloof, and integration requires first contact between these aspects of self.

The dream highlights my desire for relatedness. E-motion. I have been asked why I hyphenate. Emotion comes from the Latin *emotio*, derived from *emotus*, meaning "moved out" or "to be moved." I am filled with e-motion. While working on my doctoral program, I decided that e-motion made more sense as the emotion causes movement. It's an Einstein thing. E-motion moves my soul. Our belief in rational consciousness is limiting; to depend on it absolutely is deeply dysfunctional.

Teaching has always delighted my soul. In 1984–85, I created an integrated social studies and language arts curriculum with my Grade 9 group. We studied root words, suffixes and prefixes using the work of Bill Sherk. Singing, dancing, imagining and creating, we made up words. The student vocabulary grew in many directions. Words like *impactipediphobia*. I remember that word and the story behind its creation. One of the boys had broken his foot and it was in a cast. One morning one of the other lads said, "Mrs. Gregor, Billy is suffering from *impactipediphobia*."

Dutifully, I asked, "What's that?"

"Oh, he's afraid of having his other foot broken." A good deal of laughter ensued. Energy in motion. That's what humans are. E for energy. E-motion. Laughter teaches a good deal.

I have learned even more about e-motion these past three years. Silencing, slicing, bottling, canning and preserving but never using. We just "put it all behind us" and "forget about it."

Trouble is, psyche doesn't forget. We have dropped our feelings of horror, fear and rage, down into the trunk and slammed it shut. The human trunk is far larger than my trunk. Trapped in the underworld.

Denial of our emotional lives must end. The world tips precariously to the right. We turn our faces away from the harassment and denigration of women's emotional lives. It may look like men have it all. That is another patriarchal lie that substitutes power for soul. From top to bottom the hierarchal system must wake up. We need to see the hidden poor, the weak, handicapped or homeless men or women. I need to see my own complicity. Gated rooms, communities and countries exist within me and everywhere around the world.

We must recover our ability to emote. E-motion underlies every thought, word and action we take. And yet, e-motion has been denigrated by the rational Western literary canon from time out of mind. I could write a whole book of family stories just on that theme. Just last Christmas I started the meal blessing by reading a story written about my grandmother during the Great Depression. It's called *Three Pieces of Soap*. I warned the assembled 35 or more family members, "I cry easily now, so just get used to it." I cried. Wet eyes in abundance. Nobody dissolved.

I am experiencing inner climate change. Icebergs are melting. Moving toward wholeness requires energy. Thus, e-motion.

February 17, 1991

A drawing arrives in the mail from our Indian foster child. The lotus. Mechanical, not beautiful as the lotus flowers of my imagination, its arrival prompts a question. Why? I too am contrived, mechanical, holding in some inner nameless void, the centre of power, wisdom and love. Fear again. Of what? My teeth are tight, aching from restraint. I try to resist the constant inner need to surrender to this journey yet deeper into myself, or toward my Self, the God within.

What is the history of e-motion in our culture? It is an aspect of *Eros* and we are a proud *Logos* culture. Believe me, I know. I was raised in a household of men. Mother enforced the patriarchal rules. When my mother wanted to silence my tears after Dad died, I experienced a flash of insight. Aha! We must show the good nun how much faith we have! Look. We so know that Dad is in a better place, we don't even cry. This is not a gender thing. It's about the patriarchal God in the Sky hierarchy and power. Who has it? Who wants it? Who gets it? And how? I wonder again what voice my grandmothers had. And what do the enforcers of the rule lose?

In a delicious twist, I am told that one Oxford Dictionary definition of Logos is "The Word of God, or principle of divine reason and creative order, identified in the Gospel of John with the second person of the Trinity incarnate in Jesus Christ." I am driven to the only few words I know in German: *Mein Gott in Himmel.*

Tears are weakness on display. My brothers, except Michael, can't cry. Won't cry. Don't cry. A tear may slide unbidden, but is quickly killed. At Dad's funeral, brother David stood in Mass, his young daughter in his arms. Kasey was puzzled. "Dad," she said, her tiny hand caressing his face. "Why are you crying? Dad?" He turned his head, stopped the tears. Brushed her hand away and stood taller. Straightened his shoulders. Brother Bob bottled his tears inside. Forever. It got far worse after the death of his nine-year-old eldest daughter. He never stayed in the church till the end of a family funeral. Ever. Not Mike's, nor Mom's, nor Dad's, nor my Bill's. I wonder about my deeply sensitive, rough, tough, brother. The rest of the story is far too long to tell.

You have heard it a million times. Maybe even said it. "Big boys don't cry." "He cried like a girl!" Turns out girls don't cry either. I cry now. This recounting feels like one continuous cry. One primal screaming wail for her children; the cry of the Earth Mother.

We hold deep in our collective unconscious the oceans of tears shed by people, often women, around the world over lost, dead, traumatized, disappeared and murdered children since the beginning of time. That is our heritage from the collective unconscious. The unshed tears of the mothers, grandmothers, and so on and so on. With thanks to Thomas King: we are all stories. It's just silenced grandmothers all the way down.

That's why, for me, e-motion is necessary.

It was days before I finally recorded *Integrating Energies*. If I don't write it, it doesn't exist. Right? Keeping the dream secret would leave superego a foothold to regain control.

This is the second of many dreams of integration of the masculine and feminine energy; I must integrate the inner patriarch.

The dream tells me my repressed feminine remains a huge issue. I am a private person. The dream points clearly to guilt, fear, and privacy as the means to bring these feelings to where I can "see" them. Keep it secret. No, write it down. The argument goes on. I know the dream is not literal. The taunting voice says, "Really?"

Sexuality is related to creativity and fulfillment; it is apparent that I am afraid of my own inner power of integrated wholeness. A simple flash back to childhood and beliefs about purity tell the story of fear of sexuality.

I am seeking inner harmony and am puzzled at how to be. I am also puzzled that the male figure is willing to embrace me when I know he is married. So even in the dream the inner/outer is confused. The ego self represses much of the dream. I do not choose to remember the second part of the dream, which is quite obviously the key. For some time now, many dreams are vaguely remembered. I have the sense of hiding from the real self.

Accepting Love

I sense Dad's presence. He has "come" to tell me that he loves me. He loves me regardless. He has always loved me but he did not speak the words because speaking was too difficult. He loves me. I have brought into his life much joy and love. He loves me unconditionally. There is nothing I could do that would cause him not to love me. There has never been any need to seek his approval for I have always had it. The peace seeps into the very deepest core of my existence. The deep fear I have of conflict with others is healed. It doesn't matter about conflict. I could have openly disagreed with Dad and he would not have abandoned me. The assault as a child caused me to fear losing Dad. Somehow, in a child's understanding, the assault happened and could happen again if I disagreed with "big" people. Big people are the church, institutions, men in my job or world of work. I was "tied" to Dad seeking his approval when I had it all along.

"You are my beloved daughter. My only daughter. You are the daughter Mother and I never thought we'd have. We love you. I love you. You even changed your name because you wanted to please me. I did not understand it then. I do now. My beloved Elaine, it would make no difference what the name. You have shown me many things these past years. You have been always a loving child. And you are free to be a child of God as He created you to be. Be open, child. Be love and continue to bring joy to your mother who in the pain of losing me on the human level walks in much fear. But she relies on you. She trusts you and she will come to understand that death is not final. Death is glorious and joyful."

The dream is much like a very deep meditation. Awe. That word does not approach the full expression, the incredible essence and feeling of the dream. Words are sickly and mute in the face of the experience of Infinite Love.

My inner world shifted another fraction. A month later, reading in Thomas Merton's autobiography, I find him speaking of his own dead father: "The sense of his presence was as vivid and as real and as startling as if he had touched my arm or spoken to me."

Although my dreams are often intuitive rather than sensate, images begin to come again.

A Nun, the Indian Man and the Tramp

A nun, black habit, pure white wimple, shoulders and head only. The third time in over two years the same image of a very serene looking Indian man with a headdress. Then the tramp with scraggly hair, beard. Incomplete image.

My inner nun is very outdated. In 1962 many North American nuns began wearing street clothes. One aunt, Sister Mary Vincent, then mid-50s, left the wimple behind for a simple veil. Another aunt, Sister Mary Augustine, 25 years younger, took back her Christian name, Charlotte, and modernized her dress. Yet, I dream of the 1950s nun, head covered, the rest of her body invisible. The questions are, "What are the veiled secrets? Where is your body?" The image does not surprise me. After this dream has steeped for 28 years, I remember an experience with a very cold, aloof, righteous nun. I was in a two-week-long catechism program at the Sturgeon Lake Mission some 10 miles from home. One nun confiscated my doll, and sent me to peel potatoes. I was six. I don't remember my transgression. I raged inside. I did not shed one damn tear. Sunday, the beginning of the second week, my family came to visit. I asked Dad if I could come home. He hesitated a moment. I went home. I remember only the sick feeling in the pit of my stomach. I don't remember if I ever got my doll back. I always said I didn't like dolls anyway. Right.

The Indian Man is truly a Wisdom figure. He has come before and says nothing. An image of inner, silent wisdom, he will speak to me when I am ready.

The tramp is more difficult. Where is the tramp in me? I am tempted to search one of those pathetic pop culture dream symbol books. I don't. In my active imagination work, the tramp in me speaks. "Look to the unclaimed aspects of yourself and you will find much of what you seek. Don't worry about acceptability. I live free of societal expectations. I am your spontaneous self. Your fears are unfounded."

Chapter Eleven

Veils of Illusion

*In order to be honest as possible with myself, I wrote
everything down very carefully following the old Greek
maxim: "Give away all thou hast, then shalt thou receive."*

–C.G. Jung, *Memories, Dreams, Reflections*

February 17, 1991

Today an image floats before my eyes. A child is held aloft by
the energy of fire. Crystal, burning, dancing, sparkling. The fires
of transformation. I expected instant miracles. Now, knowing
the glacial pace of soul repatriation, I laugh at myself and resolve
anew to write this process as it happens; this is not "Made for
Television Evangelism."

Diving Deep into the Pool of the Unconscious

I continue to practise active imagination. For months, as I meditate, I imagine myself diving off the high diving board into a deep pool of water. Then surfacing, swimming strongly, triumphantly, calmly, to the side. I am able to "dive" into the unconscious and emerge in transformed victory.

I have never actually put my head under water since I was 12 or 13 years old. Yet in my worst depressions a swim or a sauna give me a peaceful night's sleep. The waters of the unconscious. The waters of the womb. Feminine symbol of healing waters. Biblical imagery gives a stamp of known inner approval to my journey. So I wash in the river of Jordan. Dive into the pool of Bethesda in John 5:1–16. Jesus effected a cure at Bethesda and archaeologists discovered a reservoir in northeast Jerusalem in 1888. A steep and winding flight of steps leads down to the deep pool and on the wall a fresco depicts an angel troubling the waters in remembrance of healing the paralytic man. Then there is Jacob's well referred to in John 4:6 to 4:21 Genesis 33:19, 48:22. Wells and water. I am reminded of the experience of the dry well on the farm in April 1988. I imagine filling the well. It's all symbolic. All metaphor.

I am open to relationship with the Other. I am open to spontaneity, creativity, vulnerability. I will shed the culturally appropriated masculine armour against abandonment, vulnerability, softness and weakness. I will merge the outward secure, confident, powerful, strong woman with the inner, crying, weary, exhausted, lonely and fearful one.

I read and read some more. Reading replaced medical or psychiatric visits. It stood in for spiritual advisors and others who might try to deter me from where I needed to go. I was uncertain enough with having to fend off authority in the guise of healers. I was sure there would come a time when others might be of assistance. For now, I continued to meet with Verna over dinner, coffee, or sleepovers. We had a bond of trust. I'd come to realize that midlife women needed Crone mentors—spiritual midwives to help us birth ourselves. We needed guidance on when to breathe or push and when to rest or breathe more deeply.

One of the most helpful books I read during this time was *The Wounded Woman*:

> But if the person penetrates more consciously into the reason for weakness, then comes awareness that the excuse of weakness was really only a way of avoiding the strength already there. What the person originally took to be weakness is now understood to be defiance, i.e., a refusal to commit. For Kierkegaard, the despair of defiance is a higher consciousness, a realization that one has the strength to choose the Self, or in Kierkegaard's terms, to make the leap of faith which requires acceptance of the uncontrollable and transcendent, but that one chooses not to do so in stark defiance against the powers which transcend reason and man's finitude. In defiance, one refuses to change. In the despair of defiance, one refuses possibility and infinitude.... The despair of defiance appears to me to be an aspect of the armoured Amazon. And yet in the end they are secretly the same—two poles of a split in self.[74]

Sadly, what I am naming as fear of ridicule, is actually refusal to accept the uncontrollable and transcendent.

There is no doubt I find great difficulty in questioning the "rules." I have been told I do question, but in honesty back then I did not question the BIG SACRED rules of family, church and society. Before 1988 I didn't even question the silence rule, or the rules against emotional expression of pain, fear, rage or even love.

---

[74] Linda Schierse Leonard, *The Wounded Woman: Healing the Father–Daughter Relationship* (Athens, Ohio: Ohio University Press, 1982), 21.

I am thrown into chaos. I teach myself that it is safe to question accepted concepts of evil, God, sin, virginity, and more. There is no violent, raging, punitive God to send thunderbolts to strike me dead. I must engage in reflective, critical thought or I will continue to live life based on the unconscious rules passed on to me through generations. I was born to question. That much seems apparent. I will die on every level if I continue to accept obedience, ritual authoritarianism, rigidity, orderliness, denial of feelings, totalitarianism and subservience.

For, as Jung said, "It should never be forgotten—and of this the Freudian school must be reminded—that morality was not brought down on tablets of stone from Sinai and imposed on the people, but is a function of the human soul, as old as humanity itself."[75]

It isn't just Freudians who need the reminder.

I will cultivate spontaneity, vitality, inner freedom, independence and feeling. I seek truth, beauty and goodness. I seek that which is far greater than I—I seek the transcendent and the uncontrollable.

As I read and write tonight, the image of a large willow tree with deep roots arises. Branches sway gently in a breeze. Then a wild storm rocks the willow, slashing and tearing at the branches. But the willow is flexible, rooted in deep ground. Ground of beingness, rootedness, connectedness. Mother Earth the Womb (Tomb) of humanity. I could draw the beautiful willow if I had crayons.

I have spent the weekend at Mom's. It is our chance to just be, with no sense of urgency to do anything. I leave Eugene and Shirley's with a load of books and tapes. Beautiful generous hearts. Shirley says I should do dream workshops. I protest immediately.

---

[75] Carl Jung, *Collected Works* (New York: Pantheon, 1966), Volume 7, para. 30.

The Big Questions

Sin. I will not record the title of the book I am reading. I hate it. The author writes *ad nauseum* about sin. So why am I persisting in reading it? My issue lies with the concept of eternity and the infinitesimally small human mind. Condemned eternally by sin? No, I am not an expert in the theology of sin. When did the concept come into being? I have a strong intuition that man has conjured up this concept in response to very early times when people were often struck down by the forces of nature. These forces, personified in gods like Zeus, for example, punished with lightning bolts and thunder. I haven't studied this, but I read in *The Compass Magazine* an article by a Jesuit priest about sin. He claims that the blame and shame heaped on Christians with this notion of offending God bears a lot of responsibility for wrecked lives. Sin seems to have multiple meanings. Misunderstanding. Wrong choices. Learning lessons. But burn in hell eternally? What kind of malevolent, misogynist, intolerable, totalitarian god is this? Betrayal. Children believe this stuff and perhaps, like me, carry it unconsciously into adulthood.

I realize why the idea of "sin" makes me crazy. My life. My life to the age of 43. Being told in Confession that praying for healing was ridiculous and I needed to get myself to a good doctor. I wanted to reach out and choke him with my bare hands. Not a very loving reaction. I wasn't a sinner because I was depressed. So, the Jesuit priest in *Compass Magazine* speaks directly to me. Man—and I say man because that's who did the writings about sin—has confused himself with God. Mary Daly wrote, "If God is male, then the male is God." A scene flashes into my mind. A young nephew is visiting. We are having a long conversation about computers. He is working to convince his mom to get him one. He really needs to figure out how they work. He is about six. As we chat, he asks if maybe he should pray for one. I hesitate. I say, "Well, perhaps She will help."

"Oh," he says casually, "God is a man. Everybody knows that! It says so right in the Bible."

I laugh and tell him we have a lot more to chat about! I do not see my own complicity. What language can I use? God is definitely a male word, all arguments to the contrary. The pronoun He is not generic as some would have me believe. For want of another word then, God/dess sees us as beautiful radiant beings of light. We see ourselves as rotten worms of existence. Why? The early writings of the church. It's time that changed. It's time to reflect, review, reconsider and cycle back to when God was a woman, as Merlin Stone wrote in her book by that title.[76] I think I need to reread Mathew Fox. Soon I would be attending lectures with deep thinkers with more theology background, like John Shelby Spong, author of *Why Christianity Must Change or Die.*[77]

March 3, 1991

If, as Jung says, the collective unconscious—a universal collection of images, intuitions, and very powerful instincts—has been with me since the moment of conception, then it seems significant to get to know myself. This fits clearly with earlier developments of Wilder Penfield whose experiments showed that we are 80–85% unaware of the context of our Self. This amuses me. Here I always thought I was so rational. Imagine. Making decisions, deciding what to do in one's life, daily, monthly, yearly, with only 10% (some say much less) of the available information. We humans really have an exalted opinion of our rational capabilities.

If this collective unconscious has always been there, the job of inner healing requires incredible trust in the Source of All as Goodness, Truth, Beauty, Love, Joy, Peace and Harmony. Know thyself, then, is not a selfish narcissistic journey but a journey

---

[76] Merlin Stone, *When God Was a Woman* (NY: Harcourt Brace Jovanovich, 1976).

[77] John Shelby Spong, *Why Christianity Must Change or Die* (NY: HarperCollins, 1998).

of heroic proportion to the centre of Self where God resides in Invisible Essence.

Sacred Support Circle

> Dad, Mom, Colin and I sit in a circle. I can "see" Mom but Dad and Colin are there in presence-essence rather than sensate quality. I am laughing, laughing, laughing. A real deep laughter that rolls up from within and spreads out till I am helpless with hilarious, spontaneous, delightful laughter. In the morning, I do not remember why.

At the time of the dream I write no interpretations or even possibilities. I wonder why? There is hope and delight in the three-generation circle of wholeness. Is that it? Is this my inner circle of support? The strong, gentle aspects of the masculine are not actually manifest in my psyche; they are present only in essence. I wonder at that too.

Walked On

> There's a sidewalk on which lies a trampled brassiere.

I awake surprised that I am wearing my bra. It is afternoon. I have much energy from this very restful nap. Am I walking on my feminine self? Trampling the concretized feminine? Trampled bodies? Or trampling on the structures that bind the feminine breast in its generative, nurturing aspect. Removing the trampling, the restrictions, the norms that say women leaders are sluts if they show a hint of cleavage? I am slowly removing patriarchal norms. I emphasize "slowly." Maybe becoming vaguely aware is more truthful.

Learning to say NO. I talk about it. Sometimes I even believe I can do it. The child who must do everything to please others emerges just when I don't want her to. When the pressure gets too high, I erupt in sleeplessness, restlessness and finally angry outbursts that leave me guilty and defensive. The Judge, that internal subcritter,[78] better known to writers as the Censor, berates me constantly. I yell angrily at a colleague at work who is wanting something now, right now. In a fit of rage, I order him out of my office and feel guilty. The fact is, he was too pushy, too demanding. However, I could simply have told him that. I am willing to say no with simple assertiveness.

I am becoming aware of the myriad ways my church and the world devalues the feminine. The invisible cultural conditioning creates rock-solid expectations of the woman's role as compliant, submissive, sexual object, caregiver, recipient of male largesse, scheming, manipulative, and weak, not to mention a bully at work. That's on a good day. These are the unconscious projections of a patriarchal society onto women. I finally begin to understand the feminine as a state of being in relationship, an inherent principle of life within humanity and the earth. Strong, active and made equal in the eyes of the Creator. I have yet to figure out how Augustine manoeuvred around the Christ's words, "neither male nor female..."

Although Dad was stern and strong, outwardly unemotional, somewhat detached, I felt a profound sense of security, stability

---

78 Complexes, subpersonalities, or as Sister Sylvia laughingly refers to them (in Maryknoll, Book II, *Authoring Self*), "subcritters," are an emotionally charged group of ideas or images within the personal unconscious formed in response to life experiences. The energy that lies within reinforced patterns of behaviour around a major trauma, when unresolved, continues to generate fear of the same thing happening again. The complex can be resolved, dissolved, through staying with feelings rather than avoiding the pain.

and structure around him—perhaps too much. It was the lack of display of emotion that led me to believe that spontaneity or sensitivity were to be avoided. That side of Dad came through much against his will, in his music and his apparent but silent joy in his family.

The preverbal early childhood assault created weird beliefs. The negative experience led to the Inner Tyrant or Inner Predator complex that robbed my energy. Depression and anxiety develop from a child's negative experiences. I read further. Preverbal childhood experiences can last a lifetime. I decide not. Dad was unable to express his feelings directly to me. I know now that he was a deep well of tenderness that he kept well capped. There are rules to being a man in our culture as well. Displays of tenderness are displays of weakness. My dad was born into the culture of 1908.

I am learning the inner dance of integration. I am changing. I am willing to flow in and with the river of life. The worst wound any human person can suffer is to be cut off at the root. Untold damage is done when the child learns to dam up the tears that would flow out as healing waters. In our hypermasculine, patriarchal society, we are estranged from our own woundedness; our own source of healing waters. I am absolutely never good enough. Have never felt good enough. I am beginning to discover that it isn't all bad that no one was able to help me with depression. In learning to do it myself, I have unwittingly created the "handcrafted" life. I am making my own world, one dream at a time. I write my self one healing cell at a time. I will learn to dance whole unto myself.

> Where there is no wind
> There is no Spirit
> No breath of life.
> Where there is no water
> There is no healing.
> Only crusted pus-filled scars.

I strongly recommend reading *In a Different Voice* by Carol Gilligan.[79] Gilligan was my introduction to feminist thought. Her book removed veils of illusion. I was stunned at the infighting among students in the all-girls' school where Gilligan did her research. I was surprised at the exertion of female hierarchy and power over actions of the female staff. It turned out not to be as simple as looking to the past for solutions. We must create a new consciousness.[80]

Jesus, how do I break loose from the chains I have forged around my own soul? In our cultural rejection of the feminine, we run the major risk of reducing ourselves to passivity or obedience to raw power, as in the wars, the military, the Nazi death camps; to self-death, to despair and utter hopelessness. I am determined that the Triple Goddess, The Great Goddess, reduced by the patriarchy to passivity, will be returned as Mother Mary, gentle steel, model of The Great All, the strong feminine.

Leonard suggests the undeveloped or distorted repressed father figure appears in dreams as the archetypal Dummling.[81] Weak, inept, bumbling. I understand that Leonard is fighting through a weak, alcoholic father. Perhaps she has failed to see this possible Dummling in women whose fathers were "everything" collective, conventional wisdom says they should be. Thus was my dad. My hero. Strong fathers may unwittingly contribute to the Dummling/Amazon life. Myss, writing in *Sacred Contracts: Awakening Your Divine Potential*,[82] presents the Dummling as an aspect of the Clown. The mask that I wear to cover my real emotions. I have prided myself on being in control of emotion. In fact, can get furious if someone suggests I am being an emotional

[79] Carol Gilligan, *In a Different Voice: Psychological Theory and Women's Development* (Cambridge, Mass.: Harvard University Press, 1984).

[80] Carol Gilligan and David A. J. Richard, *The Deepening Darkness: Patriarchy, Resistance, & Democracy's Future* (NY: Cambridge University Press, 2009).

[81] Linda Schierse Leonard, *The Wounded Woman: Healing the Father–Daughter Relationship*, 1982.

[82] Caroline Myss, *Sacred Contracts: Awakening Your Divine Potential* (NY: Three Rivers Press, 2001), 375.

woman. The Dummling may pull such tricks as having me forget the details of directions, assignments, get lost, drive through lights and generally get me in trouble with collective mind for being just a dumb woman, thus pushing me to recognize my inner archetypes. Or he could cause the bodily rebellion—tired arms, aching neck and back—anything to force me to stop and be spontaneous, youthful, playful. Is it the Dummling who blurts out answers to non-existent questions and draws blank looks and stares from others? Often lately I find I am not listening to others and answer in inappropriate ways. We westerners mostly avoid letting anyone know our feelings. It is through jokes and intimidation—the role of the Court Jester, the Clown—that we hide our vulnerabilities. Where is my Court Jester?

Maybe this deserves another look. Rabbits, frogs, the Lamb, dwarfs, Jack and the Beanstalk and the goose who laid the golden egg. How is it that myth is filled with the weak who solve life-threatening situations? I have never understood the figure of the red-haired adolescent in the *Four-Storey Motor Home* dream. Is this the repressed father image? The playful boyish side? I have spent many years too serious to laugh. The father's daughter caught in Amazon armour?

Leonard tells me that,

> Rage is often hidden in the body. Many women suffer from hypochondria, experiencing physical weakness and illness that really cover up pent-up energy. Headaches, backaches, ulcers, colitis, and stomach problems frequently disappear when anger is accepted. Depression, a state in which all one's energy seems to disappear, is still another subterfuge for rage. Anxiety attacks often cover up anger that leaves one shaking in helplessness. Suicidal tendencies veil a murderous anger

turned toward oneself and in the form of emotional blackmail, veil anger towards the other.[83]

The Wounded Woman was published in 1982. I suppose it is a form of defence to say that the father-daughter wound is a condition of our patriarchal culture. Both men and women suffer the wounding. Women are just automatically considered inferior, weak, passive and dependent. Men, on the other hand, are put down if they show any enculturated feminine qualities such as gentleness, or, now in 2016, respect for the earth and protectiveness toward the environment. Gender is totally confused with masculine and feminine principles. And so, when I behave as Dame Rebecca West said, in ways that differentiate me from a doormat, I am accused of being aggressive, having balls, being domineering or pushy. The same behaviour is seen as strength in men. And that is the problem. I have no wish to be a man. I do, however, wish to be able to make my own decisions, be independent, have a career that satisfies my soul, have children and not pander to the requirements of making beds for my growing sons. I need to protect Mother Earth. I am an Earth Mother whose soul purpose is learning, writing, and living on the land with deep respect. This systemic confusion impacts me, my family, my workplace and the entire society known as the Western world. I do what I can to change it but this is a collective pattern that requires deep work by many. I am deeply afraid when I read back over the biographic records of my life that my part of the work has only just begun in a serious way.

I have shed enough tears since April 1988 to create a new ocean. Redemptive tears, ancestral tears, tears of transformation, rage and grief. Sorrow is necessary, culturally speaking, as a part of the seasons of life. Raining tears nurture the seeds of inner

---

[83]   Leonard, *The Wounded Woman*, 124.

growth just as the sun ripens the seeds to harvest. Jesus wept. Mother Mary wept.

March 9, 1991

Daughters who have had "too positive" a relation to their fathers have still another aspect of the father to redeem. If the relation to the father is too positive, the daughters are likely to be bound to the father by over-idealizing him and by allowing their own inner father strength to remain projected outward on the father. Quite often their relationships to men are constricted because no man can match the father…. To redeem the father in themselves, they need to acknowledge his negative side. They need to experience their father as human and not as an idealized figure in order to internalize the father principle in themselves.[84]

Indeed, my idealized father must be redeemed. I can clearly see the idealization growing as a simple survival technique. Of course, Dad had faults. He was alive. I recall being furious with Mom if she ever contradicted him. I labelled the most necessary conversations as "nagging."

It happened several times a week. Dad trucked cattle, pigs or grain to, auction markets, elevators or whatever, four times a day. Mom would hand him a list of groceries, or some item she needed from Grande Prairie. He would grumble. In retrospect, of course Mom was right! It was a necessary part of running a large household as well as my mom did! She was at home with no transportation. How in hell was she going to get small grocery or household items that cropped up during the week?

---

[84] Leonard, *The Wounded Woman,* 166.

I point to my strength and courage as coming from Dad but does it? I have the necessary courage and strength. I am my own oak tree. I grow my own roots. I crown my own willow. Yes, I could count on Dad for total unspoken acceptance. Now, I must pull that projected courage and strength back and place it squarely within me.

I am learning patience with the labyrinth, circles, dance and cycles of the feminine. Healing is a spiral dance. I am weaving. In October my Inner Christ voice, or soul voice, spoke of waiting for the new seeds to grow to harvest. I think I understand a little now. In winter's dark days of death, I must wait patiently and descend once more into the darkness to await the joyful rebirth of resurrection to new life. I will hibernate and rest. Integrate and synthesize. I will await the new healing potential and possibility of spring secure in the knowledge that love stored in harvest will enable me to endure the darkness of winter. The sunflower will return, more resplendent than before, rooted more firmly in Mother Earth's wonders. I am joyful in the creativity of spring's fresh green growth. Later, I realize that the promise Spirit has given in John 16, is the same Scripture verse given to me in meditation December 29, 1990, the night before Dad died.

May your tears be turned into dancing.

For the Lord, our light and our love

Has turned the night into day.

The song comes to mind strong, fresh and singing beautifully within.

Chapter Twelve

The Darkness Light

I begin this chapter with a four-act dream that moved my old house totally off its foundations!

Renovations, March 15, 1991

Act I

I am in the living room of Mom and Dad's farm house. It is a total mess. My cousin, Kathy, walks by the picture window, smiles, waves and comes in the front door—to the right of me. It is summer outside but the Christmas tree is still in the corner. I am horrified that company would come and see the tree still up. Kathy comes through the door, which pushes the tree behind it. The tree is bedraggled and brownish, dead looking. She picks up an ornament from the top of a shelf or television, looks at it, smiles, puts it back. I am mortified—the dust and grime are clearly visible on the ornament. Kathy is here visiting from Vancouver. Bob, her husband, stands behind her, says nothing.

Act II

I am still in the house but now the gyproc is hanging loose from the walls and about a foot too long. The edges are cracked several inches up. I am in another room of the house on the left side with a hacksaw. I pull the gyproc out toward me and cut off at least a foot including the broken edges. I can see a crack of light around the edges of the window, which also is covered with gyproc. I do not cut the gyproc that covers the window. I trim the left side by the wall.

Act III

My brothers, Bob and Jerry, are hauling hay, I think. As we head around the corner by the driveway Bob says, "The big guy isn't gonna make it this time. He's going too fast." The tractor and trailer swerve dangerously as we fly around the corner and off the trailer bed into a huge ditch filled with water. Bob climbs out first, very fast, the water is very deep. Just as he stands up on the edge, I think he may fall backward and then we will be in 12 feet of water. He stands clear, I grab his leg and get out. Jerry follows.

Act IV

I am back in the house. I have the messy, left side room pretty much cleaned up. The gyproc fits smoothly. I am somewhat concerned at my craftsmanship. Some "kids," seemingly Colin and Jason, are busy cleaning up the other parts of the room. Bob comes in and says something like, "The house is dirtier than it has ever been." I am upset and think, "It would be clean if everyone helped out." I say nothing out loud. Kathy appears and also my cousin, Ralph. I ask Ralph if he is on holiday. Kathy picks up the same ornament, a dog figurine, now clean and shiny.

The dream takes place in Mother and Dad's house in my teenage time, yet the dream ego is adult. I am rebuilding my inner world. The massive changes since 1988 clean and activate the healing dog. My dog Rascal appeared in *The Bridge* (August 1989). This seems another invitation into the inner healing chamber of the ancient temple of Asclepius (you cannot enter the temple until a healing symbol such as a dog or snake appears in your dreams).

There are several repeated dream motifs such as the living room, the tree, the vehicles. My cousin appears to my right. Then, I am in another room, to my left. After the scene in the 12 feet of water, I return to the house where the messy left side is cleaned up. If left is feminine and right is masculine, and my inner house is immersed in such deep healing, it seems possible I am less reliant on authority and thus enabling Eros.

The Christmas tree is an old earth people symbol of everlasting life. As body, the dead evergreen branches represent my central nervous system. The dream tells me I have pushed or repressed my brown and bedraggled nerves and capillaries behind the door to my living room. I am feeling guilty that it is still there in summer. The dream surely tells me how dead my nervous system is. I have been avoiding the reality of my body's need for healing.

No doubt, I am still concerned and worried about collective groupthink. "What would people think if they knew the mess my inner life is in?" Or, I am afraid of the many inner changes.

Bob, an older brother, is my childhood protector and my rescuer in the dream. He could be there to show me the masculine relational aspect ready to assist me in the journey into the dangerous corners and waters of the unconscious. He provides a "leg up" out of the depths of the unconscious. Bob also represents safety in rebellion. I have always admired him because he simply lived his own life without seeming regard for the opinions of the collective group mind. Always somewhat of a rebel, he represents male kindness, gentleness, and acceptance. It appears that both older brother aspects will help.

Bob taught me many things in childhood. We once rode our old white horse around inside the classroom at lunch time. He led the way on my first and only school walkout when some folks showed up at school to give us the Gideon Bible. "We're Catholic," he told the teacher. Out we went, my brothers and cousins, returning only when the coast was clear. Going with Bob was always an adventure. He was a fighter against the norms, rules and regulations. I suppose I wanted to be just like that but didn't have the nerve to give free rein to the masculine energy that urged me to take a risk—jump in—and let the chips fall where they may.

Kathy might symbolize a positive aspect of my helpful self. She is a cousin, a close friend, a childhood confidante and an important part of my adult life. She and Bob both question the state of my inner house. I think the dream is encouraging since I have closely related aspects of myself coming to help. Kathy presents me with the dog figurine, clean and shiny, at the end of the dream.

Apparently, I would like the Ralph aspect of myself to return from "holidays." What does Ralph represent to me? Our family was seven and our cousins were eight. Ralph is a couple of years older than me. A non-talker with a shy, quiet grin. Shuffles his feet when I say hello or ask about his day. I hardly know a thing about this cousin. A little-known aspect of myself.

My inner children are helping to clean up, to figure out, my life. I am enlarging my world. The picture window might just be exactly that. Finally, I get the picture, I can see my life changing. I welcome the small crack of light. The windows allow me to see inside and outside. The dream tells me more change is occurring.

Hacksaws are a useful tool for cutting metal; the dream hacksaw is not a pretty image but it gets my attention. I do employ hacksaw techniques, sawing away at myself in never-ending tapes of self-criticism. Perhaps after two years of relentless changes, I have cut my way out of the gyproc trap of ego.

The literature says that BIG dreams most often arrive at critical impasses. This long and complicated four-act dream ends with a plasticized lifeless dog figurine. That's not good. Except all dreams bring healing. I commit to bringing my instinctive, feminine energy to life.

There are many references to a foot, which I can think of as 12 inches—gyproc a foot too long and also a foot from the wall. Twelve feet of water.

I recently attended a teacher development conference in Vancouver. The focus of the conference was story as teaching tool and teacher as writer and reflective practitioner. I am tranquil there in the green, growing peacefulness and rain. I spent three days on my own simply attending the conference and walking miles in Stanley Park. Dream re-entry through writing gets at *story*; it also seems the most appropriate technique to bring the energy and power of this dream into focus in the outside world.

Change or No Change

In a semicircle is an unknown man, a pushy aggressive female, me, and a male principal. We are involved in a discussion in a school. I am trying to explain why it is necessary to try to change a timetable early in the year so the students—Grade 10—know well in advance and are not upset at the changes. The person beside me on the left is a woman known to me with whom I am uncomfortable. There is some kind of competition.

The dream shows the potential for wholeness with the unknown, my shadow self, my dream ego and the masculine principle of the inner world. Four is a reoccurring theme in healing dreams. Four directions, four seasons, the square around the circle. Perhaps in the school of life I am arguing with my own repressed feminine and feeling particularly uncomfortable as the negative feminine argues against any changes to my timetable. I am willing to change.

Inner Closet

> Somewhere Mom and I are looking in a closet. It is empty.
> We have cleaned it out, I guess. "It's perfectly dry. That's
> wonderful," I tell Mom. I have a sense of being happy that
> the closet was not flooded. The walls of the closet were very
> clean and smooth.

Jung recommends honour and patience in the dream world.
I make no sense of the dream until sometime in January, 1993,
when I come to understand that the closet may represent a
sepulchre, a whitened, dry and sterile space I have hidden within.
The presence of Mother (mater) indicates unconsciousness. The
unconscious is trying to tell me something important. The next
dream tells me I am not getting the message, not making the
connections.

Garbled Connections (the dream comes twice)

> I am speaking to Faye by telephone. A garbled voice comes
> on the line speaking nonsense. The dream ends without the
> telephone connection becoming clear.

Faye is a teacher friend and part of our meditation circle.
Apparently, my inner road-blocks are effective. Estes provides
some clarification:

> The malfunctioning telephone call is one of the top
> twenty most common dream scenarios that humans
> dream. In the typical dream, the phone will not work,
> or the dreamer cannot figure out how it works. The
> phone wires have been cut, the numbers on the keypad

are out of order, the line is busy, the emergency number has been forgotten or is not functioning properly. These sorts of telephone situations in dreams are very close in timbre to the misstated or overwritten message in letters, such as in the folktale *The Handless Maiden* when the devil changes a celebratory message to a malicious one.[85]

It seems clear that I have hijacked my own celebration of inner healing by falling prey to doubts, fears and desires. Our culture strives to ensure that all women conform to patriarchal, scientific, positivistic, hierarchical thought forms. I work to convince myself while I meekly shout to those around me.

Crippled Feminine

Several sequences in which Dad is alone. I remember only the last one in which Dad has his suit on and is tying his tie, ready to go somewhere, or coming from somewhere. I run crying to Auntie Anne who is sitting in her wheelchair.

I awake still sobbing. The dream is incredibly intense. I get up at 5:20 a.m. Once in the bathroom washing my face, I realize Mom was not in the dream. Why am I crying? At first, I think something may have happened to Mom and I have run to Auntie Anne, my mother's sister, for comfort. This is far too literal. Is this then my crippled inner feminine? I could use some help here.

I slowly begin to admit to myself that the "paralysis" of the wheelchair is reflective of my attitude to healing. It has been such a very long path and still I am unhealed. I seem to be facing the ultimate inner paralysis. The wheels on the chair are symbols of possibility, symbols of change and turning. Apparently, some part

---

[85] Estes, *Women Who Run With the Wolves*, 474.

of me does see me as whole and perfect, while the rest resists and wants to pretend paralysis rather than living fully on my own two feet. My father complex is getting ready to leave, symbolized by the formality of Dad and his tie, which he wore only to church, weddings, funerals and on special occasions.

I am willing to listen to my soul voice and be an integrated whole person.

Recognizing Feminine Power, March 21, 1991

There is a strange man. He directs a whole "play" and does it very well. I do not "see" the play. I am not even sure it is a play but I know, or sense, he is a good actor.

The man is a drunk. His daughter is terrified of him. He and I fight verbally. A large crowd mills around. Rachel and I are leaving. I tell her to go on her bicycle. She has seven minutes to get there. It is 10:23 a.m. She wants me to come with her but I say she can go alone. I think she wants me to carry her. In any case, we are looking at a map. There is a LARGE building, a power station.

I see a round, large building like a seaport terminal. I am watching the man and staying away from him on the other side of the crowd. I am afraid he will harm Rachel. His daughter returns. I put my arms around her; she is shaking. "Be sure and come to our house if he is really bad." She goes to find the man, her father. He begins to circle again. A buzzer or something signals the crowd. Everyone starts to leave. The man lurches, strangely pointing and trying to say something. I stumble backward—into a dead dog with a large knife or hatchet still buried in it. The dog is very small. The dream ends. I wake up. Conscious, I am sickened by the memory of the dog. I am afraid. Later I realize the man is wearing a brown suit.

I have been circling these dream images for days, months and years. I must remember that every single aspect of this dream is me. My beliefs. My values. Dreams tell me stories about myself. I must listen and integrate the teaching; I don't have to like it. This is the pedagogy of discomfort. Unconsciously I have chosen these symbols to give me a truer picture of my own beliefs. And sometimes dreams aren't pretty. The knife, the hatchet, the dead dog. The dog, again. My small daughter, seven minutes, 10:23 a.m. The frightened daughter. The power station? Seaport? My fear for my daughter. The brown-suited man appears. Again.

Finally, I break through to some understanding about the repressed feminine. The dream may be asking me, "Where is the patriarchy in you killing your feminine soul?" Behind the scenes, I am unaware, unconscious. The frightened, trembling child is an idea that wants to express itself but I refuse to hear. Within me there are crowds milling about. I should be grateful the milling or grinding has not stopped since it means there is movement within. My young feminine wants to be dependent but I refuse, thinking she has movement, escape, available. Another cycle symbolized by the seven minutes is ending and beginning.

I have both a map and power. The round seaport symbol could point to storage, a place of safety for the feminine. I have the promise of safety. And the animus can be transformed as the man in the brown suit from my *Pushed and Pulled* dream makes another appearance. He circles around until he can point out the axed, hatcheted dead dog. The axe, a deeply feminine symbol, is often confused as masculine by dreamers. The knife is symbolic of masculine clarity and insight. The axe the feminine. Where have I been chopping away my insight? Where am I killing my own healing? What am I pruning? It is time to confront my own inner negative repressed feminine—the negative animus, as termed by Jung, or the inner paralyzing, deadly patriarchal beliefs. Where have I silenced myself? Repressed myself? I must have the courage to see what I see and not look away.

I sincerely wish I had been much more knowledgeable in 1991. I may have saved myself years of angst. Now, as I look around at the fingers of blame pointed at men, I realize I had to come to understand my own complicity in my powerlessness. I must take my own power. I recommend every woman, every daughter and every man, study the story of The *Handless Maiden* and let it seep into their bones. The father, the patriarchal god, chopped off my hands. I am growing them back by crying over the stumps all these years.

Transformational Fire

I am with two others, we are talking. The place seems to be outside in a grassy area. A hill with a ditch, a gully. I sit peacefully. Suddenly a fire begins to burn under my feet and the flames shoot up around my legs. I take off my coat to cover the fire and stop it but flames come around from beneath. Still no burning and no fear. "We will have to stop it or the whole place will go," I say.

Since this is Passion Sunday, the fire seems symbolic. Catholicism has adopted the ancient custom of blessing the new fire struck from flint, a natural substance. The new fire starts the Christ life anew within me. In the dream, the fire is spontaneous, transformative, rebirth. It washes away any misunderstanding. My armour, coat, tries to keep the entire place from burning. If I play with this idea, it seems possible that my inner fire will indeed burn away my "place." I continue to ask to change my life. And, then, am afraid of the changes. Who will I be if I change? I am a strange person. Asking for miracles; refusing to change!

The Trickster

> I am in a large hall or room in a bed with a male figure who I think is The Director. His silver white hair gleams. I am doing very "kinky" things with/to this person. The covers are over both of us. As the covers come away, I see behind me, through a doorway, the male figure who I thought was with me. He is laughing. Then I realize the figure in the bed is not anyone I recognize. I realize the whole office staff is there but I don't really see them. They are all laughing at the "joke." I am appalled, sick at heart that people I trust would trick me this way. I get up and wander aimlessly around the hall. I don't remember anything except a sense of humiliation and sick shock.

The dream is filled with emotion. Strange as it may seem, I now understand that this is a pivotal dream. The covers are my attempts to hide my emotions, vulnerability and creativity. Who am I becoming? This is my animus ridiculing my birthing, transforming self. Animus is loath to accept my newly forming unconventional, unacceptable, nonconformist faith in creation as Divine Mother. There are many aspects of my repressed feminine patriarchal director self that fear humiliation. I recognize the dream is bringing these fears to consciousness. Naked in public and inappropriate sex are both common motifs in dreams. There is nothing kinky about becoming whole in generative creativity.

Some months later as I read this I am reminded that I have always felt different. I have been afraid to do anything out of the ordinary for fear of laughter. I have used enormous amounts of energy to repress these feelings. The fact is, I am different. Now, finally, I think I may have come to an understanding. Hiding is not innate to my personality nor to my feminine soul or my life. It is a complex formed from a variety of unpleasant experiences and lodged in psyche as a subcritter.

I remember one Saturday morning after I had been at a community dance where Dad played his banjo with the band. "I noticed that no matter who asked you to dance last night, you said no," he said. "Why?"

"I don't like people watching me," I said. "I feel like everybody is laughing."

Dad shook his head. "No, Blink," he said. "Everyone is so focused on themselves they don't even notice anyone else. Just like you were. Don't worry. Dance. Nobody will even notice."

I tried to listen. I still felt people were watching. But, since I was assured they were not, I danced in the outer world. I danced with Bill. That is my children's favourite memory of their dad. Dancing with their mother.

Now, 30 years later, I still force myself to do things. Sometimes I shake so badly, I am absolutely certain someone will notice. A few times they have. At graduation in high school as I sang in the large auditorium, a young man from the class the year before commented, "Your dress was shaking. Were you that nervous?" Yes.

So, when I read *Feel the Fear and Do It Anyway*,[86] I agree. If you think that doesn't cost, you will be wrong. "Do it afraid." Another cliché that I followed. My body is clear on the consequences.

Is it any wonder that my central nervous system wants to shut down? This spring my body is achy, tired. I want to do many things, like walk, ride the bike, clean the house, ride the horses. I do nothing but work. Even reading or meditating is done only with pushing effort. The body weeps the tears the eyes refuse to shed. *I* don't cry. Well, I have shed an ocean of tears this last three years. All the tears held in rigid control come spilling out with little provocation. I don't cry. Turns out, yes, I do. I find it very embarrassing. Some people have commented. I try not to hear them. I have frozen my unexpressed emotions in the muscles of my body. No wonder they ache. I know that somewhere

---

[86] Susan Jeffers, *Feel the Fear and Do It Anyway* (NY: Random House, 1987).

underneath all the masks and layers of social conditioning is the REAL ME. I wonder if I have the energy to continue the process.

April 4, 1991

I meditate before going to bed. Sending love and light to all those unknown, unloved souls on earth. It is 11:38 p.m. when I retire. Bill has been asleep since 9:00 p.m. He gets up for tea.

The Presence

It begins in our bedroom. I am passionately trying to make love with Bill. Someone comes and opens our bedroom door. Bill gets up, against my wishes, to lock the door. He gets into bed and a small nephew comes out of the closet. I am becoming very angry at the interruptions. There are several, at least three, more interruptions. Bill is not responsive to my passion and whereas I want to ignore the interruptions, he continues to get up to attend to each problem. I try all manner of inventions. Finally, he gets up and leaves. I am devastated.

A different dream begins. I leave my body, seemingly, and have a sense of rolling off the bed and around not exactly but sort of on the floor in a circular movement, then back to the bed. I know my body is on the bed but I am not in it. Again, I leave my body. There is a dark, hissing, sinister presence. I "fly" around the room, hands extended like claws and hissing or spitting at the unseen presence. I am then in the kitchen at ceiling height and notice that the pictures on the dining room wall of the peasant man with his loaf of bread, Jesus standing at the door, and the crucifix over the hallway door, are not there. In their place are the yellowed images of where they once hung. I begin a one-way dialogue with the presence.

"Let's be friends."

Hiss, spat.

"Let's be friends."

Hiss, spat.

"Jesus, you come."

Once more I repeat, "Let's be friends."

Somehow during all this I realize I am dealing with an extremely angry part of myself. I continue to repeat, "Let's be friends. Jesus, you come."

Bill, in reality, came back to bed at 12:30 a.m. So the entire dream was very short. At 6:15 a.m. I awake very refreshed.

Again, I am forced to tell the unflattering truth. That dream scared me so deeply I stopped meditation for many months. Every warning I had ever read or encountered flashed right through me. The words, "Your healing might be from the devil," returned and stayed for days.

The second truth is, I had an excellent day. High energy. Positive feelings. I won't know it for many years, but this was pretty much the final gasp of the negative father-god complex.

By evening I am wondering if it is "safe" to tell the dream. Surely some will see occult in it. Again, I am voicing my own fear and projecting it on to others. My intellect knows the devil, the hissing and spitting force, is really the dark forces of introjected rage against the feminine in my own psyche. This is not my father, but my animus-driven, misinterpretation of God, my denigration of the feeling values of feminine relationship.

[The liberated woman] ... [may] become identified
with her animus and lose the vital link with her feminine
identity, living in a false (for a woman) masculine level.

Such a woman will then find herself in a double-bind situation, where her idealization of the masculine leads her to denigrate the feminine. Considering the thousands of years of the patriarchal inflation of the male principle it is hardly surprising that women who introject this find themselves in the grip of a tyrannical, powerful and judgmental force that undermines their individual identity.[87]

For women such as I, first-generation highly educated, working against the cultural norms outside the home, invaded by inner angry raging males, the risk of identification with a Tyrant animus is very high indeed. I have much to be thankful for if I can avoid this.

I reread the *Screwtape Letters*. My entire concept of hellfire, evil and the devil is fraught with fear. No wonder the patriarchal Christian church has been able to keep its captives. The printing press helped. That was 500 years ago. I have read, prayed, experienced miracles. What else will it take? Much more is the answer.

In 1991, resistance to healing comes from the animus, my inner oppressed, repressed, deeply angry feminine. There are deep, dark forces in my psyche that are spitting angry. I am reassured by C.G. Jung's statements about integrating the whole, light and darkness, into the personality. I am reminded of the dream of the black cats and yellow chicks. Is it that the inner child, the nurturing values of the feminine, are left behind and abandoned while the adult Pearl is "always busy"? There are those activities that the child in me loves to do. She loves to pick and arrange the flowers. Yellow flowers in particular. The earth is her first real love; she loves beautiful trees, hills and

---

[87] Jasbinder Garnermann, "Rescuing the Feminine: The Problem of the Animus in Women," *Inside Out*, Issue 7 (Winter 1991), https://iahip.org/inside-out/issue-7-winter-1991/rescuing-the-feminine%e2%80%a8-the-problem-of-the-animus-%e2%80%a8in-women%e2%80%a8 retrieved February 6, 2018.

meadows. She wants a kitten. She likes to write poems. Poetry is a side of my personality that I neglected in my pragmatic attempts to survive. I suppose poetry might have brought too much emotion with it. The child within is available to help the adult see the world from her perspective—fresh, green, loving, whole.

Yes, I feel abandoned. The knife of insight can be sharp. Truth? I have abandoned myself. I let my fear rule far too often. Not on the outside. It is in my rational, logical mind where themes of betrayal and fear of regression back to depression raise hell. I have rationalized staying away from healing groups because of their "narrow-minded" attitudes. It may well be that I am projecting my own narrow-mindedness onto others. I have used the excuse of Bill and the kids needing me at home to prevent going out to serve others and so am "wasting" the love energy that the Christ pours out to me. In the past few days thoughts of avoiding a particular friend have pestered me. Avoiding conflict is another lifelong theme. So I have been "hermitting" myself and feeling more and more listless.

I am trying to come to relationship with the animus. Both *Trickster* and *The Presence* dreams deal with this theme. The dream tells me to relate to myself. Animus figures include father, lover, brother, teacher, judge, wise friend or priest or parson. Sometimes, unknown figures such as magicians, artists, priests, monks, a young boy or a stranger appear as the unrecognized animus figure. How does one come to relationship with Self? I am deep in uncharted waters.

I am confronted with an interesting problem. I am a woman; but as a woman, I live in a patriarchal society dominated by Logos[88] or reason. I have instinctively known that to be "just like a man" is not the answer. Actually, the physical strength of my

---

88 The Oxford Dictionary defines Logos as 1. Theology: The Word of God, or principle of divine reason and creative order, identified in the Gospel of John with the second person of the Trinity incarnate in Jesus Christ; 2. (in Jungian psychology) the principle of reason and judgement, associated with the animus. Often contrasted with Eros

brothers was easy to understand. I knew we were equal. I also knew we were different. I think I know that woman must bring her unique gifts—perceptions, acute sensibilities and feelings, feminine values of tenderness and gentleness, nurturance and instinctive discernment of relationships. If we all knew what Eros[89] was, it would help. I am in awe at the ignorance ingrained even in the Great Oxford Dictionary definitions! If we knew Eros as the principle of love and relationship, an ethic of care could move to balance the Logos that is so predominant in this culture. Part of the tragedy of enrolling in the feminist movement is being caught in patriarchal values and believing that in order to be successful, woman must function as pseudo-man. Being economically competitive, assertive and "bringing home the bacon" satisfies the patriarchy. It will not satisfy the needs of woman for relationship; neither will this balance the planet, which wobbles dangerously in rational, dry, competitive wars; these death structures refuse to see the feminine values of strength, courage, death-birth-rebirth, love of environment, art, music and philosophy as valuable. Woman must function as strong woman in relationship with her whole Self. Then the planet can be balanced and not whirl off her axis into oblivion.

I persist. In a bizarre twist, working with this dream material in the winter of 2018, I finally notice the small nephew who comes out of the closet. He represents my newly emerging youthful animus figure, a small, kind, gentle, delightful child. I must enlist this child in my service.

---

[89] The Oxford Dictionary definition of Eros is 1. Greek Mythology: The god of love, son of Aphrodite. Roman equivalent Cupid; 1.1 Sexual love or desire; 1.2 (in Freudian theory) the life instinct. Often contrasted with Thanatos; 1.3 (in Jungian psychology) the principle of personal relatedness in human activities, associated with the anima.

April 19, 1991

Yesterday, Joan stops by my office to bring back my dream journal and "Journey to the Light" story. We have talked about me presenting dream workshops. I told her that I felt like a proud hypocrite even thinking about it. She insists she has dreamed a dream for me.

A Friend Dreams for Me?

She sees me lecturing to a large group of people. I am wearing a beautiful, shimmering, green outfit with a luminous glow surrounding me. I am speaking about learning logs and reflective writing.

I tell her that dreams are seldom, if ever, for someone else. She is emphatic, "Pearl, this dream was given to me because you are refusing to see it." She quotes Goethe and says I should start planning now!

> Whatever you can do, or dream you can, begin it.
> Boldness has genius, power and magic in it.
>
> —Goethe

I have been to Dr. Z., kinesiologist, four times in the past ten days. She speaks of the paralyzed inner will. Her treatments have removed the steel bands around my back and chest just below my breastbone as well as the pain under my wishbone and through my back. In September, Sally gave me a reiki treatment and was amazed at how "cold" and "frozen" I was even with the energy from her hands.

Today after craniosacral therapy, I am emotional, faint and nauseous. I am very low in energy. Dr. Z. says my central nervous system is not functioning well due to the years of repressed trauma and stress. All part of the process, I am told. This inner psychic numbing is creating a scary, dissociated feeling.

With the distance of 25 years of learning I finally "see" the issue of language. I was steeped in patriarchal language. In 1991, even after all the dreams, the miracles and the mysteries, I was still holding tightly to dependence, perfectionism, fear and *of course, the Father God*. In 2018 I adjust the paragraph below.

April 29, 1991

The ways of the Father [of the Divine Mother] are inexplicable, mysterious and wonderfully filled with awe. There are no words available in the language of mankind [humans] at this time to adequately define [the Mother] God. [Mother] God is. (The minute I make these changes I know I can stand accused of heresy and the sin of presumption.) Presuming to know [Mother] God is totally fantastical. Actually ridiculous. Just look for a second at the diversity of the earth. What person alive or dead has a clue how to create this universe in its complexity?

Of course the language of Father God will continue for many, many years.

In Mark 8, Jesus prayed twice for the healing of sight. With the first laying on of hands, the man saw people and thought they were trees. Again Jesus laid his hands on the man's eyes. Then, the man saw clearly. Healing is an incredibly complex process; *even the Master prayed twice*. I know. I have been told. By humans. Just declare it done and it is done. Sure. And have I done it? Have you done it? I would like to believe in instant miracles that result in 100% ever-after perfection. My experience shows me that there are many layers of logic, patriarchy and religion and I am growing ever wearier. My experiences are not supported anywhere except in mystical theology and the little-known writings of the mystics. Experience is what I have. Experiential religion.

Recently, I went with a friend to a charismatic group. After some prayer and meditation, the group prayed over an older woman who was having never-ending shoulder pain. When the healing prayer finished, the leader asked expectantly, "Are your shoulders healed?"

The older lady thought for a bit. Tentatively, and very, very quietly she said, "No. Not really. They still hurt."

The attack was swift and lethal. "You just don't have enough faith. You need to believe in the healing or it just can't happen."

I shall never forget that scene. I watched, infuriated, as the older lady crumpled in tears. I am ashamed to admit, I said nothing.

I see the lady in Mass the next Sunday so I go up to her afterwards. Tears fill her eyes. "I guess I just don't have enough faith," she says.

I speak quietly. "No. Neither do I."

I have a million questions regarding my own beliefs. The questions never quit. "Is suffering redemptive?" The answer comes: "Ask someone who has been tortured." Perhaps it might be. I think back to the inner promptings when I received the gift of compassion and forgiveness. Yes, it might be redemptive. Just not alongside the concepts of sin and hellfire. Or as the result of punishment from God.

Is death the ultimate healing? Is my dad healed? What about the uncles who died of cancer after incredible pain? I seek clarity and wisdom. I know I must "let go of the rope" regarding Dad's death. Tears are so near the surface. A flower, a song, a word, a look, a memory of Dad with the kids, pictures. Everything so easily brings tears. I feel weak and helpless. Will I ever grow up and accept life and the transformative process of death that is part of it? I don't know. This spring is a difficult one. Rootless. Blown by winds of emotion. Going nowhere while the world around glows in incredible beauty. Sometimes I can see the beauty. Sometimes it is all black, mouldy and ugly. Jesus said,

"Mourn in joy." Reading the *Power to Heal*[90] for the second or third time, I think I feel a glimmer of understanding.

Finally, in May 1991, my month and the month of my forever devotion to Mother Mary, the darkness light begins to dawn. It is truly the darkness of the feminine that nurtures me. My desire to understand the feminine/masculine energies within me deepens. Darkness. Darkness absorbs the entire colour spectrum. The feminine creates through darkness.

I work deeper to understand the role of the feminine in my changing world. I notice that Jesus shows a most radical love in His speaking, touching and healing with woman. I reflect on His ground-breaking radical ministry with the Samaritan woman, His mother Mary, Martha, the widows, Jairus' young daughter, the Syrophoenician woman and many others who are faithful, strong, courageous, soft, gentle, enduring. These are the powerful figures who lead the disciples to faith. Who is first at the foot of the cross? Who is at the tomb early in the morning? Who is rather insistent that Jesus begin His healing ministry at the wedding in Cana? How can my church continue its insane exclusion of women from the priesthood?

The issue of inclusive language is reflective of the power struggles inherent in hierarchical, paternalistic structures. Jesus paid scant attention to such Pharisaical exhortations except to chastise. He healed the haemorrhaging woman who should not even have been in public since a bleeding woman was considered unclean. He touched the 12-year-old daughter, a woman of marriageable age. These were acts of healing from no self-respecting Jewish rabbi. How is it possible to reduce the ministry of the Christ to divisive argumentation over the anthropomorphic maleness or femaleness of the Creator? How have I been so blind? More prayer. More meditation. More reflection. More stitching, weaving, knitting. Creating a full garment to clothe my soul.

---

[90] Francis MacNutt, *The Power to Heal* (Notre Dame, Indiana: Ave Maria Press, 1977).

Merger Attempts

I come into a very large room like a giant gymnasium. I am with someone from a group session from the first scene of the dream, which I cannot remember. The figures are all feminine. The rest of the group is in the far right-hand corner.

"This is the biggest room I have ever been in. It is very large for such a small group," my companion answers, then goes to my left where I have a sense there is a square table in the corner. I go over to take a spot in the group, which feels (room is in darkness) like a circle. As I move to the circle the leader is speaking. I stand still. "Someone" tries to come "into" my space. I am very uncomfortable with the sensation of invasion of my body from behind my back. I exclaim, "There is only room for one spirit in this body." A voice is speaking. I begin to wonder if I am to integrate with this something. I ask for guidance. The scene shifts.

The leader introduces four other people who are late in joining the group—two couples—and lastly, she announces my name as joining the group. I am relieved when my name is called. I thought for a second I would be left out and wonder how I feel about that. The group breaks for some reason I am not clear on.

Finally, a dream that shows I am truly becoming part of the dance of creation. I am called by name. I decide to go back into the dream and begin by praying to the Holy Spirit, Jesus of Nazareth, Mother Mary and Joseph to guide this experience and assist me to integrate feminine energy.

I am reading Julian of Norwich several months later when I realize that I never did go back into the dream. I have "forgotten" all about it. I am a slow learner. Don't I know that the simple act of recording the dream can suffice to advance my progress?

The gymnasium may be symbolic of the enlarged room within my being. Round tables, square tables, both symbolic of wholeness. One question is, "Why choose the gymnasium for this encounter?" The dictionary of etymology is useful. The word comes from the Ancient Greek term *gymnós* meaning "naked." Of course the dictionary, a product of patriarchal times, goes on to say the competitions were means to encourage the aesthetic appreciation of the nude male body and a tribute to … the gods. Great Inanna! Help! Perhaps the dream is suggesting that I learn to recognize my own creativity, the power of four, wholeness.

Julian's writings show me mysticism as a deep development of the feminine. I find a definition of *locutions*: Julian views locutions as "silent" words from God more clearly understood than those words heard by the outer ear. I find the reference to ear as significant for no reason I find … until many years later. Locutions carry authority, persist in memory and produce a change in the soul. I understand better, in my rational consciousness, why I resist. There is no "scientific" evidence. Only the writings of those whom our world might consider slightly insane. Promptings. Channelling. Locutions. Inner Voice. Words. Voices? Deep inner words are forming in my conscious understanding. They prescribe phenobarbital for that. There are asylums for crazy midlife women.

Some time ago in meditation Jesus "said" His agony and passion were experienced in joy. I have struggled long and hard with this. I have tried to ignore I ever heard the words. But I know clearly that I heard them. Joyfully, I read of Julian's experience in which she explains the terrible suffering of Jesus' passion and the joy He experienced in his love for us. And now I read Julian's words, *Revelations to one who could not read a letter. Anno Domini 1373*. Of course, the language has been domesticated and the English translation reads:

"It is a joy and a bliss and an endless delight to me that ever I suffered my Passion for you, for if I could suffer more, I would."

"But all will be well and every kind of thing will be well."

"Know it well, it was no hallucination which you saw today, but accept and believe it and hold firmly to it, and you will not be overcome."[91]

Where did I find this book? The Ursuline Sisters of Mary, Stillpoint House of Prayer, Edmonton, Alberta, Canada. I was deeply comforted. Perhaps I am not insane after all. Perhaps this work I do will lead me to myself. And all things shall be well.

Reflections on transformation, the life of the mystics and shamans, and the lives of saints tell me that inner transformation is marked with trauma, dismemberment, and terror. So far, then, I am a fairly normal person whose life is in the midst of deep and significant transformation. And all things shall be well.

May 19, 1991

I am slowing the healing process. Since I last wrote of inner images, I have dreamed and remember only fleeting images. I am being more patient (I think) and focusing on growth in slower stages. My steps into the labyrinth are measured. Jesus has promised oneness in the pyramids of time. I am patient. The pyramids of time? A phrase that holds promise but what can it mean?

Wisdom and Integration

A man appears in moccasins, with a beaded belt and soft turtleneck pullover. He is an ancient inner guide. He smiles gently and with great compassion. Wisdom appears written on the lines of his face. The wrinkles on this ancient man are not wrinkles but softly chiselled life.

---

[91] Julian of Norwich, *Showings*, ed. Richard J. Payne, trans. Edmund Colledge and James Walsh (New York: Paulist Press, 1978), 144, 149, 164.

Sometime in the night I am dreaming of making mad passionate love to Bill. My whole body reacts in loving passion. The dream image is very brief. I have my legs wrapped around Bill.

The dreams are simply reaffirming the patterns of unification in motion within me. I am reading Morton Kelsey, *The Other Side of Silence*[92] for the second time. He speaks of differences in inner personality. Somehow my fear of being ostracized is stronger and stronger. Why? There is not one shred of evidence to support the fear.

I continue to learn about the workings of dreams. I find that the ordinary rules of life don't apply. Dream language is contradictory. There is nothing literal. I can be two different people, or many different aspects of myself at once since time does not apply. Time may expand, contract, change. Space is no limitation either and often one place merges into another as the scenes unfold. There is no beginning, middle or end. Years of developing rational and logical thinking must be laid aside as I learn the non-rational, symbolic language of the dream. I wonder how many years it will take me to be fluent in the language of the soul.

Meditation and dreaming are closely linked. When I meditate regularly, I dream more clearly, remember the dreams more explicitly and understand their meaning more easily. Dreams are another part of the wheel of spiritual experiences. Without all the spokes the wheel does not function. Dreams have brought me to question doctrines, ideas, and any human pretension to understanding the mystery of the Godhead.

---

[92] Morton Kelsey, *The Other Side of Silence: A Guide to Christian Meditation* (Mahwah, New Jersey: Paulist Press, 1976).

Chapter Thirteen

The Elusive Feminine

*When we don't listen to our intuition, we abandon
our souls.*
*And we abandon our souls because we are afraid if we
don't, others will abandon us.*

–Terry Tempest Williams,
When Women Were Birds

Red Fires of Insight

As I lie down to sleep I feel a ring of dark faces around me.
An Indian appears with a knife. I pray. Mighty Infinite God
guide and protect me. Prayers of childhood surface. I realize
I have a mound of fear left inside of me. Most Sacred Heart
of Jesus, I place all my trust in you. Then the circle of dark
faces disappears and around a dark centre, like the sun from
behind clouds, a beautiful fiery red light flows. I feel flooded
with this light and am very peaceful.

I dream of a young girl, Rachel, in my favourite red suit, the zipper in the skirt is open. I ask, "Does it fit?" I am amazed Rachel can wear the suit. In reality she is younger, much smaller and shorter than I. I tell her, "The zipper is open."

As I drive the 160 km to my morning appointment, I am struck by the image of the red ring of fire and the fiery red suit. I'm elated that this dream image has come back. Filled with incredible energy. The day is wonderful. I accomplish every task in love.

In the evening, I am grateful for the quiet time alone. The house is calm and peaceful. And red is the colour of blood, the vitality that keeps me living. Blood red, the colour of woman, menstruation, childbirth, transfusion to life. Red. And also the colour of raging anger.

"Red … is the archetypal color, the first color humans mastered, fabricated, reproduced, and broke down into different shades.… It dominated visual culture.… With the advent of the Protestant Reformation, however, people began to view the shade as gaudy, even immoral, and its pre-eminence began to fade."[93]

Red. The oldest colour. I am reminded of the fears and the warnings that I could "lose" my way. At some deep, unconscious level, I found the guidance I needed. The psyche, soul, is far beyond the feeble efforts of the written or spoken word's power to capture. Steeped in the traditions of childhood, a loving childhood home, I prayed. Sick truly unto death, in depression as an abscess on the soul, mired in the pus of anger, shame, hurt, rage and abandonment, I turned, sometimes in anguish and sometimes in peace, to the goodness that dwells within every aspect of Divine Creation. And as I asked questions, love medicine drained the pus within that was poisoning my life. And my spirit rejoiced. But not in the sticky, sweet, syrupy saviour

---

[93] From Abigail Cain, *The 20,000-Year-Old History of Red Pigments in Art* (www.artsy.net, February 13, 2017, retrieved February 15, 2017).

I heard about on the televangelist programs on which people seemed to have absolutely no responsibility nor any authority. I had no desire to be a puppet.

Red, the fire of transformation in the deep psyche. Somewhere I read that the psyche is formed in fire at the root of the soul.

Now, 27 months after the awe-inspiring experience of cellular transformation when the very marrow in my bones was revitalized, flowing with new blood, I find no less a Christian authority than Morton Kelsey writing of the scientific, religious affirmation of my experience. Kelsey clearly states the pitfalls to be avoided, the critical processes I must apply to any thought or idea that comes into my life. For, indeed I can CHOOSE, in free will, how to use the gifts of the Spirit. Although Kelsey does not invoke hysterical fear and threats of eternal damnation, sin and evil, the word *choice* looms large. Choice has become hugely complex. I need some basis of experience for my choices. I learned very young to believe in faith and miracles. Any idea, thought or power can be used for personal gain, to wield power and control people and earth. Or for good.

This is not the prerogative of religious leaders. Look around at political, economic and social leaders. How to choose? Carefully. Very carefully. I have chosen to view life through a lens of spirituality, Jungian psychology and dreams. Although this life is far from perfect, the depression has been gone for three years. My world may be challenging; it also is intensely interesting.

Meditation, intuitive knowing, dreams, the inner voice, Zen, TM—these are not instant gratification. These are the disciplines and ways of the lifelong journey. Surely no more can be lost here than in the dead rituals of Pharisaic beliefs. Surely Jesus told the parable of the talents to illustrate that I must use what gifts I am given. Yes, there may be dangers of ego inflation in turning inward. There may be dangers of being overwhelmed by the darkness of the dark side, the shadow, of myself. Surely these dangers are less to be feared than the living death of depression and ignorance of love. Kelsey outlines the dangers as expressed throughout the ages. In modern times C.G. Jung spoke of the dangers of losing contact with reality, being overwhelmed by the contents of the collective unconscious. I wonder often that I was able to avoid psychosis. I am deeply grateful for my friend Verna throughout this turmoil. The gift of trust, the affirmation of faith in goodness, in God, in the power of Jesus' love dwelling in me—that is my continuing daily prayer.

May 25, 1991

Today I attended the evening healing Mass at Our Lady of Perpetual Help church in Sherwood Park. The Mass focused on healing the family tree. I went to the front where a man prayed over me as he had in February 1989. He saw a vision of four laser beams penetrating through my head, two in the front, two in the back, and travelling through the body. I claim healing of my central nervous system. I am open to healing every cell, fibre and muscle. Jesus, integrate every aspect of my being. In the Mass, during the Eucharistic celebration, I offered and asked for healing for our family. As usual, the energy of Spirit brings tears. Warm, pulsing tears. This has come to mean for me great depths of healing. I claim all the healing for families on my prayer list, both living and deceased. Jesus, radiate through me the beautiful light. Make me a perfect channel of peace, love, joy, harmony, faith and trust.

A pamphlet about the conference on spiritual direction arrives. The doubts begin. I immediately begin to notice the name Assagioli in the books I am reading:

Italian psychiatrist, Roberto Assagioli, who speaks of talking with the Inner Christ in an unabashed way that would make most Christian ministers blush. He finds that this kind of meditation, called psychosynthesis, often produces profound changes in both the inner and outer lives of his patients, and he tries to help them achieve spiritual psychosynthesis as well as spiritual development.[94]

So, after two years of struggling to believe, to have faith that Jesus really does talk to me in meditation and in promptings as I work and as I drive, that the Inner Christ is real, alive and lives within me, I find the words of Kelsey. Would that everyone I have ever known could experience the loving words of the Christ spoken beautifully right inside them. Jesus, how is it that I insist on visible proof? Why is external authority necessary?

I begin to hope and pray that psychotherapy becomes more holistic and that I find the necessary guts to hear what Assagioli has to say. I am just beginning to live according to the purpose of my soul. A little. The pain in psyche resolves one tear at a time.

May 28, 1991

I am centred in light. Within me a deep centre of peace radiates from a small still point. The million facets radiate out to reach into the Peace of Christ, which surrounds and protects the entire universe.

An image of four directions forms. In the east are the gifts of wisdom, love, inner consciousness, beauty, the abundant riches of eternity. From the west comes the knowledge of the heart but this image is unclear, unfinished. From the north blows cold hard logic and rationality, whereas in the south is the warmth of intuitiveness, grounded knowing, feminine darkness of the womb, and rebirth.

---

[94] Morton T. Kelsey, *The Other Side of Silence: A Guide to Christian Meditation* (Mahwah, New Jersey: Paulist Press, 1976), 151.

Four Directions

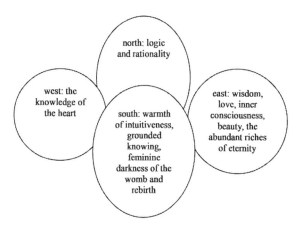

Prompting

> *Beloved child, you have uncovered a new level of rootedness in your being. Be gentle as the new roots seek nurturance in the soil. Remember soil, seed, warmth and light nurture the seed to spread its roots in greater depths of knowing. The simple things you love so well nurture you. Speak to the flowers, trees, grass. Follow your Rascal in new adventures. And we will guide you. Be gentle. Be firm and be love. For the roots are deep.*

And once again the tears flow. I pray for much, but mostly courage.

Sometimes I wonder why in all the years of depression, I did not come across a medical person who understood spirituality. And even more often I wonder why, raised in a Catholic family of deeply rooted tradition, I missed understanding that God speaks to each and every person since He lives within His creation rather than "up there." Now can I have faith outside the hearth? Faith without walls?

"Psychiatrists had to get into the act for just one reason: people with Christian backgrounds had backed out, and God will apparently raise up sons of Abraham from stones when it is necessary."[95]

The hand is stretched forth to help me. To pick me up so I can start again. For there is no map for the soul journey of life. There are signs that I may recognize and signs that I may misunderstand. I am also coming to realize that it is impossible to close the door on that which brought me to this threshold in the first place.

New Connections

I am in my office but not in my office. The Other appears, puts an arm over my shoulders, needs reassurance. Two secretaries are there. I feel their disapproval but ignore it. The Other wants to go to his office where there will be no one to hear our conversation. As we leave my office, I ignore the disapproving glances. His office has two parts. Bluebeard sits at a new computer. I am surprised he is there and also somewhat envious of the new Mac computer, which does more than mine. "It is more powerful," he says. We don't stay long since someone else is there. As we leave, The Other again puts his arm around my shoulders. I am very conscious he is shorter than I am. He guides me through the office—I am conscious of the stares—he doesn't seem to care. We go to yet another office. The Director is there playing the piano. He is singing and so is someone else. I sit on the edge of a large chair and join in the singing. I know The Director likes my singing since we sing together at many office functions. He always invites me to come. The song is beautiful and he is an excellent piano player. The last notes of the song fade away. The Director turns toward me, smiles and says something.

---

[95] Kelsey, *The Other Side of Silence*, 189.

The dream moves through three different rooms in my psyche and brings to consciousness the disapproval that I have projected onto others. I realize I have made some poor bargains with my inner predator, negative animus or repressed feminine. I have said "yes" when I really didn't want to in order to be loved or to win approval. Maturity requires self-approval. The Other has placed a great deal of trust and confidence in me. The disapproval really comes from the oppressed feminine, the Tyrant, Top Dog or negative animus. Call it what you will. The fact is I constantly criticize, judge and censor myself. "Who do you think you are?"

Our singing I take as a clear expression of harmony of integration. Singing plays a major part in my healing, as does music. I loved to sing in my childhood church. The nuns loved music, taught me a lot and were very encouraging. I went to a private school to take up voice lessons.

The Other and his wife are great gifts to me. Their dream questions prompt me to read, study, try different techniques, reflect, meditate and pray for wisdom and understanding. I am not sure if they realize how much more they help me than I help them.

The offices and the powerful computer are interesting. Bluebeard is a deeply patriarchal user who has attempted to bully me into working on his teams. I have refused because he gives "orders" when we are equals. He shows me my own negative animus again. The Other is the precise opposite. We work well together. Have deep and searching conversations. I enjoy his deep intellect, knowledge and respect for everyone.

I recognise The Director from *The Trickster* dream in March. In life I trust The Director completely. A musician, widely experienced in many leadership roles, wise beyond his years, I have deep respect for him. He hired me and, in order to ensure a permanent contract, he mentored me on several teams. He came to my office every several weeks to "chat," which was his way of doing performance evaluation. Once, very seriously, he asked, "Do you think Alberta Education is sexist? I don't see it but I thought you would tell me straight out."

I smiled, "Sexist? No kidding. You watch at the next directors' meeting how the lone woman director is treated and how she responds. You will see what I mean."

He nodded. "I don't understand it." We talked for a long time. He left shaking his head. A few weeks later, he was back. "You're right. It is. Far more than I could ever have imagined."

The three office scenes move from disapproval, to new knowledge, to joyful, peaceful singing.

I am reading and struggling to understand the masculine and feminine in relationship. I am aware of a gentle feeling of release and harmony after I write this dream down and read a bit from *Woman in Sacred History: A Celebration of Women in the Bible*, which is unusual in that it is written by a woman.

But soon I am listless and my legs and feet feel core pain. I realize how much energy surfaced while working the dream. I listen to *Pachelbel's Canon* and *Gentle Mother* playing softly on CD. Then I realize I have cleaned the kitchen, bathroom and bedrooms and am ready to go outside. A lovely rain is glistening on the grass as I hoe and play in the dirt. I am reminded yet again of Mary, Mother of Earth, Mother of the Seasons.

June 5, 1991 Warning: Rant Ahead

"You can keep digging it up, the black shit, or you can quit it and be healed."

So feelings, pain, fear and black goop—I could just have ignored and declared it all out of existence. So says another avant-garde leader and member of the so-called New Age community who is done with organized religion. Funny. Sounds like the same old religion to me. Just give it to Jesus. The same compost as the charismatic group and the lady with the painful shoulders. This time, I am that woman.

I fill many journal pages with my ranting. Then hit delete when I finally get to the realization that I am angry at myself and my need for approval, acceptance or perhaps unconditional love. Spewing rage everywhere may make me feel better. It is even necessary to write the anger. Writing is a healing process. When I started writing to heal, I promised myself I would not use whitewash. This is excruciating pain interspersed with unimaginable joy. To pretend otherwise is to live a lie.

June 11, 1991

Unification

> I am in a workout gymnasium. The Other is there. We go up from a basement via an elevator with steps. Upstairs the Other attempts a physical relationship but I reject him for fear of condemnation from those figures who are watching from the shadows in the room.

The fear never seems to abate. I am doubly determined to awaken fully my feminine soul and integrate my inner world.

Unshed Tears
There are rivers under
Desiccation.
Water locked
Bedrock, black walls
black walls.
Thought walls.

Her walls.

June 14, 1991

I am looking for C.S. Lewis, *A Grief Observed.* I understand that death often brings us to new understandings of love. My dad's death is raw and painful. My brother Tony says he can't seem to move past the depression that has settled on him since December 30. Even as I type I cry. Does one ever grow up? When I look back, I am amazed at my own stupidity. Dad died December 30. In two weeks, June 30, we would have been celebrating his 83rd birthday. Patterns. Seasons. How little I understand.

June 16, 1991

Come home. I continue to hear the whispers within me. I attend a healing service at the Edmonton Convention Centre with Judith and Francis MacNutt. Francis draws on his understanding of the New Covenant. God within each of us, awaiting our turning in loving relationship toward him. He speaks of God as neither masculine nor feminine but more than both. He identifies precisely where I began this journey, believing somewhere within myself that I was in danger of being found by an angry, vengeful, punishing God. But I couldn't run from the divine within me. His wife Judith tells stories of the people she has worked with in spiritual therapy, or psychotherapy.

I went to the healing service by myself. I experienced the most intense warmth and heat burn through me. Raw, inflamed heart burning deep inner intense fire. Quiet tears flowed eternally. Deep inside I let go and tears poured. The story unfolds and unfolds.

Perhaps I can understand it if I write it through. Francis speaks about the approach to God the Father depending on the relationship with one's personal father. It makes sense at the moment but later doesn't work for me at all. I had a fine relationship with my dad. It was my childish interpretation of external Father; all I had were patriarchal words. My children have the same language in their unconscious. Where is the language mother? Francis and Judith MacNutt do fine work. I certainly learned a good deal from his writing. Still, gendered language makes a gendered God; makes a gendered unconscious.

I have been privileged in my wounding. I have received the gifts of forgiveness and compassion. I intend to change the patriarchal language haunting my soul until I reach beneath the bedrock to the feminine. I am uncovering and claiming the divinity gifted to me at birth. My soul journey experience is multifaceted. C.G. Jung echoed Meister Eckhart, who says, "It is not outside, it is inside: wholly within."[96]

I am slowly, ever so slowly, inching my way deeper. More than once I heap scorn on my head for the microscopic pace. Then, again, in *The Portable Jung*, I find comfort: "People will do anything, no matter how absurd, in order to avoid facing their own souls."[97] He lists many of the current crazes deemed spiritual while ensuring personal wealth. I must slow down. Write. Reflect. Dream. Reflect. Read. Pray. Repeat. Rant. Agonizing depth work. I think of my earlier pages of ranting.

Soon after the service with the MacNutts, I attend a video presentation of Joseph Campbell's book, *The Hero with a Thousand Faces*[98] led by Jo Nelson, International Cultural Association (ICA). The book is heralded as the common story behind all religions, all cultures. When I finally reach some awareness, I will recognize that the *Thousand Faces* are, hmm, male.

In the fall of 2016, I am reflecting on various structures for my story. What shape will it take? How long will it be? Will it take one book to tell or two? This is a creation story. It is an archetypal exile story. It is my exodus story out of the patriarchy and patriarchal structures within my being. It is the story of death, birth and rebirth. It cycles. It is a labyrinth. I am born and born yet again. There is a constant folding, refolding, an implicate order that turns back upon itself. Then just yesterday, in a webinar conversation, someone

---

96 C.G. Jung, *The Portable Jung* (NY: Penguin, 1986), 363.
97 Jung, *The Portable Jung*, 363.
98 Joseph Campbell, *The Hero with a Thousand Faces* (Princeton, NJ: Princeton University Press, 1988).

says we need to write a new book for woman's myth. As women, we need a new myth. I gasp. I wrote that in my dissertation published in 2008. In her novel, Carol Shields' character tells her patronizing new male editor, "How is it I can so easily be seduced back into patriarchal thinking? How do I remember what I have forgotten? How many more times will I forget?" I ask myself the same question again and yet again. Will this writing follow the lay lines of the new myth? Is part of the journey approaching its end?

In June, 1991, I am reading *The Man Who Wrestled with God*.

> To be forced to undergo a journey through the wilderness is an archetypal experience. Perhaps everyone who is called upon to a higher psychological development must undergo such a wilderness experience. There are many ways we are forced to undertake such a wilderness experience. People can be plunged into a psychological wilderness, a dreadful time of doubt, anxiety, or depression and never leave their doorstep. Looked at purely clinically, the journey through the wilderness seems to be a sickness or breakdown; looked at spiritually, it may be an initiation or rite-of-passage we must undergo in order that a change of consciousness may be brought about. Egocentricity dies hard in most of us. Often only the pain of a wilderness journey can bring about the desired new attitude.[99]

Yes, I realize it is written by a very patriarchal Christian man about a man. Perhaps I could just rewrite it from a feminine perspective as a woman on an archetypal journey to her own spiritual development? Plunged into a descent to the goddess,

---

[99] Sanford, *The Man Who Wrestled with God* (Mahwah, New Jersey: Paulist Press, 1981), 16.

Inanna, initiation, through depression—without ever leaving my living room, job or family? Liberating my inner world from the negative masculine and the oppressed feminine is certainly the work of midlife and seemingly many of my Crone years as well. The story will continue. This is one woman's soul-seeding journey.

Chapter Fourteen

Insights

Carving Out My Story

The image of exodus, the pain and the wrestling compel me. People, says Sanford, people. I would like to write the story as hero. It seems so easy. The clinically depressed perimenopausal Catholic woman in a transcendent flash of soul healing discovers dreams; she uncovers the roots of depression lie in molestation when she was a preverbal child. She learns to work with her dreams, to dance, to write and to sing her story. She lives happily ever after.

Except that **isn't** my story. Mine is a story of the search for soul healing and the lost feminine. It must be an open-ended, self-organizing story of co-creation and evolution of the feminine. A complexity science story; a story of doubt, uncertainty, lost beliefs, heresy and transformation. This story spirals all at once and time after time. I would like to skip to the end. Or maybe not. What is the end? In the Christian myth, it begins in the Garden of Eden. My *Garden of Eden* dream comes in the middle of the labyrinth. It comes shortly after the *Red Fires of Insight*, the sacred fire in my heart. I lie down for a nap, asking for total rest, mental, physical, emotional and spiritual.

The Garden of Eden

I am at a rodeo/fair grounds with my horse—one like Dunfor. I have no place to tie her up so I leave her outside the trailer. I am a bit worried she might wander off but there are lots of horses around. I assume I will find her.

Sometime later I realize the horse has indeed wandered away and I go looking for her. With me is a small child of eight or 10 years. As we search the area, many people are exercising their horses and changing tack. One young man has a sulky; he and his horse are practising turns. We—my younger self stays with me throughout the dream—cannot see my horse anywhere, so return and go in another direction along a lane of some kind. At one point an older woman stops me to ask for a cigarette. As I give her one, I comment about not giving too many cigarettes away these days. The expression on her face is indescribable.

There is a store somewhere close by. I am unsure if I have been there or not. We head off along another lane, which seems to have a lot of very nice houses and an open field. Suddenly I am in a very, very beautiful back garden filled with fruit trees and flowers. I am so surprised to find this beautiful garden. There are huge, luscious peaches and other large gorgeously coloured fruits. Two women, one older and one younger, about 30, are on the back patio. A fence separates it from the fruit and flowers. I speak to them over the fence. "This is a very beautiful garden. We can't grow fruit like this in Alberta." The older woman tentatively offers me some fresh fruit. I "sense" the younger woman is reluctant, almost angry. Immediately I say something like, "Oh, no thank you, that's not why I stopped. I just wanted to tell you how lovely this garden is."

This dream asks many questions. Why not accept the fruits of my labour offered from the beauty and wonder of creative, fertile spaces within? When will I accept wholeness? When will I learn to trust my instinctual feminine energy and find my inner gardens? Clearly, I have misunderstood the inner feminine based on my misunderstanding of the story of Eve's temptation, the fall of man and loss of Eden forever. I am invited into my soul labyrinth; I walked these tunnels as my younger self. This dream asks many questions.

The dream also has many feminine symbols. Horses, my dream ego, and the three ages of woman as Maiden, Mother and Crone. The masculine, the sulky driver, is practising turns with the feminine. Apparently, I either still need practice to understand my natural feminine soul or I do not recognize that I am still driven by patriarchal consciousness that devalues my abilities. The garden, the fruit, peaches and tunnels are all symbolic of the deep feminine. The sulky driver? Dreams love a pun.

Robert Bly writes that if a man or woman has been sexually abused in childhood they will eventually need a "heaven haven," a garden walled off within to cultivate precious plants, flowers, vines, trees and a fountain. The flowering peach tree is an ancient Chinese symbol of wholeness and completion.

The walled garden image has a long history. I think of the Christ's grief in the garden of Gethsemane's *hortus conclusus*. I have not yet learned the rich world of archetypal grief in the inner world. The notion of holy grief will return to me in the fullness of time.

A Pearl Myth

Deep in human consciousness a new myth is birthing one person at a time. Outside the rodeo/fairgrounds, we recognize our instinctive self can roam freely and has much to teach. A woman and a girl child lead the way. But they are not quite ready for the journey. They walk past the storehouse of wisdom and knowledge. They do not recognize its presence or its free wisdom.

The old myth lives. Only by the sweat of their brow, through pain and sorrow, will they reach their goal. They stop to share their smokescreens with an old woman in the shadows. She keeps the smokescreens in place even if only briefly. Old mother continues her work quietly for She knows that humans someday in time emerge like ants or bees to consciousness. Through tunnels and the lure of things like beautiful houses in an open field, the maiden and her older self continue their ancient seeking.

A perfect luscious peach appears. Bursting richness. Alas, the tree is enveloped in the smoke. The two women politely decline.

The woman is grateful and gives thanks to the Goddess. She does not realize the essence of goddess includes birth, death, rebirth. Nor does she see that the anger and rage are hers. She ascends back to the world of the Sky God. Mother sighs. Soon. Perhaps soon. Soon.

My farm gardens have beautiful trees, including one which I have deemed the Sacred Saint Flowering Crabapple. She practises the radical hospitality of the Christ. Her blossoms feed the earth and Her crabapples feed the birds in summer and again in spring when the cedar waxwings and the early returning male robins feast on the dried berries. One winter four partridges roost in her bones. Her arms reach the sky. Her roots reach down and pull life up from earth to the sky. Her love of social justice sends her roots so deep and her arms so high that passers-by come off the road to find her gifts: children for their wives, lovers and mothers for their children. Saint Flowering Crabapple dances freely, sacred and black against the sunset. She understands that death is transformation through her annual All Souls descent of leaves and she creates the earth.

At the end of June, Bill and I spend a few days at Moose Lake, Alberta. I write little but reflect a lot as we sit often in silence on the dock. A short poem arises as I sit by the campfire.

Escape

War. Fighting. Imprisoned. The Director is there asking me to explain our escape. Speeches of Catholic philosophy. "Don't separate family from home."

Fire in the hearth

Motion on the lake

Strange dichotomies of

modernity

Yearning for a past this wasn't and a

future that isn't

Notice the use of the word *our*. There are so many selves inside a self. When I finally realize the deep significance of this dream, I see links back to *Broken Church*, my second-ever dream, in May 1989. There have been many dreams since then of Catholicism, church, nuns, priests, and philosophy. I am imprisoned by my own philosophy. I am at war with my beliefs. My positive masculine is trying to help but my unhealed ego does not want to lose top position. I thought I had toppled the ego in *Holy Shit* and *The Gold of Transformation* dreams. I warn myself, as I do often, don't separate your family from home. I still wonder what home might mean in the dream. Is it my inner self? Is it a spiritual meaning? I don't know.

I am birthing self.

Worlds Inside a World

I do live a normal life. This summer Bill and I are redoing our hopelessly outdated and very scruffy kitchen. Sanding, painting, replacing worn baseboards, stippling the ceiling, installing a new kitchen fan and lights. Washing, scrubbing, cleaning and sorting out the accumulation of five years of living back on the farm.

For two summers I have had neither the energy nor the desire to refresh the house. This summer it is an obsession. I am cleaning the inner and now deeply desire to clean the outer. I gain energy as I "clean my house." Often people in healing call me to say, "Guess what? I'm cleaning my house. I have this obsession …" Another friend, early in her process, kept hearing an inner "clean your house" message. I have worked to clear out the unexamined fears, issues and attitudes of 45 years of living on this planet. I now work to clear dust and cobwebs from the living room. I am amazed at the energy level. Bill also is amazed. He is working with me and would prefer that we slow down a little.

When we finally finish the kitchen project, we go out for dinner. We laugh a lot. "Next time we decide to do this," Bill says, "we are hiring someone and going away on holidays! I would really like to stay married!"

A New World Emerging

I awake hot and uncomfortable. It is a very warm summer night. As I lie, restless, I begin to remember a dream, then it slips away. I arise, go to the bathroom, brush my teeth, have a glass of water. I sit down on the edge of the tub enclosure and run cold water over my feet and legs. Bits of the dream come back. As I begin to write, the dream returns in a flood.

In spring of 2014, I will be diagnosed with scleroderma. The diagnosis is wrong; I return a couple years later when the burning, aching, hot, cold, inner itch, redness and skin sensitivity become unbearable. A new diagnosis, erythromelalgia, is unheard of except by one myofascia massage therapist in 2017, Parksville, British Columbia. She thinks about it for a couple hours and suggests I do Gabrielle Roth 5 Rhythms dance as healing. This may seem a bit strange, however further investigation proves her to be absolutely correct. The shamanic rhythms of the dance originating in the world of the feminine will begin the healing of the vestigial remnants of childhood trauma. In due time this will become the Foot story.

Labyrinthine Birth

I am talking with several people. I leave the group, go into a darkened room. One person goes into a second room. As I start toward the back of the darkened room, I feel very afraid. I can hear voices through the darkened hallway connecting the two rooms. I walk rapidly, forcing myself not to run, through the connecting tunnel.

I join the other person, a woman I think. We take seats at a round table close to the room entrance, which now seems like a small restaurant.

"Do you mind sitting here? We have no lights," says the waitress who comes by the table. Strange—it seems light to me. We sit down. The other person sits to the left of me. In a few minutes, a Chinese/Oriental girl appears at my right hand. She is crying. Her eyebrows are arched high almost invisible and I am very aware of one eye. "He asked me what I am. Who does he think I am? I am a waitress. He asked 'Is that all?' Of course not. I am more than just a waitress. I am a student of the '50s." My companion whispers to me, "Good Guy is a principal of the '50s too. He knows better. He would never say anything to hurt her feelings." The girl rushes away. I can hear her crying, wailing, "He has no right to hurt my feelings."

Somewhere in all of this I crouch low and have a fragment of whispered conversation with Jackie, an acquaintance from my brief charismatic experiences. Jackie is very vivacious. She tells me that sermons are sometimes very boring. "Yes," I say, laughing, "when we were kids and complained about boring sermons Dad always said, 'Life's sometimes like that. You have to put up with the boring to get to the good part.

> God probably has to do some pretty boring stuff He doesn't want to do either.'" God putting up with "boring stuff" is hilarious. "Especially the last few years," Jackie says, "some of the sermons are pretty bad." I don't tell Jackie my thoughts, which run along the line of now that I have read and studied so much I often find the priest's words have a whole new meaning and if they don't, I just "wander off somewhere inside myself."

One aspect of my being knows the experience of deeply healing miracles. Why haven't I spoken up? Whispered secrets. I find Dad's explanation of God's boredom hilarious. It worked when I was six, but at 46 I need to learn to stand and speak from my soul, my deepest place of feminine power.

Many years after the dream, I post a computer-generated sign on my study wall just to the right of my computer: **I will follow the agenda of my soul.** To honour the dream, I write a short, short story.

A Birth Story

I was born a matryoshka doll, self nesting in self nesting inside self. One day, a crack appears and seeds fall in, are watered with grief and bathed in sunshine. The harvest is late and the leaves decay. The seeds are planted, grow, and are replanted many times. Much of the growth is underground. Water still pours out onto the richly composting soil. The wails of women are heard bringing a new world into being. The old world still calls from time to time through the walls of the birth canal. Encouragement whispered. Laughter shouted. A circle of women assists each new birthing. Midlife women, women of the '50s birth themselves. Birthright reclaimed.

My *Escape* and *Labyrinthine Birth* dreams tell me clearly there is an inner war going on. I thought it was childhood misunderstanding of Catholicism. It was. It is also so much more.

July 16, 1991

Finding Self-worth

A large room. The Director. Another area. I am looking for a less expensive way to get transportation to somewhere. A man I only know about but don't know offers to help. He goes off somewhere and comes back with a paper. The paper has perhaps six names of elected officials.

There are three columns, two with numbers.

<u>Name</u>	Amount	Amount
	75	15

He explains that I could raise money by sponsoring/advertising. "I won't contact these people. They are far too important." As he walks away I wonder how he has time to help with so many community projects. I think he has told me before that he just enjoys helping.

An almost unknown aspect of myself shows me I need to ask for help. I need to say what I think. I must accept my own self-worth and step up.

I do enjoy helping. I serve on many community boards. I have co-edited the local community history, *Looking Back, 1979*. Served in probably every position on Alberta Teacher's Association Local #63, including president. Where have I served myself? Accepting my self-worth on the inside is apparently more difficult than just talking a good game. But my coming trip to New York is for me.

Whenever my inner critic yells, "You are being selfish, you shouldn't bother important people," or other criticisms like, "You're too stupid to do…," then I need to recognize it is my own superego afraid of losing control. I have to complete my own birthing process.

This *Self-Worth* dream is quite possibly related to my trip to New York. I have most surely thought, but not said, that the people there will be much smarter, mature, more educated than I am. More brilliant, more gifted, much more everything. I wonder where I got the nerve to book a ticket and why I am not excited. I wonder about the horrendous cost in dollars to the family budget. I am promised abundance, so my fears and I are going to New York. My legs and hips are driving me crazy. I pray. Thaw the inner will that I may serve my soul.

Sally gives me a reiki treatment this evening. Christos. During the reiki, a song plays through me. It's like a garden of roses and shimmering violet raindrops. I soar over mountains and look down through the eyes of an eagle. Piano key vertebrae play a soul rhapsody through my spine. Peaceful, calm serenity washes through me.

High Places

I am in the high school. There is a cafeteria/workroom where people are eating. There are disorganized shelves of books. I am a little uncomfortable, not knowing how to get what I need but afraid to ask. I see where I can order food. I put in a number two on a fax machine for some kind of message. It is unclear where the message will come. Later, as I wander around, I see a fax and looking through find what I am looking for (what it says on the paper I am not sure) under some other messages on the machine.

I want a Coke. There doesn't seem to be a clear system to order one. Then I find one but wonder if I can have it or if it is someone else's. A student comes. He is to be in my classroom. I gather he has been in some trouble. Later I meet his mother. He was kicked out of school in the fall and "came back when Brownies were finished." She seems unclear and reluctant to explain.

Again later, I am wandering through another part of the school and see a cinnamon bun. I see no place to order one so like the Coke I take it and eat it as I walk along. A female teacher I have spoken with earlier rushes up and asks where I got it. I tell her but I am feeling guilty for not asking how to get a bun properly. She says it must be hers since she ordered one. "Didn't they tell you in the office how to order?" "Not really," I say. So she rushes off. I am guilty and embarrassed. A thief. She returns with an office clerk. "Didn't she tell you we all order our own?" The clerk looks guilty, "No, I didn't." It seems there is no organized system for making sure people get their own orders. The clerk looks downcast.

Suddenly I am in another corridor. A former assistant superintendent of schools is standing there. I am standing up on something. He reaches up, puts his arm around my waist, lifts me down. "We're in pretty good shape for almost 50," he says as he holds me close. Then he begins to explain that he didn't get the job of superintendent in Drayton Valley. "Some woman, wife of some other superintendent, got it."

I am sure I know who got the job and so I say, "I think she is a pretty good superintendent." "Oh no," he says, "she got the job because she is a smooth talker." I turn away to greet some other administrators who have just come up.

As I write, I remember putting my hands on each side of the superintendent's face and telling him, "You just be yourself and everything will be fine." Such good advice, Pearl. Take it. I am intrigued by the theft of Coke, the troubled student and disorganization. Plus, of course, the superintendent's smooth-talking wife. My animus figure put-down echoes my fears about inadequacy in New York or anywhere else for that matter.

I stumble into more material about Hermes as trickster, prankster, thief, and symbol of transformation. He is the wise old man in the unconscious. He provides me with encouragement, protection, principles and containment. I recall *The Wise Old Man* dream. Dreams present koans. Mysteries. I read again about the origins of hermeneutics, the art of interpretation from beneath the text. What underlying meanings are present in my writing, in ancient writings, the art and sculptures of ancient times?

The dream points to my inner fears. I am too staid, too risk-averse. This transformative aspect of self, the patron god of thieves, remains deeply unconscious. An interpretive glance ensures risk, not certainty. According to Campbell, Hermes guides souls to the underworld. Hermes has become a deeply composite symbol: winged horse, winged dragon, and bird symbol of transcendence. The dream is so much more than I knew. I hope it is not too late. Perhaps Hermes will return in my deep dreaming and enable me to find the meeting point between "containment and liberation" as suggested by Jung in *Man and His Symbols*. I need to unite these opposing forces within me: my need for security and a risk-free life together with my need for inner freedom and liberation. I do not need to steal the sweetness of life. It is freely available if I follow the path of my soul.

I need to break out of old patterns, inhibitions. Hermes is pushing me to move into the contradictory side of my personality, to travel between consciousness and the unconscious. There are still many hidden parts I could learn about if I would "just be myself."

Friday night, July 26, 1991, two days before my flight to New York, I gather my courage and begin to read, *The Three Faces of Eve*.[100] I become nauseous. Fighting the desire to vomit, tears streaming down my face, guts rolling, I put the book down and go to bed.

The book haunts me for days and years. Then, I was encouraged by the ending. But working through my journals in 2016 and searching the web for bibliographic details, I learn that doctors falsified Eve's healing. The original book was written by her psychiatrist in 1957. There is false information and his claims to have cured the patient are greatly exaggerated. She has now written her own story, *I'm Eve*.[101]

There are several conflicting reports. My interest lies in the fabrications, mistreatment, exploitive and immoral, chauvinist and paternalistic behaviours of the doctors associated with her treatment. Eventually, yes, Chris Sizemore, the patient Eve, was able, with the help of seven different psychiatrists over the years till she was 51, to put together a stable personality. That required painstakingly integrating 22 subpersonalities. Originally, there were three. Chris Sizemore attempted to complete her identity by reclaiming her own life story. Actress Sissy Spacek announced she would like to make a documentary about the final and true story. This plan came to naught when 20th Century Fox threatened Sizemore and Spacek with a lawsuit claiming the movie mogul's rights to every version of Sizemore's life.

Historically, the publication of *Three Faces of Eve* makes more sense. It was 1957 post-war America. I was 12 years old. Psychiatry was very raw. Mental illness horribly misunderstood. Multiple Personality Disorder known mostly in lurid stories. Chris Sizemore went on to be an activist in mental health. My

---

[100] Corbett H. Thigpen and Hervey M. Cleckley, *The Three Faces of Eve* (NY: McGraw Hill, 1957).

[101] Chris Costner Sizemore and Elen Sain Pittillo, *I'm Eve* (NY: Jove Publications, 1983).

life experiences, from my first visit to the psychologist in 1966 to my last with a psychiatrist in 1985, are testament to the little we really know. By 2015 I will have one last psychiatric experience with a sleep disorder specialist. Nothing has improved.

The field of mental health is still questioned, still viewed by many people as pandering to lazy, dim-witted people with no self-discipline who could "snap out of it" if they chose. Choose. Choice. The word zinger aimed by the individualistic culture we live in. "Poor choices." I have come to understand the weaponry beneath those words. Choices are fully dependent on the knowledge and experience we have available to us. As children, that knowledge may be rather limited by time, place and culture. Not to mention gender, which starts with blue and pink at birth.

Patriarchy defined Eve. Women are all Eves in a world caught by the archetype. Lest you think I am out of touch, my own daughter in about 1998 was told, "You are inappropriately dressed to go to church. You will need to cover up." It was summer. She wore a tank top. Woman, the temptress. The underlying myth is alive and living through institutions of certainty. Recently, in a closed online webinar group, I learned the deeper story of Salome and John the Baptist. The hypersexualization of 12-year-olds is alive and well and living in your basement.

Why did Dr. Corbett give Chris Sizemore the archetypal name, Eve?

The Garden

In the very first days in life, as well as in utero, my encounters with cultural layers of shared tacit knowledge began to shape me. I learned the tribal family gestures, styles, language, identities, community norms and expectations. I think I can safely say that for most Canadians, dream conversations are not part of those first cultural encounters. In my cultural conditioning, dreams were just not part of living. I knew about some Bible story dreams like Joseph being told in a dream to flee Egypt. Responses to the dream, in relation to the Western canon, are conditioned from the moment we begin to go to school. We learn mimetic, mythic, and theoretic cultures.

When dreams came into my consciousness, I awakened to the knowing that there is more than my simple reality and yet my reality is all. In years of dreamwork, house dreams and renovation dreams have played a major role. *The Living Room* dream (1988) starts my knowing of the beauty of my inner world. But psyche never rests. If the Jungian concept of the collective unconscious is correct, there are many more deep transformations to come.

The drive within me that energized language since infancy has become an even deeper drive to understand the experiences. I write dreams for the same reason language was invented; that is some kind of intermediating impulse seeks clarity with others in my world. As my dream world unfolded, words became the tool for making images on a page. Images that I could share with others as a word artist, for I am not a drawing-pictures artist. Dream writing is a way to broaden my understanding of the cultural universe beyond the parameters of religion or science, to deepen my understanding of the dark forces within my psyche. According to Estes, writing in *Untie the Strong Woman: Blessed Mother's Immaculate Love for the Wild Soul,* a single dream can be the touch of the Divine that will rearrange the very atoms of mind and body.[102]

Renovation dreams are my inner world response to "becoming." I learned from infancy to age 43 how to be Catholic, a woman, a teacher, a mother, aunt and sister. Then when I took up the study of dreams and healing, psychic renovations were necessary. Think of children as mime artists. As dreamer, I am again a child in a continuous world of mimetic learning and unlearning. I have looked into *The Garden of Eden,* been in *High Places,* and soon will be in New York.

---

102 Clarissa Pinkola Estes, *Untie the Strong Woman, Blessed Mother's Immaculate Love for the Wild Soul* Colorado: Sounds True, 2011.

Afterword

This concludes Book I, but my story is a woman story of Sarah's circle, not Jacob's ladder. I had to leave home to heal depression. What is home? I didn't know depression's source. After that, another and another spiral. I made sacred agreements. I met agreement holders along the path. I came first and foremost to learn forgiveness and compassion. It is my personal journey through meditation, healing, the world of dreams, depression, becoming whole through journaling and study of the world of the feminine. In Book II, *Authoring Self*, I will start in the Garden, Maryknoll Centre, New York, and learn more clearly who I am. In Book III, *Cauldron of the Feminine*, I will leave the sky gods and travel down below to find the Sacred Feminine, the Dark Goddess, buried naked, broken, beaten and tortured under layer upon layer of rock. I will wash her wounds with my tears, clean away the dirt with my hair and rearrange the atoms composing mind and body, bring her slowly to consciousness. I will stand rooted, rounded and free, one woman coming to feminine consciousness. I hope my journey speaks to you. What I have written has a coherence, a sort of interconnectedness. Space between the spaces. Bridges of connection. I have come to know that I agreed to be Servant and Midwife as teacher, mother, writer, healer, guide and deep learner. I hope you might imagine our connections through the archetypal patterns, the study of dreams and self. The story emerges slowly, agonizingly slowly from the depths of the unconscious where there may be no more shape than a flock of cedar waxwings in a feeding frenzy around the ornamental crab tree I see outside my kitchen. And sometimes it smells like the manure pile in spring and summer heat, or potatoes unknowingly touched by frost, unwittingly rotting in the basement.

I survived the descent and return. Now I must learn to live yet again, differently. The Great Mother will inexorably teach me about "… the power and passion of the feminine [that] has been dormant in the underworld … in exile for five thousand years."[103] I will be required to sacrifice my identity as a spiritual daughter of the patriarchy.

I know and know yet again the beauty and terrifying anguish of the journey which shines through, revealing deep chaos, coherence and complexity. I am given to believe this work will feed the soul of women; the soul of the world. I hope this contributes in some small way to the to the birthing of a new consciousness. I encourage you to write, draw, dance, sculpt and stitch your own dreams.

---

[103] Perera, *Descent to the Goddess: A Way of Initiation for Women*, p. 8.

References

Bacovcin, Helen. *The Way of a Pilgrim and the Pilgrim Continues His Way: A New Translation.* New York: Doubleday, 1978.

Butler, Alban. *The Lives of the Saints.* New York: Benziger Brothers, 1887.

Cain, Abigail. "The 20,000-Year-Old History of Red Pigments in Art." www.artsy.net.

Campbell, Joseph. *The Hero with a Thousand Faces.* Princeton: Princeton Univ. Press, 1988.

Clare, Sister Francis. *We, the Bride.* Green Forest, AR: New Leaf Press, 1991.

Clift, Jean D. and Wallace B. Clift. *Symbols of Transformation in Dreams.* New York: Crossroad, 1984.

Estes, Clarissa Pinkola. *The Red Shoes: On Torment and the Recovery of Soul Life.* Louisville, CO: Sounds True, 2005.

———. *Untie the Strong Woman: Blessed Mother's Immaculate Love for the Wild Soul.* Boulder, CO: Sounds True, 2011.

———. *Women Who Run With the Wolves: Myths and Stories of the Wild Woman Archetype.* New York: Ballantine Books, 1992.

Fox, Matthew. *Original Blessing.* Sante Fe, NM: Bear & Company, 1983.

Fromm, Erich. *To Have or to Be?* New York: Harper & Row, 1976.

Garnermann, Jasbinder. "Rescuing the Feminine: The Problem of the Animus in Women." *Inside Out*, no. 7 (Winter 1991).

Gibson, David. "Jesuit Pierre Teilhard De Chardin's 'Conscious Evolution' Plays Role in American Nuns Vs Vatican Debate." *Huffington Post*, June 1, 2014.

Gilligan, Carol. *In a Different Voice: Psychological Theory and Women's Development.* Cambridge, MA: Harvard University Press, 1984.

Gilligan, Carol and David A.J. Richard. *The Deepening Darkness: Patriarchy, Resistance, and Democracy's Future.* New York: Cambridge University Press, 2009.

Groothuis, Douglas R. *Confronting the New Age: How to Resist a Growing Religious Movement.* Eugene, OR: Wipf and Stock Publishers, 1988.

Houston, Jean. *A Mythic Life: Learning to Live Our Greater Story.* New York: HarperCollins, 1996.

———. *The Search for the Beloved: Journeys in Mythology & Sacred Psychology.* New York: Tarcher/Putnam, 1987.

Jeffers, Susan. *Feel the Fear and Do It Anyway.* New York: Random House, 1987.

Johnson, Robert A. *We: Understanding the Psychology of Romantic Love.* San Francisco, CA: Harper & Row, 1983.

Jung, Carl Gustav. www.jungcurrents.com.

———. *Collected Works.* Bollingen Series. New York: Pantheon Books, 1966.

———. *The Portable Jung.* New York: Penguin, 1986.

Keating, Charles J. *Who We Are Is How We Pray.* Mystic, CT: Twenty-Third Publications, 1987.

Kelsey, Morton T. *Discernment: A Study in Ecstasy and Evil.* Mahwah, NJ: Paulist Press, 1978.

———. *The Other Side of Silence: A Guide to Christian Meditation.* Mahwah, NJ: Paulist Press, 1976.

———. *Prophetic Ministry: Psychology and Spirituality of Pastoral Care.* Rockport, MA: Element Books, 1991.

Leonard, Linda Schierse. *The Wounded Woman: Healing the Father–Daughter Relationship.* Athens, OH: Ohio University Press, 1982.

Lerner, Gerda. *The Creation of Feminist Consciousness: From the Middle Ages to Eighteen-Seventy.* New York: Oxford University Press, 1993.

Lewis, C.S. *The Screwtape Letters.* New York: HarperOne, 1942.

"Lives of the Saints." Our Lady of the Rosary Library, http://www.olrl.org/lives/.

London, Scott. "The End of Rationalism." *Ottawa Citizen,* December 16, 2001.

MacNutt, Francis. *The Power to Heal.* Notre Dame, IN: Ave Maria Press, 1977.

Maloney, George A. *Indwelling Presence.* Locust Valley, NY: Living Flame Press, 1985.

———. *Uncreated Energy: A Journey into the Authentic Sources of Christian Faith.* Rockport, MA: Element Books, 1987.

Merton, Thomas. *The New Man.* London: Burns & Oates, 2003.

———. *The Seven Storey Mountain.* San Diego, CA: Harcourt Brace, 1948.

Meyer, Ann P. and Peter V. Meyer. *Being a Christ!: Inner Sensitivity (Intuitional) Training Course.* San Diego, CA: Dawning Publications, 1983.

Molloy, Dara and Tess Harper. *The Globalization of God: Celtic Christianity's Nemesis.* Aran Islands, Ireland: Aisling Arann Teoranta, 2009.

Myss, Caroline. *Sacred Contracts: Awakening Your Divine Potential.* New York: Three Rivers Press, 2001.

New, Chester W. and Charles E. Phillips. *Ancient and Medieval History.* Toronto, ON: Clarke, Irwin & Co., 1941.

Noddings, Nel. *Women and Evil.* Berkeley, CA: University of California Press, 1989.

O'Connor, Peter. *Dreams and the Search for Meaning.* Mahwah, NJ: Paulist Press, 1987.

O'Donohue, John. *Eternal Echoes: Celtic Reflections on Our Yearning to Belong.* New York: HarperCollins, 1999.

Paludi, M.A. and G.A. Steuernagel (Eds.). *Foundations for a Feminist Restructuring of the Academic Disciplines.* New York: Haworth Press, 1990.

Payne, Richard J. (Ed.). *Showings by Julian of Norwich.* New York: Paulist Press, 1978.

Perera, Sylvia Brinton. *Descent to the Goddess: A Way of Initiation for Women.* Toronto, ON: Inner City Books, 1981.

Rainer, Tristine. *The New Diary: How to Use a Journal for Self-Guidance and Expanded Creativity.* New York: Tarcher/Penguin, 1978.

Richardson, Laurel. "Getting Personal: Writing Stories." *International Journal of Qualitative Studies in Education* 14, no. 1 (January 2001): 33–8.

Ronnberg, Ami and Kathleeen Martin. *The Book of Symbols: Reflections on Archetypal Images.* London: Taschen, 2010.

Rossetti, Stephen J. *Slayer of the Soul: Child Sexual Abuse and the Catholic Church.* Mystic, CT: Twenty-Third Publications, 1990.

Russell, Peter. *The Global Brain: The Awakening Earth in a New Century.* Edinburgh, Scotland: Floris Books, 2007.

Sanford, John A. *Dreams: God's Forgotten Language.* New York: Crossroad, 1984.

———. *The Man Who Wrestled with God: Light from the Old Testament on the Psychology of Individuation.* Mahwah, NJ: Paulist Press, 1981.

Saul, John Ralston. *Voltaire's Bastards: The Dictatorship of Reason in the West.* New York: Simon & Schuster, 1992.

Savary, Louise M., Patricia H. Berne, and Strephon Kaplan Williams. *Dreams and Spiritual Growth: A Judeo-Christian Way of Dreamwork*. Mahwah, NJ: Paulist Press, 1984.

Sharp, Daryl. "What Is Active Imagination?" AROPA: The Romanian Association For Psychoanalysis Promotion. http://www.carl-jung.net/active_imagination.html.

Sizemore, Chris Costner, and Elen Sain Pittillo. *I'm Eve*. New York: Jove Publications, 1983.

Spalding, Baird T. *Life and Teaching of the Masters of the Far East*. Camarillo, CA: DeVorss & Company, 1996.

Spong, John Shelby. *Why Christianity Must Change or Die*. New York: HarperCollins, 1998.

Starhawk. *Truth or Dare: Encounters with Power, Authority and Mystery*. San Francisco, CA: Harper & Row, 1990.

Stone, Merlin. *When God Was a Woman*. New York: Harcourt Brace Jovanovich, 1976.

Storoy, David. "David Bohm, Implicate Order and Holomovement." https://www.scienceandnonduality.com/david-bohm-implicate-order-and-holomovement/.

Thigpen, Corbett H. and Hervey M. Cleckley. *The Three Faces of Eve*. London, UK: Pan Books, 1960.

Tillich, Paul. *The Courage to Be*. New Haven, CT: Yale University Press, 2000.

Vanderdorpe, Florence. "When Myth Shows What the Mind Does Not Reach." *Storytelling, Self, Society: An Interdisciplinary Journal of Storytelling Studies, 1932-0280* 7, no. 2 (May 2011): 91–109.

Walker, Barbara G. *The Woman's Encyclopedia of Myths of Secrets*. Edison, NJ: Castle Books, 1983.

Whitfield, Charles L. *Healing the Child Within*. Deerfield Beach, FL: Health Communications Inc., 1989.

Woodman, Marion. *Leaving My Father's House*. Boston, MA: Shambhala, 1992.

Woolf, Virginia. *A Room of One's Own*. London, UK: Hogarth Press, 1929.

Dream Index

I, the Woman, Planted the Tree (Book I)

Made in the USA
San Bernardino, CA
18 December 2018